Jeanne Riou, Mary Gallagher (eds.)
Re-thinking Ressentiment

WITHDRAWN
UTSA LIBRARIES

Cultural and Media Studies

WITHDRAWN
UTSA LIBRARIES

Jeanne Riou, Mary Gallagher (eds.)

Re-thinking Ressentiment

On the Limits of Criticism and the Limits of its Critics

[transcript]

This publication was made possible thanks to the generous support of a University College Dublin Seed Funding grant for publications, a National University of Ireland publication grant, and financial support from UCD's School of Languages, Cultures and Linguistics.

Bibliographic Information published by the Deutsche Nationalbibliothek
The Deutsche Nationalbibliothek lists this publication in the Deutsche Nationalbibliografie; detailed bibliographic data are available on the Internet at http://dnb.d-nb.de

© 2016 transcript Verlag, Bielefeld

All rights reserved. No part of this book may be reprinted or reproduced or utilized in any form or by any electronic, mechanical, or other means, now known or hereafter invented, including photocopying and recording, or in any information storage or retrieval system, without permission in writing from the publisher.

Cover concept: Kordula Röckenhaus, Bielefeld
Cover illustration: view7 / photocase.com
Typesetting: Martine Maguire-Weltecke, www.mmw-design.com
Printed in Germany
Print-ISBN 978-3-8376-2128-0
PDF-ISBN 978-3-8394-2128-4

Library
University of Texas
at San Antonio

Contents

Acknowledgements

The editors not only would like to acknowledge generous financial support for this publication from University College Dublin, both from the Seed Funding Scheme and from the School of Languages, Cultures & Linguistics. Our thanks also go to the NUI, National University of Ireland, for funding received under its publications scheme and to Martine Maguire-Weltecke, who typeset the manuscript.

Introduction

The first task of this volume, which aims not only to re-think Ressentiment, but to situate it in relation to criticism, the limits of criticism and the limits of criticism of criticism, is to define the word 'Ressentiment'. The very fact that the term is typically not translated into the language in which it is being conceptualised or analysed (English or German, for example) should alert us to its unusual linguistic status. The first systematic theories or analyses of Ressentiment were written in German and, in deference – or at least with reference – to that fact, this Introduction retains the capitalisation of the term in the German language. This special treatment is intended to foreground the fact that the untranslated importing of the French term into discourses in German and in English affects the extension of the concept, suggesting that its inception coincides in some way with its translingual migration, most notably and most seminally into the discourse of Friedrich Nietzsche and Max Scheler.

The project of the volume as a whole focuses on the relation between Ressentiment on the one hand, and criticism on the other. Arguably, Ressentiment involves, above all, hatred and criticism of that which is desired or envied, but out of reach. Ressentiment is a reactive emotional response which undermines the value of that which, although desired, cannot be attained. Clearly, however, the charge of Ressentiment could then operate as a strategy for undermining any criticism, opposition or dissent, articulated within a given system. We could thus approach it, even though it is – arguably – an emotional phenomenon, from the perspective of Systems theory, showing how, much like intimacy, it is produced in particular ways by the codes of a particular system. In this volume, several contributions address the relationship between Ressentiment, power and criticism. Discussion of the concept in the various essays of the volume thus pursues (discourse on) Ressentiment in a number of directions, beginning with its latency in certain late eighteenth-century commentaries on competitive envy. In the various essays of the volume, some authors examine the lineage and historical associations of Ressentiment, while others look more to its traces in contemporary discourse. For, in today's world, the charge of Ressentiment is often used, less by traditionally conservative forces than by the neo-positivist discourses underlying and fuelling contemporary liberalism, in order to undermine the rational credibility of political opponents, dissidents and of those who critique the status quo.

Towards a History of Ressentiment
Early Theories, from Nietzsche to Scheler

As a translingual term, 'Ressentiment' has a relatively short history. As Friedrich Nietzsche and then Max Scheler conceptualised it, Ressentiment is a reactive disposition, based on the subject's perception of its lack, or falling short, of certain positively connoted qualities, attainments, etc. The resultant feeling of envy is suppressed, however, as such and converted into criticism or indeed denial or negation of the value of the lacked qualities or attainments (this operation is described by Nietzsche as 'transvaluation'). It was Nietzsche who, in a foundational moment of conservative cultural criticism, first turned the spotlight onto the concept referenced by this French term in his *On the Genealogy of Morals* (*Zur Genealogie der Moral*). According to him, Ressentiment is the real driver of Christian theories of morality. The kernel of the argument is that repressed hatred and envy, allied to a sense of subjective powerlessness, give rise to Ressentiment in multi-faceted symbolic guises.[1] On the one hand, Ressentiment-critique was aimed at the metaphysical tradition and along with this at the intellectual roots of Western culture. On the other, however, it carried over into a theory of political protest as first Nietzsche and then Scheler viewed the movements of protest and dissent that emerged in the nineteenth century as products of Ressentiment. Before looking to the presence of the term Ressentiment in a range of discourses and contexts, as the individual contributions to this volume will do, it may be useful to begin with a more detailed account of its conceptual history.

Most of Nietzsche's later writings on culture, but especially *Beyond Good and Evil* (1886), [*Jenseits von Gut und Böse*], and *On the Genealogy of Morals* (1887), [*Zur Genealogie der Moral*], are characterised by a searing critique of the Judeo-Christian tradition. For Nietzsche, the liberal idea of the common good, a product of the Enlightenment, is in fact a late outgrowth of this tradition. At the heart of the Judeo-Christian tradition, he sees a narrative of victimhood, an aesthetic rendering of (originally Jewish) peoplehood as a story of subjugation. Arising from the oppression of the Jewish people, an aspiration to freedom becomes embedded in a certain aesthetic identity based on an acceptance of suffering. Nietzsche believes an aesthetics of suffering to have intertwined itself both in Judeo-Christian morality and in neo-Platonic Christian teachings on redemption, all of which de-privileged the senses and preached a morality based on an afterlife that would lend *post factum* meaning to suffering.

From his own perspective of late nineteenth-century thought on physiology and on evolution, adaptation and metabolism, Nietzsche was convinced that life

---

1 | In a compelling study of Nietzsche's concept of Ressentiment, Esam Abou El Magd writes that envy, alongside a longing for revenge, contributes to the sense of existential powerlessness that fuels Ressentiment. See: Esam Abou El Magd, *Nietzsche. Ressentiment und schlechtem Gewissen auf der Spur*, Würzburg: Königshausen & Neumann 1996.

should be conceived of in relation to its physical processes and that to ignore these would be anti-scientific and anti-intellectual. To this extent, his attack on metaphysical thinking *per se* is based on a belief that it ignores or even rejects the physiological reality of life and invents to this end the intellectually cowardly alternative of an interior, spiritualised ideal. Life, real life, for Nietzsche, is the "will to power" ["Wille zur Macht"], as he puts it in *Beyond Good and Evil*.[2] This concept has little to do, however, with an aspiration towards power or dominion in the political sense. It concerns above all the way in which all processes of life are engaged with each other and more specifically it emphasises the fact that affective nature, desire and the will towards individual development are all intrinsic elements of the life-force. When, as a result of cultural forces, the individual is prevented from realising his or her potential, when vitality is curbed by a submission to belief systems that are hostile to life or development in this sense, an inherently corrupt public morality is the inevitable by-product. This is the state of moral corruption in which Nietzsche believes European philosophy to have colluded, to the signal benefit of the various vested interests of Christian religion.

Critically, he extends this rejection of any morality founded on hostility to the life-force to include an attack on narratives of political emancipation, which he accuses of fostering aspirations that undermine the individual's lifeforce. Instead of striving for self-development and instead of embracing experience, those individuals who submit to political calls for group solidarity (whether these concern early Jewish emancipation or nineteenth-century oppositional movements) insidiously suppress their own vital development, in Nietzsche's view. Where there is no individual achievement or mastery of adversity, the triumph of a group identity is altogether suspect, then, for Nietzsche. Hence, both in *The Geneaology of Morals* and *Beyond Good and Evil*, references to struggles for political emancipation tend to be very critical.

As we shall see, Nietzsche has recourse to the notion of Ressentiment principally with reference to an individual (or group) hiding behind an ideal or a set of values which it has itself done nothing to produce or bring about. Ressentiment is, for Nietzsche, a product of a certain revelling in achievements that are not one's own. An individual or collective subject driven by Ressentiment is mediocre, in Nietzsche's terms, but regards itself as superior to others by virtue of the fact that it does not conform to an ideal that it belittles as soon as it realises that it, unlike others, cannot attain to it. Not only has the claimed superiority of Nietzsche's "man of Ressentiment" nothing to do with real achievement, but it has everything to do with failure, or at least negative capability.

Concurrently with his critique of both Jewish and Christian values, Nietzsche articulates a critique of metaphysics, not merely because of its association with

---

2 | Friedrich Nietzsche, *Sämtliche Werke. Kritische Studienausgabe in 15 Bänden*, Giorgio Colli and Mazzino Montinari (eds), Munich: DTV de Gruyter 2007 (=¹1980), Vol. 5. *Jenseits von Gut und Böse. Zur Genealogie der Moral.* (=²1988), 35, p. 54. References to this volume will be abbreviated in the following to *KSA*, Vol. 5. *Jenseits von Gut und Böse*, 36, p. 55. References to the English translations will, however, appear first.

a belief in transcendence, but because of what he perceives to be its didactic morality, a morality opposed to life and to nature. In Nietzsche's view, systems of ethics such as those proposed by Aristotle ignore something very fundamental to human life, namely an urge to do good that can stem from uncurtailed "natural" life. In fact, Nietzsche sees life in its pure form as quite distinct from a subjectivity bound up in identification with, or self-measurement against, external ideals. Whether such ideals are associated with Aristotelian ethics or with Christian teaching on the status of the weak and the sick, both predominate and intermingle, in his view, in Western cultural and political history. Moreover, the Enlightenment association of truth with the political notion of the common good is something that Nietzsche holds in contempt. Like all rationalist ideas, it severs the link with what is natural and therefore (for Nietzsche) good in humanity: namely, the celebration of life itself. It is in this context that he dismisses and indeed ridicules Voltaire's perspective on truth:

> O Voltaire! O humanity! O nonsense! There is something to "truth," to the *search* for truth; and when a human being is too humane about it – when *"il ne cherche le vrai que pour faire le bien"* (he looks for truth only to do good, Translator's note) – I bet he won't find anything![3]

Truth, for Nietzsche, is an illusion, since – conflated as it is with notions of the moral good – it has become a cultural ideal underpinned by passivity. Rather than allowing for growth and experience, the individual life becomes stupefied by this passivity which he describes as a "herd morality". From this critique, it is only a short step for Nietzsche to draw the conclusion that liberalism, not unlike German nationalism, is both a product of intellectual laziness and a characteristic of democracy itself.[4] Ressentiment flourishes in a liberal climate wherein individuals aspire to rights and privileges that they do not deserve or merit and thus easily fall into the begrudging mentality that Nietzsche believes to be so very central to Christian morality.

Nietzsche does not view social inequalities or hierarchies as inherently problematic. Instead, he takes issue with what he regards as the artificial denial of inequalities or hierarchies. In other words, he rejects the call for equality in so far as this involves a denial of the fact that individuals have different talents and different degrees of talent. From Nietzsche's perspective, it is equally mistaken to ascribe an intrinsically positive value to, or bestow privileged status on, culture itself. His view of a "healthy" culture can be inferred from what he sees as positive for individuality, namely allowing life (nature) within oneself to flourish.

---

3 | *Beyond Good and Evil*, ed. Rolf-Peter Horstmann/Judith Normann, trans. Judith Normann, Cambridge: CUP 2002, p. 35. [F. Nietzsche, *KSA*, Vol. 5. (35), p. 54: "Oh Voltaire! Oh Humanität! Oh Blödsinn! Mit der 'Wahrheit', mit dem Suchen der Wahrheit hat es etwas auf sich; und wenn der Mensch es dabei gar zu menschlich treibt – 'il ne cherche le vrai que pour faire le bien' – ich wette, er findet nichts!"]

4 | See also Christian Emden, *Friedrich Nietzsche and the Politics of History*, Cambridge: CUP 2008, p. 257.

Since one's nature can only be experienced from within, the idea of culture as a valid external expression of personhood is problematic. For Nietzsche, individuals are not equal and what one should strive for is not equality but rather individual growth, development or self-realisation. Whereas this latter aspiration is based, according to him, on intrinsic values, political struggles for freedom or social struggles for equality are, on the contrary, contingent or circumstantial. Not only does Nietzsche regard political emancipation movements as suspect, then, but he links his theory of master-slave morality to a particular interpretation of the Jewish political struggle that he holds to be foundational in Christian moral thinking. For Nietzsche, the struggle that emerged from Middle Eastern oppression of the Jews combined a desire for political liberation on the one hand and an expression of political suffering and victimisation on the other. In *Beyond Good and Evil*, he puts it as follows:

> The Jews – a people "born for slavery" as Tacitus and the entire ancient world say, "the people chosen of all peoples" as they themselves say and think – the Jews have achieved that miraculous thing, an inversion of values, thanks to which life on earth has had a new and dangerous charm for several millennia: – their prophets melted together "rich," "godless," "evil," "violent," "sensual" and for the first time coined an insult out of the word "world." The significance of the Jewish people lies in this inversion of values (which includes using the word for "poor" as a synonym for "holy" and "friend"): *the slave revolt in morality* begins with the Jews.[5]

What followed this historical Jewish "inversion", namely the Christian identification with the poor and the sick, had begun, according to Nietzsche, with the early positioning of Jewish political identity and, more specifically, in the lamentations of a suffering, victimised people. It is the subsequent valorisation of such laments that Nietzsche sees as having produced profoundly negative effects. The Jewish "inversion" embraces suffering at the same time as lamenting it. What in this way comes about, he argues, is a new form of slavery, one linked both to Jewish notions of moral uniqueness and to Christian notions of suffering and of redemption based on a belief in transcendence. This is a particularly negative form of slavery, for Nietzsche, because the assumption of a collective identity prevents the individual from striving to make the most of his or her own existence. Nietzsche does not believe that the late-Enlightenment notion of political equality and the burgeoning nineteenth-century social equality movements understood human freedom in anything other than a superficial way, and did

---

5 | *Beyond Good and Evil*, Rolf-Peter Horstmann/Judith Norman (trans.), Cambridge/ New York: Cambridge University Press 2002, p. 84. [*KSA*, Vol. 5, 195, p. 117: "Die Juden – ein Volk 'geboren zur Sklaverei', wie Tacitus und die ganze antike Welt sagt, 'das auserwählte Volk unter den Völkern', wie sie selbst sagen und glauben – die Juden haben jenes Wunderstück von Umkehrung der Werthe zu Stande gebracht. [...] In dieser Umkehrung der Werthe (zu der es gehört, das Wort für 'Arm' als synonym mit 'Heilig' und 'Freund' zu brauchen) liegt die Bedeutung des jüdischen Volks: mit ihm beginnt *der Sklaven-Aufstand in der Moral*."]

not avoid the valorisation of victimhood which he perceived in the Jewish "inversion". Hence, the ideal of equality – a cornerstone of democratic principles – was highly suspect to him.

But what, one could ask, makes Nietzsche's viewpoint so significant for re-thinking Ressentiment in the early twenty-first century? After all, should Nietzsche's objections to equality not be seen simply as his personal response to his nineteenth-century environment and to the political formations he so clearly disliked? *Lebensphilosophie*, an eclectic philosophical movement in which he, along with Bergson, can retrospectively be called a key figure, was instrinsically disinterested, after all, in "group" formations, and could be called subjectivist, or, in Nietzsche's case, solipsistic and therefore profoundly individualistic. Can Nietzsche's views not, then, simply be placed in their historical and philosophical context: why should their analysis of particular ills of protest groups concern us today? The reason is this: the significance of Nietzsche's views on Ressentiment is that they are linked to an understanding of freedom and to the question of whether subjective freedom has an intersubjective dimension. If subjective freedom indeed turns out to be part of something that cannot be understood without recourse to something that is not reducible to, or capable of being contained in, an individual act or understanding, then Nietzsche's analysis of Ressentiment is worth returning to in order to re-evaluate how we can or, as the case may be, cannot think past societal formations.

Some years after writing *On the Genealogy of Morals* and *Jenseits von Gut und Böse*, Nietzsche returned to the theme of Ressentiment in *Ecce Homo* (1888). Reflecting autobiographically, and weaving, in so doing, a web of ironic self-stylization on the one hand and grotesque self-aggrandisement on the other, Nietzsche describes overcoming, and narrowly escaping, Ressentiment. Strikingly, Ressentiment is linked here in more personal (albeit self-consciously so) language to his own recently experienced illness (in all likelihood the onset of the illness that would cause his early dementia and eventual death). It is likened to an inability to heal.[6] The essence of illness is therefore not so much in keeping with the nineteenth-century bacteriological paradigm which tends to construe illness in terms of invasion of the discrete organism from the outside. Here, in *Ecce homo*, illness is at its most threatening not just by "being", but by the organism's own acquiescence, i.e. whether or not it can mobilise its inherent powers of healing, or instead simply succumbs to something more powerful than itself.[7] The spiritual analogy is of Ressentiment as a paralysed state, a heightened, but unproductive sensitivity, an inability to take revenge against the perpetrators of perceived wrongdoings, an overall sense of being or having been "hurt", and of thereafter being powerless, ontologically or otherwise, to alter this existential reality. Freedom from Ressentiment, on the other hand, means not being laid

---

6 | Cf. Friedrich Nietzsche, *KSA 6, Der Fall Wagner, Götzen-Dämmerung, Der Antichrist, Ecce homo, Dionysos-Dithyramben, Nietzsche contra Wagner*, eds Giorgio Colli, Mazzino Montinari, dtv: Munich 2011, =²1988, p. 272f.

7 | Ibid.

low by the consciousness of such extreme states of weakness, and Nietzsche adds that this freedom can only be known if its opposite – in other words paralysis – has also been experienced.[8] As Martin Seel has recently argued, there is a paradox worth noting in Nietzsche's *Ecce homo*. On the one hand a textual enunciation of radical individualism and of self-referential authorial freedom, this text, on the other hand, in its very proclamation of autobiographical, individual rootedness, is appealing to the horizon of its readership for recognition of this and thus, paradoxically, moves beyond the individual.[9] It situates its claim within a social or, perhaps, intersubjective sphere, since without the reader, who is part of this, the authorship would be either self-contained or in the equivalent to a vacuum. It is not, however, and Seel is right in suggesting that the urge to exemplify (Nietzsche's elucidation of how he has avoided Ressentiment and thus avoided being spiritually broken by illness) has to be seen as an aesthetic gesture and thus as part of the social world in which such gestures take on meaning in a way that is at least partially shared.[10] The question of Ressentiment, therefore, is more than strictly personal. It is not a matter of personal triumph or personal failure. This brings us back to the starting point for several of the attempts in the contributions to this volume to analyse Ressentiment as it is sometimes construed in contemporary discourse. All-too-often encountered as the limit of speech in a hostile environment, the onset of Ressentiment could be the moment where a subject senses that its grievance will be construed from the perspective of more powerful parties in the social world as irrelevant, and, if anything, evidence of an ailing mentality that cannot meet with the demands of its environment. At such moments, the limits of criticism are defined: personal grievance, not rationally legitimate concerns, are thought to be the cause of a person's failure to endorse the values of his or her more dominant environment. Some of the essays in this volume will give examples of this. Looking at the con-

---

8 | Ibid.

9 | Cf. Martin Seel, *Aktive Passivität. Über den Spielraum des Denkens, Handelns und anderer Künste*, Fischer Verlag: Frankfurt/Main 2014, p. 140. The paradox, for Seel, is that Nietzsche cannot escape the specific rationality of philosophical speech. Precisely the heightened claim to self-referentiality proves, for Seel, that as an example of autobiographical discourse, Nietzsche's text shows itself to participate in aesthetic discourse and, moreover, to exemplify the fact that the aesthetic discourse belongs to rationality.

10 | Ibid.: "Auch die Selbstfeier als eines schlechthin einzigartigen Individuums bleibt – schon weil es sich um eine Feier handelt – eine exemplarische Handlung. Mit ihr weist der Autor doch immer wieder über sich hinaus. Eine Rhetorik der Singularität ist in der Philosophie – wie wohl auch in der sonstigen Literatur – nicht durchzuhalten, nicht einmal von Nietzsche, dem ungehemmtesten und selbstbezogensten Ich-Sager aller Zeiten." [Even the self-celebration of an utterly unique individual remains – simply because it is a celebration – an exemplary act. With this act, its author again and again refers to something beyond himself. A rhetoric of singularity turns out in philosophy, as in other literature, not to be sustainable, not even by Nietzsche, the most uninhibited and self-centred I-sayers of all time. (Trans. J. Riou)]

ceptual history of the term Ressentiment can help foreground those recurring features which may turn out to apply to both contemporary discourse and the origins of the concept in the late nineteenth- and early twentieth centuries.

In two of his most important philosophical writings from 1913 to 1922, the philosopher Max Scheler concurs in many respects with Nietzsche's analysis of Ressentiment.[11] These writings are *The Nature of Sympathy* [*Wesen und Formen der Sympathie*], a 1922 revision of his 1913 publication, and a longer essay from 1915, *Ressentiment* [*Über das Ressentiment im Aufbau der Moralen*]. Scheler argues that Ressentiment is not a specifically Christian phenomenon, even though at times it has crept into Christian ethics. For both thinkers, however, Ressentiment is at the root of the "protest movements" (the term is Scheler's) of the nineteenth century and both focus in particular on the Ressentiment that they see as driving socialism, while Scheler takes issue additionally with feminism. As products of an unacknowledged envy of the more (naturally or socially) talented or highly-ranked "Other", these and a whole range of other movements are discredited for Nietzsche and Scheler. And for Scheler, the critique of Ressentiment does not stop there. Instead, it carries over into his countering of criticism itself, into his dismissal of the whole theoretical basis of the critical demand for social change as being based, fundamentally, on Ressentiment.

In his 1915 essay on Ressentiment, Scheler contends that Nietzsche's theory of Ressentiment as the root of Christian morality is based on a number of misreadings of Antiquity.[12] He argues persuasively as to why this is so. Overall, however, he agrees with Nietzsche that the modern industrial Age is characterised by the tendency to produce protest movements that try to lessen the inequality between people by "weakening" the "strong". Where he differs from Nietzsche is that he does not believe Ressentiment to be a product of Christian thinking. Whereas Nietzsche had described the Christian ideal of love as a product of pure Ressentiment in *On the Genealolgy of Morals* [*Zur Genealogie der Moral*], I,8, Scheler claims that with the rise of the bourgeois classes from approximately 1300, a morality of Ressentiment emerged that reached its pinnacle in the French

---

11 | In a longer study, I have discussed how Scheler's thinking relates to early Phenomenology, incorporating the notion of Intentionality set out by Brentano and developed further by Husserl. Alongside others such as Theodor Lipps, Alexander Pfänder and Edith Stein, Scheler's writings made a significant contribution to empathy theory in the early twentieth century. Some of the ideas which will be mentioned in the following in relation to Ressentiment have been examined in a different context in this longer study. See: Jeanne Riou, *Anthropology of Connection. Perception and its Emotional Undertones in German Philosophical Discourse from 1880–1930*, Würzburg: Königshausen & Neumann 2014, pp. 90–131.

12 | Max Scheler, *Ressentiment*, Milwaukee Wisconsin: Marquette University Press, trans. Lewis A. Coser/William W. Holdheim with an introduction by Manfred S. Frings. [*Das Ressentiment im Aufbau der Moralen*, ed. Manfred S. Frings, Frankfurt/Main: Klostermann ²2004 (¹1978).] In the following, references will be made first to the English translation and secondly to the German text.

Revolution.[13] Scheler's essay is at least as searing in its critique of emancipatory social movements as is Nietzsche's *On The Genealogy of Morals*. Moreover, his arguments, both in relation to what he sees as Nietzsche's misunderstanding of Christian asceticism and his underestimation of Greek "fearfulness" of death show greater differentiation and precision than Nietzsche, the language becomes no less rhetorical than Nietzsche's and the dismissal of what Scheler regards as protest movements no less vituperative: "The man of *Ressentiment* is a weakling; he cannot stand *alone* with his own judgement."["Der Mensch des Ressentiments ist ein Schwächling, er kann mit seinem Urteil nicht *allein* stehen."][14] Calls for equality and social solidarity are, according to Scheler, nothing other than a desire to bring somebody else down – someone more naturally entitled, or entitled by the fruits of their labour, to enjoy greater privilege, advantage or luxury. A person capable of advancing by their own means, he claims, does not need to demand equality. To call for equality as a political right is therefore based not only on weakness, but on moral cowardice in the face of this weakness – Ressentiment: "Nobody demands equality if he feels he has the strength or grace to triumph in the interplay of forces, an any domain of value!" ["Niemand fordert Gleichheit, der die Kraft oder die Gnade in seinem Besitze fühlt, im Spiel der Kräfte – auf irgendeinem Wertgebiet – zu gewinnen."][15]

Compared to his arguments elsewhere, including over long stretches of his essay on Ressentiment, Scheler's conclusions in this respect are somewhat glib. He makes no effort to substantiate the claim, for instance, that all advocates of socialism or feminism hold these convictions as a result of envy or Ressentiment. No attention is given to the respective thinkers and ideas accused by Scheler of being motivated by Ressentiment, and the result is conservative political thought that defends what it sees as a natural status quo. At the same time, in contradiction, many aspects of the status quo are rejected by Scheler himself, either in this essay or elsewhere. For instance, in *The Nature of Sympathy*, he is capable of being very critical of what he sees as masculinist, patriarchal and anthropocentric positions. And he is highly critical of the industrial Age, particularly towards the close of the essay on Ressentiment, elsewhere also of capitalism, but overall defensive of the conditions of capitalist economy. The crux seems to be that change, where Scheler regards this as necessary, is best brought about by individuals in a stronger position making the sovereign decision to improve the conditions of those less fortunate. This is in keeping with his understanding of "giving" as an act of Christian love.

Far from being an act of self-sacrifice, the individual who is able to give is strong, according to Scheler's reading of Christian morality. Here, he differs from Nietzsche. Where Nietzsche speaks of Christian asceticism and self-denial that turn into a form of hypocrisy, Scheler sees instead a Christian view of

---

13 | *Ressentiment*, p. 53. [*Das Ressentiment im Aufbau der Moralen*, p. 36].

14 | *Ressentiment*, p. 103. [*Das Ressentiment im Aufbau der Moralen*, p. 89.]

15 | *Ressentiment*, p. 102. [*Das Ressentiment im Aufbau der Moralen*, p. 87.]

ascetic practice that can only be exercised by a strong individual. Asceticism, and the self-control involved, are therefore not what Nietzsche regards as a weakening of the individual, but are instead possible as a result of the individual's vitality and strength.[16] This "strong" individual, we can extrapolate, has the power to choose whether, for instance, to give or retain, to indulge or abstain, to withhold or knowingly and positively "give" to another.[17] As such, this sovereign individual does not differ greatly from Nietzsche's conception of the medieval knight whose notion of justice is built on an understanding of personal honour.

Scheler also believes that Nietzsche's reading of antiquity is flawed in one crucial respect. He believes that Nietzsche overlooks that certain periods of antiquity, citing Epicureanism as an important example, are marked by a great fear of death. Their favouring of indulgence is, according to Scheler, not so much a by-product of a natural vitality as a last-ditch attempt to defy the limits of mortality.[18] It is therefore driven by fear rather than fearlessness and is, as such, the opposite of what Nietzsche holds it to be. Related to this, he criticises Nietzsche's reading of the Christian morality of self-diminution – wanting to bring oneself "down" to the level of the weak, or the sick, or the poor. The Greeks, he points out, saw weakness and sickness etc as a sign of diminution, whereas the major change that Christianity brings about is that to "give" to the weak or to turn towards the sick is regarded as the property of a life that is full and "healthy".[19] He makes the further distinction that Christian morality does not hold the weak-

---

16 | See *Ressentiment*, p. 95: "It is quite ridiculous to hold up 'serene Greek monism of life' against 'gloomy and dismal Christian asceticism.' For the asceticism which deserves this name is precisely 'Greek' and 'Hellenistic.' The feeling that the body as such is 'sordid,' a 'fountain of sin,' a confinement to be overcome, a 'dungeon' etc., has its source in the decline of antiquity. From there, it sometimes penetrated into the Christian Church. Christian asceticism is serene and gay; it is a gallant awareness of one's power to control the body! Only the 'sacrifice' made for the sake of a *higher positive* joy is agreeable to God!" [*Ressentiment im Aufbau der Moralen*, p. 80: "Es ist sehr lächerlich, wenn man die 'düstere christliche lebensfeindliche Askese' dem 'heiteren griechischen Lebensmonismus' entgegenstellt. Denn gerade 'griechisch' und 'hellenistisch' ist die Askese, die jenen Namen verdient. Das Gefühl, dass der Leib als solcher 'schmutzig' sei, 'Quell der Sünde', eine zu überwindende Enge, ein 'Kerker' usw., hat seinen Ursprung im Niedergang der antiken Welt, und drang erst von hier aus in die christliche Kirche zuweilen ein. Die christliche Askese ist heiter, froh: ist ritterliches Kraft- und Machtbewußtsein über den Körper! Nur durch das höhere *positive* Freude geweite 'Opfer' ist in ihr Gott genehm!"]

17 | In chapter three of the Ressentiment essay, "Christian Morality and *Ressentiment*", Scheler cites other examples of what he sees as ethical impulses within Christianity that appear to stem from ascetic renunciation, but should be seen instead as an individual's free choice and one which strengthens vitality in a positive way. See *Ressentiment*, p. 61. [*Das Ressentiment im Aufbau der Moralen*, p. 44.]

18 | See Ibid., p. 60. [*Das Ressentiment im Aufbau der Moralen*, p. 43–44.]

19 | Ibid.

ness, sickness itself as the phenomenon worthy of "love", but the spiritual reality behind it.[20] Accordingly, it is from an underlying inner health that the stronger person is able to give. In this way, Christianity avoids an equation of the essence of human life with "outer" properties such as weakness or strength, sickness or health. Rightly, Scheler shows that this is a distinction missed by Nietzsche in his definition of Ressentiment.

At this point in his essay, Scheler switches from his analysis of antiquity and the Christian notion of love to a derisory comment on nineteenth-century Realism in literary writing and painting. Realism, he argues, shows quintessential signs of Ressentiment in: "[...] the exposure of social misery, the description of little people, the wallowing in the morbid – a typical *ressentiment* phenomenon. Those people saw something bug-like in everything that lives, whereas Francis sees the holiness of 'life' even in a bug." ["die Aufdeckung des sozialen Elends, die Kleineleutemalerei, das Wühlen im Kranken, – eine durchaus aus Ressentiment geborene Erscheinung. Diese Leute sahen in allem Lebendigen ein Wanzenhaftes, während Franz noch in der Wanze das 'Leben', das heilige, erblickt."][21] Scheler's dislike of the social conscience of the Realist movement is, as has been shown elsewhere, echoed in other Vitalist tendencies which are quite pervasive in philosophy and psychology around 1900.[22] A good example of this is Else Voigtländer, whose doctoral dissertation, *On the Different Types of the Sense of Self* (1910), [*Über die Typen des Selbstgefühls*] engages with both Nietzsche and Scheler. An important theme in her analysis is the Nietzschean trope of "declining life", something which she sees as having been falsely celebrated in fin-de-siécle art. The opposite to vitality, "declining life" is, for Voigtländer, given inordinate attention in art and literature. She is referring not least to the German stage, where Ibsen's 1892 play, *The Master Builder*, dramatises lost vitality.[23] Although she does not mention Ibsen's other dramatic works, it is clear that Voigtländer does not accept Ibsen's critique of alienation and social stratification in his plays, and that the comments directed specifically at *The Master Builder* apply to Realism in general (although Ibsen is a dramatic forerunner of Modernism rather than purely an exponent of naturalist drama). Paying undue attention to the negative effects of social hierarchy gives rise to what Voigtländer, Scheler, and, before them, Nietzsche saw as a damaging preoccupation with weakness.[24] Scheler, as the above quotation illustrates, opposes the "weakness" of declining life to the perceived vitality of Christian acts of "giving" such as

---

20 | Ibid.

21 | Ibid. (Scheler is referring to St. Francis of Assisi).

22 | Cf. J. Riou, *Anthropology of Connection*, p. 103.

23 | Ibid.

24 | As I have argued elsewhere, these three exponents of Vitalism, in their privileging of vitality over so-called "declining life", share a certain common ground with populist movements of late nineteenth-century Germany such as *Lebensreform* (Life Reform). See Ibid., p. 100.

those demonstrated by Francis of Assisi, who was proclaimed a saint by the Roman Catholic Church shortly after his death in the thirteenth century. To give should be a choice based on freedom (Francis had freely chosen to forfeit his inherited wealth, and to tend to lepers, among other deeds), and not something that should be brought about by persuasion. Scheler's (along with Voigtländer's) dislike of Naturalism and Realism centres on the urge within these movements to persuade theatre audiences and readers of the necessity for social change. Realism, for Scheler, adds to the mistakes of socialists, feminists and altruists in justifying Ressentiment, adding fuel to a metaphorical fire. Not least this dismissal of Realism places him firmly in the ranks of a burgeoning conservative theory. While he would later grow disillusioned with Christianity, at this point in Scheler's career, the engagement with early Christianity is central to the form of intentionality developed in this essay and in his other major early work, *The Nature of Sympathy*. Arguably, the intentionality of love in a re-reading of Christian ethics is something which is idealised by him in this essay. The somewhat incongruous juxtaposition of St. Francis of Assisi and nineteenth-century Realism is an example of this. Scheler's dismissal of artists and intellectuals who, as was sometimes the case in Realism and Naturalism, drew attention to suffering caused by the social world is unreservedly Vitalist, and indeed, adds a political tone to Vitalism, in saying that they "saw something bug-like in everything that lives". In other words, they focus on life that is diminished, less than human, and abject – and these qualities are directly associated by Scheler with Ressentiment.

The emotional content of the notion of Ressentiment in its nineteenth-century and early twentieth-century readings first by Nietzsche, then by Scheler, and by others such as Else Voigtländer is central to the development of the concept. Emotional attributes often place the phenomenon close to other concepts that can inspire disgust, revulsion or simply condemnation. Scheler's metaphor of the bug, far from being incidental, calls to mind the abjection of Gregor Samsa in Kafka's 1912 short story, *Metamorphosis* [*Die Verwandlung*]. Samsa has become both a bug and an image of human waste, and he has lost the power to partake in human language.[25] But Ressentiment first and foremost delivered a theory of envy. Its theorists tended to see at the heart of political dissent and artistic protest not legitimate intellectual stances, but an emotional cry for help. In the aftermath, it is not difficult to see how Ressentiment has become a trope of other discursive formations. From the viewpoints of its critics, it represents the limits of criticism, more precisely the point of its descent into a prediscursive, emotional terrain that has no place in rational discourse. Far too close to a non-verbalised, non-intellectualised, reactive cry of envy, Ressentiment is dismissed in this perspective as a collective call for equality where this equality is not merited.

---

25 | Franz Kafka, *Sämtliche Erzählungen*, ed. Paul Raabe, Frankfurt/Main: Fischer, pp. 56–99. See the discussion of abjection in relation to Gregor Samsa in: Anne Fuchs, *A Space of Anxiety: Dislocation and Abjection in Modern German-Jewish Literature (Freud, Kafka, Roth, Drach, Hilsenrath)*, Amsterdam: Rodopi 1999, p. 72.

While its place in contemporary discourse connects it above all to theories of envy, the genesis of Ressentiment discourse also shows close conceptual ties with notions of pity. In the understanding of mimesis in Aristotle's *Poetics*, pity and terror are part of the cathartic process unleashed by the art of tragedy.[26] Famously, Plato in Book 10 of the *Republic* banished the artists from his ideal Republic since art was capable of arousing emotions stronger than rational thought. Conversely, Aristotle sees a purifying role for the pity and terror inspired by witnessing tragic occurrences in drama. The purifying value attributed to pity in Aristotle's theory of catharsis has a certain resonance in the Judeo-Christian tradition, and, when Aristotle's *Poetics* is rediscovered in the Renaissance, it combines with a new, seventeenth-century connotation of purifying as purging.[27] Eighteenth-century Enlightenment thought adds to the theory of catharsis a dimension of moral improvement with Lessing's acclaimed argument that the compassionate person is a better person, and that the purpose of art should be at least in part to arouse this improving emotion of compassion (or pity).[28]

However, at the close of the nineteenth century, Nietzsche takes issue with Aristotle's definition of catharsis, and departs in no uncertain terms from the Enlightenment paradigm of universal moral understanding. Art should not purge us of the experience of fear and of a sense of danger, in Nietzsche's view. On the contrary, the Dionysian anti-hero exposes himself to danger rather than seeking to purge it, and his is thus an aesthetics of withstanding and of experiencing – rather than of distancing through mimetic processes. In Nietzsche's later writing, the anti-Aristotelian aesthetic is developed into a theory of cultural weakness. *Beyond Good and Evil* and *On the Genealogy of Morals* unreservedly associate Ressentiment with the "false" morality of the Judeo-Christian tradition, one built on cowardice rather than Dionysian courage. In the spirit of this cowardice, Nietzsche infers, Ressentiment emerges as the plea for mercy and appeal

---

26 | The concept logic of catharsis was not, of course, invented by Aristotle, but has a long history in ancient Greek and other mythologies. As Mary Douglas has emphasised, it can be seen at work in rituals of scapegoating as a form of purification. See Mary Douglas, *Purity and Danger – an Analysis of Concepts of Pollution and Taboo*, New York: Praeger 1966. For a discussion of catharsis in the pre-Socratics, see: Bernd Seidensticker/Martin Vöhler (eds), *Katharsis vor Aristoteles. Zum kulturellen Hintergrund des Tragödiensatzes*, Berlin/New York: Walter de Gruyter 2007.

27 | Aristotle's *Poetics* undergoes a revival in the Renaissance but the connotations of purifying and purging change in the course of the seventeenth century. The notion of a clear conscience becomes a moot point and purging, arguably, a dividing line between Lutherans, Calvinists and other reformed Protestant sects. John Milton's evocative portrayal of Lucifer, and the temptation of Adam and Eve in *Paradise Lost* represent an emotional sharpening of the "purifying" and "purging". See John Milton, *Paradise Lost*, ed./introd. John Leonard, London: Penguin 2000.

28 | For a discussion of Lessing's notion of pity, see Martin Vöhler, "Die Ambivalenz des Mitleids. Käte Hamburgers Lessing-Kritik", in: Nina Gülcher/Irmela von der Lühe (eds), *Ethik und Ästhetik des Mitleids*, Freiburg i. Br. et al: 2007, pp. 33–45.

for pity from the centre of a weakened and corrupted core. Right up to today, this critique continues to resound in cultural theories of Ressentiment. As a result, dissent – whenever this is voiced by a minority group or isolated viewpoint – all too easily falls under suspicion of a false appeal for mercy. It is inherently under suspicion of looking for unwarranted advantage, undeserved leniency, unmerited protection. Ressentiment, in this way, can be dismissed with the contempt which Nietzsche showed for any social movement, any call for justice, any sense of protest not in keeping with Dionysian self-celebration. Moreover, in line with Nietzsche's use of the term to attack what he saw as the "herd morality" of a culture weakened and "perverted" by a false morality, Ressentiment has been an often unspoken charge at the heart of politically conservative cultural theory.

Later Theories of Ressentiment:
From Carl Schmitt to more Contemporary Perspectives

From its origins in antiquity and philosophical anthropology to today's intellectual and political landscape, the discourse on Ressentiment is intrinsically linked to thinking on equality. The degree to which the concept is reified as a theory of envy frequently relates to positions adopted in relation to the question of equality. To put it simply, although perhaps somewhat polemically: if, on the one hand, there is a view that inequality is natural or inevitable, then there is likely to be less Ressentiment, since hierarchy is accepted as being intrinsic to the social order, and the lower positioned will be less inclined to dispute their position. Where, on the other hand, equality is espoused by the culture concerned, Ressentiment is more likely to emerge, since equality, however notional, becomes a driving aspiration permeating the entire symbolic order. In other words, individuals or fractions are more prone to feeling envy or resentment because of their perceived exclusion if the potential for equal achievement (or, perhaps, attainment) is not regarded as being unjustly impeded. As Karl-Heinz Bohrer and Kurt Scheel have quipped, Ressentiment is directed against perceived "winners"; postindustrial capitalist society is, in other words, a globalised field of comparison and competition, in which the "losers" do not take their places readily.[29] Indeed, prefacing their 2004 special edition of the journal *Merkur*, a collection of essays entitled *Ressentiment! Zur Kritik der Kultur* [Ressentiment! On Cultural Criticism], Bohrer and Scheel remark that the charge of Ressentiment is particularly hurtful because the accused stand charged not just with entertaining various ignoble emotions, but also with displaying lesser powers of intellectual discernment. Ressentiment is dismissed as offering would-be critics or protesters the means of hiding behind something similar to mass protest, and as requiring neither individual distinction nor suitable qualification to argue a critical case. Those deemed to bear the mark of Ressentiment are thus judged (a pri-

---

29 | Karl Heinz Bohrer/Kurt Scheel (eds), *Ressentiment! Zur Kritik der Kultur. Sonderheft Merkur. Deutsche Zeitschrift für europäisches Denken*, 2004, cf. 9/10, 58, Preface.

ori) not to merit intellectually the "just" treatment to which they lay claim.[30] This dismissal is founded on the conservative argument that finds strong expression in the thinking both of Nietzsche and of Scheler, for whom the movements of political protest of the nineteenth century were, as we have just seen, anathema. Articulated in the late 1930s, Carl Schmitt's theory of power posits that calls for equality are under certain circumstances misplaced and are little other than envy-led or at the very least pointless. In *The Leviathan [Der Leviathan]*, his account of Hobbes' theory of the modern state includes comments on the emergence of this state as part mythical-machine (the Leviathan), part rationalist intelligence. He notes, for example, that whereas the medieval right to protest against an unjust feudal overlord was seen as God-given, this legitimate right disappears in the Modern age.[31] In other words, the Leviathan state is a colossus that subsumes individual resistance within fully rationalised structures with the result that, effectively, resistance becomes impossible. Dissidence henceforth becomes superfluous; dispossessed of any practicality, it will, at best, fuel utopian ideals which will, in turn, remain extrinsic to the controlling institutional powers. It is not difficult to imagine how this understanding of power in modernity construes Ressentiment as the futile disgruntlement of the utopian dissident. As such, it is disregarded, not necessarily as unreasonable or incorrect, but as inherently unproductive or futile. And although Schmitt does not say so, the next logical step is to conclude that if disgruntlement is already a sign of protest at a state of affairs that is factually irreversible, then it is little other than an impotent expression of envy of the authority that the dissident does not possess. Since this authority or power is never within the reach of the utopian protester,

---

30 | "Ressentiment gehört zu den Wörtern, die man als Vorwurf am wenigsten auf sich selbst beziehen möchte: Gemeint sind die anderen, und zwar die besonders Kleinkarierten. Jemanden vorzuwerfen, er habe Ressentiments, heißt ihm zu sagen, er sei ein Mensch ohne Selbstbewußtsein, der sich dafür rächen will. Ressentiment ist unter den negativen Eigenschaften wie Neid oder Haß der niedrigste und der Vorwurf daher besonders verletzend." [Ressentiment is one of those words which one would least like to hear used about oneself. It refers to others, therefore, who are particularly smallminded and petty. To accuse someone of Ressentiment is tantamount to telling them they are a person who lacks a sense of self and wants to take revenge for this. Amongst those negative characteristics such as envy or hatred, Ressentiment is the lowest form, and the accusation therefore particularly hurtful. (Trans., Jeanne Riou.)]

31 | Carl Schmitt, *Der Leviathan*, Stuttgart: Klett-Kotta 1982, (11938), p. 70–71: "Die Entfernung, die einen technisch-neutralen Staat von einem mittelalterlichen Gemeinwesen trennt, ist weltenweit. Das wird nicht nur in der Begründung und Konstruktion des 'Souveräns' sichtbar, wo der Gegensatz des göttlichen Rechts der Könige als sakraler 'Personen' gegen den rationalistisch durchkonstruierten Befehlsmechanismus 'Staat' zutage tritt." [There is a world of difference between the technical, neutral state and the medieval commune. This can be seen not least in the foundation and construction of the 'sovereign', and the contrast which emerges between divine right of kings as sacred 'persons' and the rationalist construct of the state as an ordering mechanism. (Trans. Jeanne Riou)], 70f.

the protest itself is, in logical or rational terms, misplaced, and the authoritarian state is vilified to no material effect. The state thrives on a logic that cannot be disputed, since its laws are the product of a rationalisation that has already taken place. Although the protestor's disgruntlement may not be unreasonable, the ground has shifted, leaving him or her nowhere to protest. The magnitude of the Leviathan is such that one small pocket of resistance will easily be overwhelmed. Taking the Leviathan to be the state, then this, for Schmitt, is a historical development rather than a universal or pre-ordained order of things. Be that as it may, there is little the weaker party can do.

In the preface to their edited volume, *Ressentiment! Zur Kritik der Kultur*, (2004), Karl Heinz Bohrer and Kurt Scheel offer a somewhat different reading of Ressentiment, one that foregrounds its utopian potential, a dimension that can be inferred from Schmitt's theory of power, but which remains inchoate and even ambivalent in Schmitt's thinking. For Bohrer and Scheel, the critical power of Ressentiment is indeed tied up with the rejection of the world as it is, in the name of something better. Indeed, it can articulate or reveal, in artistic as well as intellectual terms, a need for radical review of power and of thought itself (they refer in this connection to the aims of Critical Theory and to the work of a large range of thinkers).

In one of the essays collected in the 2004 *Ressentiment*-volume, Hans-Peter Müller gives an account of the major cultural transition towards an equality paradigm. For thousands of years, as Müller puts it, inequality was sanctioned by what almost appeared as natural law, innate differences and distinctions being assumed to stratify society naturally.[32] With the shift towards modernity, this presumption was gradually subjected to revision, notably by the Enlightenment, the French Revolution and then, not least, by Marx'/Engels' publication of the *Communist Manifesto* [*Manifest der kommunistischen Partei*] in 1847. Indeed, the tables were turned to the extent that, as Müller suggests, it was not the call for equality but rather the defence of inequality that became increasingly morally suspect, even though – as the emergence of anarchy, socialism and communism clearly showed – the discrepancy between the ideal of equality and the social reality of modernity was immense.[33]

Müller cites the work of Alexis de Tocqueville from the first half of the nineteenth century, who, in the wake of his travels in America observed that the freedom and mobility associated with bourgeois capitalism brought with them a persistent striving and loss of security as accompanying features of the rise of the middle class. Rather than being content with their places in a status quo, the inherent sense of possibility in a society where upward mobility was no longer foreclosed meant that any achievement or potential achievement for the citizens brought with it equal potential for loss. Indeed, such a loss of status would be far more difficult to accept than the static condition of the lower-classes in the

---

32 | Hans-Peter Müller, "Soziale Ungleichheit und Ressentiment", in: Bohrer/Scheel: *Ressentiment!*, pp. 885–894, 886f.

33 | Ibid.

pre-modern age.[34] Therefore, according to de Tocqueville, a constant sense of restlessness and aspiration are features of democracy.[35]

De Tocqueville's sense of foreboding and of the ambivalence of the desire not just for equality itself, but for advancement, is not far removed from Nietzsche's distrust of democracy. Clearly, however, de Tocqueville is more interested in the comparative ethnographic observation of Ressentiment than in providing a critique of its morality, as Nietzsche would towards the end of the century. De Tocqueville observes a fundamental openness in American democracy that distinguishes it from forms of society with either aristocratic structures or caste-systems. Theoretically, every American citizen can aspire to social mobility. De Tocqueville sees envy and Ressentiment as inevitable by-products of meritocracies, since the aspiration to achieving higher status and greater wealth, and to securing a better position in society leads to a certain vulnerability, "defeat" being as distinct a possibility for the individual as "success". Müller then cites Max Scheler's notion of Ressentiment, in particular the sense of helplessness Scheler believes can result from an individual's holding an unequal position in a society where equality is an aspiration. In Scheler's essay, the helplessness in question fuels the desire for revenge. This appears an almost inevitable consequence of the dream of equality which de Tocqueville finds so ambivalent in early American democracy.[36] Nevertheless, compared to the social closure of feudalism, the utopian dimension of a society that no longer entirely constrains individual movement is difficult to overlook, even if Ressentiment is the occasional by-product.

As a counterpoint to the argument for the utopian potential of Ressentiment, Norbert Bolz presents a negative reading in his essay on Adorno in the Bohrer/Scheel volume. Adorno's Critical Theory contains, as Bolz contends, a dialectical movement of negation in which the "appearance of the artistic object", perhaps better described as its phenomenality, defies either the terms of the fetish-character which Marx ascribes to consumer-capitalism or the totalizing tendencies of instrumental rationalism.[37] Art is therefore for Adorno the locus of Ressentiment; it refuses to be pinned down, resisting the terms of what Marx described as the illusionary structures of capitalist fetishism. The very freedom within aesthetic discourse that allows for the creation of an appearance can also provide a means of expression for troubled and, indeed, alienated subjectivity

---

34 | Alexis de Tocqueville, quoted from *On Democracy in America*, in Ibid., p. 887.

35 | In a similar vein, Georg Simmel would later describe the ceaseless competition and the striving for attainment within a constantly shifting and fluid set of value-driven objects as a feature of modern culture, indeed, as its defining psychological feature. This is evident in many of his writings, not least the lesser-known essay, "Sociology of Competition", [Sociologie der Konkurrenz], (1902). For a discussion of this, see: Jeanne Riou, *Anthropology of Connection*, pp. 195–217.

36 | H. P. Müller, "Soziale Ungleichheit und Ressentiment", p. 889. Müller refers to Scheler's *Ressentiment*.

37 | Norbert Bolz, "Lust der Negation", in: Bohrer/Scheel (eds), *Ressentiment! Zur Kritik der Kultur*, pp. 753–761, 757f.

that does not otherwise have ready access to self-translation. Along these lines, Adorno pins his hopes on art for the articulation of disenchantment with modernity. The aesthetic ubiquity of art makes this possible without art's falling back into the "trap" of Hegelian dialectics wherein all temporary states of being, no matter how politically undesirable, can be resolved. The latter are, after all, only phases in the teleological movement towards progress in history.

Bolz' argument proceeds along the lines that Critical Theory is a manifestation of Ressentiment. What he means by this is that the view of modernity espoused by Critical Theory is one that allows for no politically affirmative vision, and also demands ongoing critique of the alienation produced by the capitalist system. Since neither capitalism nor the instrumental reason of the modern world seem able to be reversed, Critical Theory is an intellectual position that predisposes the critic both to suffering and, perhaps, to melancholia. Adorno is critical of Hegel's teleological view of history and equally critical of earlier attempts at utopian synthesis such as that ventured by the Romantics. Beyond both Romanticism and Hegelian dialectics, Adorno holds the aesthetic as the only possibility of non-falsified, non-reductionist and non-dialectical expression.[38] And this expression must be *of* a certain suffering occasioned by the inadequacy of the modern world. Whether this leads to any possibility of change or of improvement, or whether Carl Schmitt's laconic insight into the futility of subjective critique of totalised power shows something indeed irreversible, is bound up with how we see Ressentiment. What does it achieve to criticise? Does it involve a negation, simply, a descent into aporia, a retreat beyond what can be realistically achieved? Bolz concludes that there is a Gnostic and a theological dimension to Adorno's conception of the work of art:

> As is the case with all Gnostic thinking, Adorno's *Aesthetic Theory* promises redemption through complete alienation. To this end, this type of thinking has a strong interest in construing the world in which we live as the worst of all possible worlds. In contrast to naïve Gnostic theology, redemption does not feature in Adorno as the unknown god who saves, rather manifests itself incognito as art. That which is wholly other disguises itself along Marxist lines in the changeability of what exists. That the world should thus be changeable is what art can show. That 'that which is is not everything' is the most fundamental formula of Gnosticism. The concept of that which exists thereby takes on a theological accent.[39]

---

38 | Bolz, in this article, refers to *Ästhetische Theorie,* Adorno's final and uncompleted work, but degrees of this stance are implicitly (and correctly) seen by him as present elsewhere in Critical Theory.

39 | Ibid., p. 759 (Trans. Jeanne Riou). ["Wie jede Gnosis verspricht auch Adornos *Ästhetische Theorie* die Erlösung gerade durch eine Vollendung der Entfremdung. Insofern hat dieses Denken ein großes Interesse daran, dass die Welt, in der wir leben, die schlechteste aller möglichen Welten ist. Im Unterschied zur naiven gnostischen Theologie tritt das Heil bei Adorno aber nicht als fremder Erlösergott auf, sondern eben im Incognito der Kunst. Das ganz Andere verpuppt sich marxistisch in der Veränder-

Tentatively, perhaps, Adorno keeps open the possibility of change. However, change is most likely to come about through that level of understanding and reflection enabled by aesthetic discourse. This is because, in Adorno's thinking, as Bolz rightly infers, there is a meta-critique (and thus non-mimetic critique) of reality in the work of art. Since its critique will always be indirect, avoiding positivist reductionism on the one hand and dialectical argument and counter-argument on the other, aesthetic discourse (for Adorno) can make of Ressentiment a critique that nevertheless holds some real transformative potential.

While acknowledging what he calls Adorno's Ressentiment-critique, Bolz nevertheless builds up to a dismissal of all other, ensuing critiques of Ressentiment. Critical theory, he tells the reader, is dead, and Ressentiment-critiques have outlived it.[40] Echoing Nietzsche's disdain for political protest movements, Bolz argues that an abundance of groupings in the modern world stake their claim to moral righteousness via rhetorical strategies which suggest that they are on the side of justice. Effectively, he seems to discredit quite an array of what he perhaps sees (along with Nietzsche) as disgruntled and outdated dissidents. Among those ridiculed are (paraphrasing Bolz) "ageing 68ers", "medieval environmentalists" (mittelalterliche(n) Umweltschützer), "feminists", adolescents who seek refuge in subcultures and critics of globalization.[41] Bolz thus groups together many shades of political opposition and protest, claiming that all are united by what Lionel Trilling has called "adversary culture". To belong to a subculture is dismissed as either a characteristic of adolescent rebellion, thus a passing phase, or a nostalgic yearning for battles which have long since been fought and lost. This line of argument in Bolz's article is worth noting, as it is indicative of broader cultural dismissals of counter-culture. Such dismissals can take many forms – for instance non-engagement with an individual or grouping accused of Ressentiment. Considerable attention has been given to Bolz's article here because its account of Critical Theory as Ressentiment-critique is particularly illuminating. It is unclear, however, whether the subsequent critique of counterculturalism offered by Bolz is, in fact, a logical extension of Critical Theory. If the latter is the case, the hypothesis would be that unlike the work of art, which is capable of complexity, counterculturalism is dialectical and reductive. The question remains whether the proposition that counterculturalism is dialectical and reductive is really consistent with Critical Theory. Bolz also argues that anti-capitalist protest can be seen as a struggle for belonging. Intellectuals, students and young people, he continues, have an abundance of time on their hands, which can result in idle or even vexatious protest. In this version of Ressentiment, protest movements are driven by the pure pleasure of negation.

---

barkeit des Bestehenden, und diese Veränderbarkeit der Welt wird durch Kunstwerke verbürgt- Dass das, was ist, nicht alles ist, ist die gnostische Minimalformel. Damit bekommt der Begriff des Bestehenden aber einen theologischen Akzent."]

40 | Ibid., p. 760.

41 | Cf., pp. 760–761.

Articulated in 2004, thus four years before the so-called economic crisis, a credit crash that tore through the social and economic layers of the European Union and, to an extent, of the USA, such an argument has a very particular ring given the political reality that would follow in the wake of this crash: a reality that took shape in the critical silence resounding from the managerialism of academe and in the apparent nonchalance of media commentators in the face of seemingly automated policies of austerity. If all forms of counter-culturalism are dismissed out of hand, it is easy to see how an intellectual vacuum might arise, of which indifference towards equality *per se* is a natural by-product.

Throughout the European Union in the aftermath of 2008, a political trend emerged with Germany as the "creditor" nation along with a small group of strongly performing euro-economies who, arguably, held the balance of power and determined the credit terms of "bail-out" nations with devastating consequences. The brutal reining-in of public spending in some, if not all of these countries (Greece, Ireland, Portugal, Spain) reflected a growing political tendency to regard the public sector, i.e. the state, as a burden on the taxpayer rather than an essential infrastructure for a functioning, citizen-led society. An example of Ressentiment in action in this broad political sense has been the demonization of the "wasteful state" with its expensive, supposedly overpaid and idle civil and public servants. In Ireland, to give one example, public sector pay was cut drastically, but along with this, rights also disappeared as unions gradually acquiesced with government plans out of fear that failure to make concessions would result in job losses. One by one, the different sectors of the large public services union in Ireland that had protested most loudly against one particular round of cuts in 2013 were granted concessions. This had the effect of offsetting opposition to the damage which overall spending cuts would do to the public sector. To protest from within would, in a climate increasingly hostile to those regarded as superfluous public servants, have been met with outpourings of public hatred. Although the banking crisis and the credit bubble as well as deeply corrupt management of these private systems were the cause of the crash, Irish newspaper and television reports bore daily witness to the fact that although the population excoriated the banks, the more immediate venom seemed directed at anyone who, in hard times, was perceived to be suffering *less* hardship than others. If those thought to be suffering "less" were state employees, in particular in education, then their salaries often seemed to be regarded as an unfair expense and a burden on "the taxpayer". As citizens were transformed in rhetorical terms into taxpayers, the culprits became those workers perceived as being paid directly from tax revenue: ie. civil and public servants, and not just the upper echelons thereof. Instead, the lower and middle scales had their wages and pensions cut and their numbers slashed. Daily laments in the media about collapsing standards of public health care, inhuman waiting lists for urgent specialist medical attention and queues in accident and emergency units, a university system that is cash-starved in the extreme and offering less and less choice to students made no difference as austerity policies accelerated. None of the all-too-evident failures of unrestrained neoliberalism brought about any sustained critique of this model. Unlike in Ireland, whose electorate the left-leaning German broadsheet

Süddeutsche Zeitung regards as historically passive,[42] there were frequent street protests in the Spanish, Portuguese and Greek capitals. However, the concerns so vigorously expressed in these countries regarding the decimating effects of mass-unemployment and reduced public service capacity were not widely debated in the EU. Therefore, protests against the demolition of what many would hold to be the two essential pillars of a functioning civil society, namely health and education, were largely dismissed as born of the Ressentiment of vested interest groups on the periphery.

Returning to Norbert Bolz's argument, it is clear that protests against the culture of austerity cannot all be seen to be driven by Ressentiment. Indeed, the suggestion that they are based on Ressentiment can itself be seen as the product of a reified notion of the existing order, for instance the order that preserves political continuity in a state like Ireland, effectively bankrupted by the greed of its banking sector and by an unshakable faith in a property bubble. What needs to be recognised here is the degree of consensus required in order to suppress alternative viewpoints. If sufficient numbers of people tacitly agree that things are "as they must be", then the likelihood of non-compliant voices being heard becomes slimmer. And the charge of Ressentiment is not infrequently a call for collusion in the suppression of unwelcome identities, communities, interests or demands.

A more nuanced approach to Ressentiment is taken by Martin Seel in the same 2004 volume edited by Bohrer and Scheel. Unlike Bolz, Seel turns to the question of morality in relation to the imperative of respect for the particular. His phenomenological approach to morality, which accords to the other the right to differ, avoids the trap identified by Nietzsche: namely morality as the idealisation of norms or as obedience to the herd instinct. In this approach, the other may not be liked or approved of and does not have to be understood either, for morality is not reduced to an obligation to conform. A homogenous community, for instance, can uphold certain traditional values, and may under some circumstances deny that different values held by "outsiders" can have equal moral status. But a moral intention to do justice to that which is neither liked nor understood has to avoid universalist aspirations. Seel's openness to relativism or at least his openness to the limits of social understanding leads him to claim that Ressentiment is often linked to a disrespect, or even an envy, of otherness.[43] This can come about when mediocre attainment, sensing its own limits, claims a higher moral ground on the basis of external value references. Effectively, such an argument follows the reasoning on Ressentiment of both Nietzsche and Scheler, namely, that an element of morality (perhaps all morality for Nietzsche

---

42 | *Süddeutsche Zeitung*, 29/30 June 2013. A translation of this article was published in the *Irish Times* on 6 July 2013, underlining the claims of this German newspaper report that Ireland had been exploited on a number of levels apart altogether from the banking crisis, and its electorate had passively accepted the corruption and mismanagement that extended in no small degree to some former government ministers.

43 | Martin Seel, "Zuneigung, Abneigung/Moral", in: Bohrer, Scheel (eds): *Ressentiment*, pp. 774–782, cf. 782.

and certainly the morality of the modern world of work for Scheler) is premised on collective Ressentiment.[44] In other words, such an argument arises, essentially, from mediocrity. On the basis of perceived shared value, and resting on collective identity, it empowers people, irrespective of their ability, to feel moral superiority and injustice at their lack of status, recognition or political rights. As Seel notes, however, both Nietzsche and Scheler themselves demonstrate an elitist morality in adopting this position. Nietzsche, for instance, considers morality to be intrinsically opposed to exceptional individual talent, so that it is a very small step indeed from morality to its by-product, Ressentiment. For Seel, on the other hand, even if morality and Ressentiment are intimately connected, morality can and should be separated from its affective tenor. Certainly, human beings are essentially driven by combinations of emotional responses: likes and dislikes, desires and repulsions inform and sometimes dictate their behaviour. There is an echo of Schopenhauer's implicit emotionality in consciousness here. But Seel, unlike Schopenhauer, tries to reconcile this emotionality with a possibility of morality that is not entirely determined by affect. Although Seel recognises that attraction and repulsion are not merely affective antipodes, but rather inherent and indeed productive forces in all human activity,[45] he avoids the more negatively-focussed "abstinence" ethics proposed by Schopenhauer as an answer to the problem of upholding morality in the face of emotional life as an inner battleground of appetites. Instead, he envisages the phenomenology of the other as a space neither reducible to, nor disconnected from, the antithetical forces of attraction and repulsion, desire and disgust, love and hate, friendship and enmity. For Seel, it would be futile to deny the existence of such dynamics of affect, and equally futile to expect rational activity to override them somehow. Instead, he emphasises the mobility of these affective forces. Attraction and repulsion are never static; and if the relation between self and other is based on an ongoing movement between attraction and repulsion, then it is possible within this relation to settle on, or for, an acceptance that the other is somehow not quite defined. In this non-definition, there is the space for the other to move, and to be accorded a saving "indifference" in the sense that its otherness negates the need for an immediate and binding emotional order, and therefore neutralises the sense of evaluation or value that can so easily lead to Ressentiment. Unlike the indifference with which Bolz pronounces (the same) judgement on subcultures, youth movements and various forms of political protest alike, Seel's "indifference" is a space which defers evaluation. Although he does not invoke the aesthetic precedent of Romanticism, its influence is, to a degree, palpable. In this way, Ressentiment can be thought of in terms of an unstable, unfixed, dynamic relation of antithetic affect rather than in terms of a fixed affective constellation with a clear identity.[46]

---

44 | Ibid.

45 | "Zuneigung, Abneigung – Moral", p. 774.

46 | The German Romantic thinker, Novalis, reflecting elements of both Schelling's

The concept of Ressentiment is undoubtedly connected to the history of subjectivity in the Western world and perhaps beyond. The point of separation between self and other, or imagined and real community, could doubtless be studied with a view to questioning whether Ressentiment, like René Girard's scapegoating, is an anthropological constant that emerges under particular sets of (sociological, ethnological and political) circumstances. Ressentiment, an emotional phenomenon in Nietzsche's reading of Judeo-Christian culture, asks questions of religious history, of Christian ideals of goodness and justice, as well as of philosophy.[47] How does morality, and the political adaptation of morality both on the "left" and on the "right" relate to the *emotional* phenomenon in its historical sense? And how might all this relate to today's world? Has Ressentiment been a trope used to offset more serious criticism of a world whose economic foundations have been called into question?

Jeanne Riou
Berlin, July 2014

---

and Fichte's thought, tended to represent life itself as a reciprocal relation between plus and minus poles, like the electrical charge of a battery. As he writes in a fragment from "Allgemeiner Brouillon" (1798–99), "Aus der Wechselsättigung eines Plus- und Minustodes entspringt das Leben". [From the mutual saturation of 'plus and minus', life emerges. (Trans. Jeanne Riou)]. This fifth fragment reflects an idea to which Novalis frequently returns. It derives from a combination of Schelling's thoughts on reciprocity, and Fichte's development of this line of thinking into the concept of an entirely antithetical relation between self and other, 'the I' and the 'not-I' ['das Ich' und 'das Nicht-Ich'].

47 | Gilles Deleuze links both Hegelian dialectics and Christian ethical thinking to an 'ideology of ressentiment' and a guilty conscience ("mauvaise conscience"), in Gilles Deleuze, *Nietzsche et la philosophie*, Presses Universitaires de France: Paris 1962, p. 183. Arguing along similar lines to Nietzsche, he sees both as falling within a tradition that devalues life, favouring a "reactive" life to one of vitality. In this is implicit the Nietzschean trope of "declining" versus "ascending" life.

The Critical Focus of *Re-thinking Ressentiment*

If the two main functions of language are naming (putting words on the world) and relating (to other beings), then the question of language, including the critical matter of linguistic difference, lies at the heart of this project. One of the reasons for this is obvious: namely the fact that *Re-thinking Ressentiment*, although written in English, focuses on a French word that was radically redefined more than a century ago by two German thinkers. Many, if not most, of the authors of the present volume reflect at some length in their individual contributions on the word "Ressentiment" and/or on its particular linguistic status. Critically, the term cannot be translated neatly into English. In any case, as Walter Benjamin memorably stated, "[a]all translation is only a somewhat provisional way of coming to terms with the foreignness of languages".[48] In drawing attention to this non-translation (and thereby to what translation is not able to do), the volume continually highlights this "foreignness of languages" and bears witness, in particular, to the relation between English and other languages.

The centrality of language to the project goes beyond this fundamental point, however. The core aim of the volume is to explore the ethics and politics of critique, specifically in relation to the position of perceived, or self-identified, "losers". Undiscriminating as the latter term might appear, and in need of scarequotes, it is an apt contemporary synonym for the Ressentiment-ridden subjects whom Nietzsche and Scheler constructed as "weak", "dominated" or "subordinate". In today's "global" world, "non-global" languages, cultures and values might quite accurately be thus identified. This is a particularly critical matter for the two editors of the present volume. Both used to work in different modern language "departments", respectively "German" and "French", in a university on a – nominally and vestigially at least – bilingual island on the edge of Europe, in the only country in the Euro zone in which English is an official language. They still work in the same fields as heretofore, but these have been institutionally re-configured or re-formed in their home university, as they have been indeed in most universities across the English-speaking world, including the United Kingdom. Most erstwhile "departments" of French and German have been integrated into larger units, in this specific case, into a "School of Languages and Literatures". The particular circumstances of this shift merit attention. Most significantly, perhaps, the "School of Languages and Literatures" does not encompass in its remit the two ancient languages, Greek and Latin (housed in a "School of Classics") nor does it encompass either of the two official languages of the Irish state: one local and national, Irish; the other global and transnational, English. Moreover, it is not involved in the teaching of the other global language studied in a separate unit on campus since 2004, Mandarin Chinese. One can only surmise that the reason for these anomalies is the exceptional symbolic importance – cultural and/or commercial – of the three languages accorded independent, sovereign

---

48 | Walter Benjamin, "The Task of the Translator" in: *Illuminations: Essays and Reflections*, ed. Hannah Arendt, trans. Harry Zohn, New York: Schocken Books 1969, p. 75.

academic status within the humanities at our university. Thus, the languages deemed non-strategic are merged under a School name that fails to identify them in any way (as modern/foreign/European etc). And yet, while this name strips the language subjects of their separate identities, the addendum 'and Literatures' does, at least, point away from instrumentalism and towards the separate symbolic riches embedded in the different languages.[49]

In what sense, however, are the "sovereign" languages more strategically and symbolically important than the five subject languages assembled and semi-asphyxiated in the contracted space of a single cost centre (German, Italian, French, and Spanish/Portuguese)? English is, of course, *the* global language and indeed Ireland's Globish currency is the country's economic trump card. The "School of English" is "out on its own" and is, moreover, the largest School in the university's College of Arts. Paradoxically, the language itself is not taught in this school, which is more concerned with the symbolic and cultural capital of literature, film, drama etc. produced in English or in historical versions of English. In fact, the university's lucrative TEFL (Teaching English as a Foreign Language) operation is taught in a separate language provision unit, an "applied language" centre, along with the other global and non-global languages envisaged more instrumentally than symbolically. As for the Chinese language provision, deemed to be of strategic importance because China is the top world economy of the future, it is part of no academic School, much less of the "School of Languages and Literatures": instead it is taught from an on-campus Confucius Institute partly gifted by the Chinese government. Irish is the third language taught as a sovereign academic subject at University College Dublin in a unit called the "School of Irish, Linguistics, Folklore and Celtic Studies". The exceptional visibility and value thereby conferred on this language relates to its local and "heritage" value.

It is worth noting that, although the structure is a legacy of the erstwhile flush "Celtic Tiger" economy, the "School of Languages and Literatures" is, predictably, in crisis. It has lost, through the recent economic recession, more than one third of its academic posts; it has also lost two actual languages along with the full academic viability of two others (Portuguese and Italian). The two definitive losses were, inexplicably, the Near- and Middle-Eastern languages, Arabic and Hebrew, which could scarcely be more critically crucial to any university aspiring to, or claiming, the status of Ireland's "global university". It needs, perhaps, to be emphasised that, far from constituting an exception in Ireland or elsewhere, the apparent erasure of linguistic and cultural diversity or divergence described above is widespread.

This book is, in its very conception, critical of the values that have driven the aforegoing narrative. It is in fundamental dissonance with the academic expansion of a narrow, economic conception of the global at the expense, less of the immediately local, than of the entire human, cultural, linguistic spectrum. Its

---

49 | Ironically, as this book was going to press, our unit was re-structured and re-named as the "School of Languages, Cultures and Linguistics". The erasure of the above-mentioned gesture towards the unique linguistic embeddedness of literature(s) speaks for itself.

very composition contests, in other words, the consensus that privileges image over word, global code over distinct language, and the transnational over the international. In respecting the non-economic and non-economical resonance of two global and two non-global languages (respectively English and Chinese, and German and French), the volume bears witness to the fact that, despite Ireland's elective affinities with the Anglo world and the economic bet that it has placed on South-East Asia, it remains for the foreseeable future located – in space and time, if not always in mind – closer to Europe than to any other continent.

In its stereo quality, this book as a whole, including this Introduction, registers the very different voices of the two editors: one immersed in German-language thought in particular, the other in French-language thought. While the individual essays of the two editors – along with this two-part Introduction – underline that double perspective, the entire volume pervasively foregrounds the play and uneconomical excess of linguistic difference and the work of translation. This reverberation comes to the fore in a singularly and simultaneously arresting and moving manner in the Mandarin symbols inscribed in the text of the very first essay, by Eric S. Nelson. However, it also resounds in the way that the entire book honours the original language of expression of the thinking that it studies. Although this respect for linguistic difference and divergence is critical to academic endeavour in the humanities, it is in crisis in the contemporary academy worldwide. It should be noted that attention to language and to linguistic diversity was not a matter of editorial policy but rather a spontaneous concern of the various co-authors. Thus, to an overwhelming extent right across the volume, although an English version of all quotations is supplied, readers can generally see, and – if they are able to, read – for themselves quotations in the original language (German, French, Mandarin). In addition, many of the authors, most notably perhaps Victoria Fareld and Mary Gallagher, focus in a particularly concentrated way on the act of translation itself.

Inevitably, the term "ressentiment" gives rise to much meta-linguistic commentary: Eric Nelson, in particular, explores in some detail the relation between "resentment" and "ressentiment". The writing of the term "ressentiment" has not been harmonised throughout the volume or even throughout this co-authored Introduction. Some authors italicise and/or capitalise it, others do not. In respect of these variations, but of course much more significantly in respect of the breadth of approaches to Ressentiment and to its re-evaluation, the guiding values of the project were not standardisation, closure or coverage, but rather suggestiveness, openness and reflectiveness.

* * *

Some of the essays concentrate on the politics of Ressentiment, and this is the case in the studies by Jeanne Riou, Caroline Mannweiler and Mary Gallagher. Others – Eric Nelson, Helen Finch and Victoria Fareld – focus more closely on the ethical stakes of the concept or on its connection with aesthetics or poetics (Dominique Jeannerod and Christine A. Knoop). However, this subdivision into political, ethical and aesthetic concerns is in many respects artificial; moreover, the three groups of essays are connected by many revealing conceptual bridges. For example, Christine Knoop's study of the dynamic of Ressentiment as it plays out in the interdisciplinary study of literature often intersects with Mary Gallagher's attempt to situate that dynamic in relation to the values of the contemporary academy as a whole. Helen Finch's commentary on H. G. Adler's views on the dangers of mechanical materialism resonate strongly with Mary Gallagher's echoing of Richard Roberts's concerns regarding the socio-political cost of the global spread of the techniques of Human Resource Management, a cost that includes the kind of "loss of self" and "self-subjugation" discussed also in Jeanne Riou's study of Contagion. Similarly, Victoria Fareld's analysis of Jean Améry's rejection of memory as closure and purification is echoed in Jeanne Riou's comments on aesthetics and catharsis. The question of literary value, while it is particularly central, of course, to Dominique Jeannerod's essay and to Christine Knoop's study of interdisciplinary approaches to literature, also underlies Helen Finch's forensic reading of Adler's post-traumatic autofiction. Most significantly of all perhaps, the relation between the ethics and the politics of equality and dissent unifies the volume as a whole. And yet, what clearly emerges from the collection is not at all a consensus, but rather a sense of divergence suggestive of the extraordinary, intellectually and ideationally generative reach of the nodal concept of Ressentiment, particularly when its significance is situated in relation to the value of criticism or critique.

In "The Question of Resentment in Western and Confucian Philosophy", Eric Nelson presents a comparative study of the way that resentment is conceptualised as a moral force in early Confucian and modern Western thought. In contrast to modern European discourse (the work of Strawson, Scheler and Nietzsche, in particular), early Confucian ethics concentrates on undoing resentment, both in oneself and in others. This stripping is indeed a major step towards becoming an ethically exemplary person in early Confucian ethics. Much Western thinking on resentment assumes that the creation or existence of inter-subjective symmetry and equality provides the means of pre-empting or undoing the fixations of resentment (and also the trap of Ressentiment into which resentment can, in certain circumstances, develop). In complete contrast to this approach, early Confucian ethics stresses that only a radically asymmetrical recognition of the priority of the other person can prevent or dissolve resentment. Nelson shows the exact terms in which the author(s) of the *Analects* recognised both the pervasiveness of resentment under certain social conditions and the double ethical requirement to counter it within oneself and to avoid provoking it in others. Self-cultivation and ritual propriety were held to be the means towards this dual ethical end. Not only does the early Confucian ethics of combined self-care and care of the other contrast with the morality of calculation, but its central value of humane benevolence could be seen as a reversal of Nietzsche's moral order. Far from valuing strength over weakness, early Confucianism prioritises the responsibility of the strong for the weak. More specifically, in a move that is somewhat reminiscent of Levinasian ethics, it makes the "superior" self responsible for preventing not just itself, but also the "inferior" other, from feeling resentment, and – even worse – from entering the dead-end of Ressentiment.

Continuing this exploration of the relation between Ressentiment and ethics or morality, two essays, one by Helen Finch and the other by Victoria Fareld, discuss the notion of victimhood in relation to the crimes of German National Socialism. For Victoria Fareld (in "Ressentiment as Moral Imperative: Jean Améry's Nietzschean Revaluation of Victim Morality"), the significance of Jean Améry's Ressentiment is intimately bound up with a refusal to let go of the past, even if this author is concerned also to conjugate the past somehow with the present and the future. Fareld argues that the Austrian Jewish Améry (formerly named Hans Mayer), a survivor of the Shoah, produced a radical re-evaluation of Ressentiment, thus conferring on this notion, so discredited by Nietzsche, a critical and even revolutionary meaning. Furthermore, Améry's thinking on the experience of the victim operates a Nietzschean "Umwertung" by revaluating the Nietzschean notion of Ressentiment itself. Améry's "Umwertung" is founded on the notion of a trans-temporal, if not anachronistic or untimely, moral responsibility. Fareld shows how Améry's Ressentiment forces the past back into the present in a temporal disorder that the author of *Beyond Guilt and Atonement* refuses to pathologise. Thus, instead of viewing victim experience as trauma from which one must recover, Améry focuses instead on making history moral. He rejects the teleology of memory as accomplishment, instead calling for the present to pursue indefinitely a continuous and perpetual remembering. If Améry's implicit critique of memory as closure is directed at all of society in the present, it is because of his radical understanding of victim morality. Crucially, he does not see this simply as a morality for those who were subordinated, powerless and victimised in the past, but also as a morality for all of those/us who, in the present, because of their/our belatedness and hence their/our powerlessness to undo what was done in the past, are subject to the same moral imperative of remembrance as the victims of past wrongs. If suffering and sacrifice are to have a positive sense, if they are to have the value of an intended action, then the experience of victimhood must not be purged or "cured"; instead it must be remembered, kept in mind, not just by the victims themselves but by all of posterity.

In "*Ressentiment* beyond Nietzsche and Améry: H. G. Adler between literary *ressentiment* and divine grace", Helen Finch studies the work of H. G. Adler, like Améry an Austrian Jewish author and survivor of the Shoah. Adler, best known as a scholar rather than as a literary writer, authored pioneering studies of Theresienstadt and of the deportation of Eastern European Jews by the German National Socialist regime. As these works show, rather than remaining stuck in the detached, distrustful or resentful stance of the victim, Adler is at pains to participate in the rebuilding of dialogue in post-war Germany. Finch argues, however, that whereas Adler's intellectual and scholarly engagement with Germany's present and future suggests a certain transcendence of his personal suffering and losses, his literary work, especially the posthumously-published novel, *The Wall*, registers the post-camp suffering of an alter-ego narrator. This fictional protagonist's predicament bears indirect witness to the resentment felt by Adler not in relation to Nazi persecution per se, but rather in relation to the short memories of his so-called friends and to the general lack of empathy shown to him as a survivor in the post-Nazi world. Finch compares and contrasts Adler's approach to Nietzsche's version of Ressentiment with that of Jean Améry. She notes the complexity, but also the ironies and contradictions of their respective approaches to the notion of victimhood, not least of which is the fact of Améry's eventual suicide. Adler's apparent willingness to participate in, or facilitate, a forward-looking, intellectual "working through" of social and political guilt might seem to have protected him to some degree from the emotions that can be surmised to have led Améry ultimately to take his own life. Moreover, the resentment inscribed in Adler's "autofiction" might suggest that the indirect revelation or exorcism of an otherwise hidden Ressentiment is not necessarily incompatible either with survival or with creative self-expression.

In an effort to relate the ethical frame of reference to the political, and to connect historical reflection on the critical value of Ressentiment to contemporary thinking on equality and on political protest and dissent, Jeanne Riou's essay, entitled "Contagion" begins with a discussion of Ressentiment as it features in the writings of Nietzsche, largely as a response to, and a repudiation of, Christian morality and more specifically early Christian asceticism (Tertullian). For Nietzsche, Christian morality is based on a contagious weakness: while it lays claim to a certain altruism, this morality serves above all the self-righteousness of the weak. The latter use it to hoist themselves up above the "strong" (whom they can then look down upon as fallen sinners). Although Max Scheler, writing as a phenomenologist, counters Nietzsche's view of Christian morality, arguing that a merciful approach to the other can reflect an ethically beneficial intentionality, there is no room in either author's thinking for "demands" for equality. For both Nietzsche and Scheler, equality can be granted or given freely, but it cannot be fought for politically. Any such struggle would inevitably involve Ressentiment. Focusing in the final part of her essay on the present political and economic world climate, and more especially on the notion of "contagious weakness" as an economic argument for the post-2008 politics of austerity, Riou explores the dynamics of the relation between "demand" and "dissent". Contagious weakness is not just an economic notion; it is understood by Riou as a metaphorical undercurrent of economic discourse after 2008. Originating in theories of Ressentiment, it takes on a new and insidious resonance in the contemporary climate.

The dynamic of political protest and dissent is also to the fore in Caroline Mannweiler's essay on political reaction to "Stuttgart 21", a major infrastructural project involving the destruction of the historic Stuttgart railway station in order to facilitate more rapid rail travel in the region. This project, spearheaded by Chancellor Merkel's conservative federal-party colleagues at local state government level, dismissed not only the bitter protests by environmentalists and conservationists, but also an unprecedented level of public outrage from all sections of the socio-political spectrum. As Mannweiler shows, the manner in which the government and supporters of Stuttgart 21 attempted to discredit anti-project protesters drew on the trope of Ressentiment. Yet so too did the mediation process put in place by the authorities after the event in order to give both sides an opportunity to listen to one another. For what the transcriptions of this process highlight is an exhaustive, not to say exhausting, effort, closely followed by the public, to demonstrate on the part of the political authorities an apparent concern to move beyond the Ressentiment trope by allowing the two sides (the expert-supported local authorities and the counterexpert-supported protesters), to demonstrate a willingness not to pre-judge the other side's arguments as being motivated by Ressentiment, or as relying on presumptions of an a priori discursive, intellectual or politico-social superiority or inferiority. In this way, Mannweiler's painstaking analysis of the transformative potential of the mediation process shows not just the contemporary discursive power of the trope of Ressentiment, but more specifically its apparently preemptive role in establishing conditions of putative discursive equality. It also shows the way in which the mass media captured/communicated or failed to capture and communicate the full import of what the analysis of the transcripts reveals. More broadly, this essay raises questions about what is at stake in the neutralisation or apparent neutralisation of Ressentiment in a polarised context where one side (more powerful in political terms) must win or has already won and the other (less powerful in political terms) must lose or has already lost.

It is the almost dizzying, specular manipulation of the trope of Ressentiment that is studied in Dominique Jeannerod's essay, "Specular Ressentiment: San-Antonio, or the Art of Faking Resentment", which is focused on the figure of the writer and on the value of literature and of the literary institution, including literary criticism. San-Antonio (alias Frédéric Dard) is the (pseudonymous) name of the best-selling French writer of the twentieth-century; his one hundred and eighty-four crime fiction volumes centre on a detective narrator-protagonist/ writer of the same name. Dominique Jeannerod shows how, through an elaborate double-cross of (distorting) mirrors, the eponymous writer/detective deploys a real/fake Ressentiment based on an apparent envy and hatred of, and contempt for, the values and the style of the anointees of the literary establishment and above all of their anointers (the critics). In so doing, San-Antonio performs not just self-parody but also bravura pastiches both of condescending literary criticism and also of canonised literary authors. He imitates above all the style and posturing of the most acclaimed popular/literary cross-over or genre-bending French writer of all time, Louis-Ferdinand Céline. The principal message conveyed by this polyphonic scriptural ventriloquism is that the consummate art of San-Antonio transcends all the writing (including Céline's) that he is able to re-produce with unparalleled verbal vigour and pyrotechnics, but that he *transcends it critically rather than creatively*. In this way, what might be read as the subversive, transgressive, anti-hierarchical instrumentalisation of a real/fake Ressentiment towards the literary establishment could in fact be regarded as lending itself to recuperation for a conservative reinforcement not just of the value of literary criticism and discrimination, but also of the value of literary style as a recognisable and thereby imitable originality. What distinguishes San-Antonio's relationship both to other popular writers and to the crime novel genre, as well as to the distinctly literary writing that he mocks, is its staged Ressentiment.

What is at stake, in other words, is the inherent subordination of secondary discourse, whether pastiche, parody or criticism. Nowhere does San-Antonio's Ressentiment resound as loudly as in his relation to Céline, a consecrated literary author who had himself used the pose of the popular writer as a cover for his literary ambition and accomplishment. It reverberates in the wide gap that separates San-Antonio's commercially enviable facility for copying the corrosive Ressentiment expressed by the critically celebrated, but deeply unpopular and impoverished author, Céline, from the "real thing". The "real thing" is not, then, the Ressentiment that the wealthy, prolific and popular San-Antonio affects in relation to his non-consecration by the gate-keepers of literature, but rather the first-degree Ressentiment that he could quite conceivably feel as a writer whose style might have been (recognised as) just as literary (i.e. genre-transcending, singular, original) as that of Céline, but is not, and partly, if not entirely, because it is "after Céline".

Christine A. Knoop's essay on interdisciplinarity and on a particular instance of the latter, which she terms the "empirical humanities". Noting the extent to which humanities disciplines have come under immense political and economic pressure in recent years to justify their *raison d'être*, Knoop takes as her starting point the question regarding the potential contribution to literary study of science in general and of cognitive neuroscience in particular. What she probes more especially is the complicated moral boundary between criticism and Ressentiment in the discursive politics of one particular instance of interdisciplinarity. As Knoop pertinently observes, the current recessionary context in the US and in Europe, which has led to the closure or merging of entire literature and other humanities departments, means that the practitioners both of discrete disciplines and of interdisciplinarity are required not just to prove their productivity and their intellectual and social value, but also to position themselves politically in order to attract or to maintain their funding. In this highly competitive context, Ressentiment is, according to Knoop, a frequent cause of what she calls an "unwillingness to accept a pluralism of methods and/or opinions". Moreover, in a high-stakes game of critical and disciplinary hierarchies, it can happen that "the simple fact of *not* belonging to a group accused of methodological or theoretical naïveté is erroneously taken for proof of the academic superiority of one's own approach."

Continuing this discussion of Ressentiment in relation to the intrinsic value of academic work, Mary Gallagher reflects – in "Ressentiment and Dissensus: the Place of Critique in the Contemporary Academy" – on the distinction between critique and dissensus. She notes in particular the radically anti-critical configuration or formatting of the global university of the twenty-first century. Referring to the thinking of Jacques Rancière, Jean-François Lyotard and Michel Foucault and also to the work of Bill Readings and various other critics of the contemporary university, she discusses the distinction, but also the possible connections, between the roles of dissensus and critique in relation to the academy. The limits of criticism and even of critique are all too evident in the context of today's almost hermetically closed economy of knowledge. While criticism, critique and most especially, perhaps, self-critique have a role in correcting error and exposing untruth, an uncomfortable dissonance risks neutralising the value of critique when it is incorporated into, or recuperated for, a closed economy. If Ressentiment pushes critique towards its negative limits, that is towards closure and stasis, dissensus attracts it towards its positive horizon of openness and action. Although Foucault presents what he terms the "critical attitude" as a (public or civic as well as a private) good, describing it in moral terms as a "virtue", dissensus might offer a more effective "virtue" for the academy of our times, a critical virtue less likely to feed into the commodification, instrumentalisation and reification at work in the contemporary academic economy of knowledge. This essay tends, therefore, to conclude that dissensus, not least because of its non-contamination by negativity or reactivity, might offer the best chance of opening up, beyond dialectics, disruptive or at least interruptive and critical spaces of true academic freedom and responsibility. Unfortunately, however, dissensus cannot be manufactured, programmed or produced, although the conditions under which it becomes impossible can be readily identified.

Mary Gallagher
Paris, July 2014

The Question of Resentment in Western and Confucian Philosophy

Eric S. Nelson

1. Three Western Interpretations of Resentment[1]

First-person social experiences of resentment, shame, and "losing face" have not been the primary focus of Western moral thought which—as Friedrich Nietzsche argued—inclines toward stressing issues concerning conscience, guilt and responsibility. Notable exceptions to this tendency are three modern thinkers who interrogated resentment as a key dimension of ethical life: P. F. Strawson, Max Scheler, and Nietzsche. Due to their concern with negative reactive affects and the social dynamics constitutive of resentment, they provide an expedient starting-point for considering resentment in Confucian ethics. I proceed in this contribution from the temporally later Western thinkers to Confucian philosophers in order to illustrate how Confucian ethics offers a unique alternative understanding of resentment and of its role in self-cultivation and in the relationships between self and other.

In "Freedom and Resentment," P. F. Strawson maintained that resentment and other reactive affects are natural and original elements of the interpersonally constituted fabric of moral life: "the reactive feelings and attitudes ... belong to involvement or participation with others in inter-personal human rela-

---

1 | A different version of this paper was published as Eric S. Nelson, "The Question of Ressentiment in Nietzsche and Confucian Ethics", in: *Taiwan Journal of East Asian Studies*, Vol. 10, No. 1/19, (June 2013), pp. 17–51. References to the German edition of Nietzsche are to: *(KSA) Friedrich Nietzsche: Sämtliche Werke: Kritische Studienausgabe in 15 Bänden*, ed. Giorgio Colli and Mazzino Montinari, Berlin/München/New York 1980. I have relied on and modified the following translations of the *Analects*: Roger T. Ames and Henry Rosemont, Jr., New York: Random House 1998; Raymond Dawson, Oxford: Oxford University Press 2000; Charles Muller (http://www.acmuller.net/con-dao/analects.html); and Edward Slingerland, Indianapolis: Hackett 2003. Chinese quotations are from the Chinese Text Project: http://ctext.org/.

tionships."[2] Without affective reciprocal relations that matter to both parties, in which they are both invested and which thus can potentially evoke negative reactive feelings in the self against the other, we would not be in the realm of the normal attribution of agency and responsibility. We usually do not resent what is considered to be outside of the other's efficacy. Despite this limitation on what we can appropriately ascribe to others, in conspiracy theories and pathological emotional conditions, we resentfully feel we have been treated unfairly even though the perceived injustice was outside of anyone's actual power and choice.

Strawson describes how resentment is a normal reaction to the other's unfairness and indifference. Resentment is experienced as a demand that the self places upon the other, demanding her or his regard or good-will, whereas shame is experienced as the demand of the other placed on the self.[3] The example of resentment serves to establish how the first-person participant standpoint of ordinary moral life relies on internal motivations and justifications irreducible to a neutral third-person perspective. The complex psycho-social phenomenon of resentment proves the necessitarian account of moral agency to be insufficient while simultaneously revealing the inanity of the "obscure and panicky metaphysics of libertarianism."[4]

An objective third-person perspective attempts to bracket the participant perspective that encompasses resentment and gratitude, condemnation and forgiveness. This neutral impersonal attitude, associated with the overly theoretical viewpoint of determinism, would not include the negative and positive emotions that help form ordinary moral life. It would also not encompass the space of reasons that includes the consideration of what is rational and reasonable to do through arguing, quarreling, and reasoning with others. In the objective attitude, which for Strawson is a useful resource to adopt as a temporary stance depending on the situation, one does not reason with others insofar as they are others. Others are not participants from this intellectualised viewpoint; Strawson describes how they become the objectivised and depersonalised objects of social policy, management, training, assessment and treatment.[5] This claim indicates that resentment is as much a social-political issue as it is a moral psychological one.

---

2 | P. F. Strawson: "Freedom and Resentment," in: Strawson, *Freedom and Resentment*, London: Methuen & Co. 1974, p. 10. Compare Owen Flanagan, *The Problem Of The Soul: Two Visions of Mind and How to Reconcile Them*, New York: Basic Books 2008, p. 305. In addition to the interpersonal character of resentment described by Strawson, Flanagan stresses how negative emotions can be self-applied. But there is nothing in Strawson's argument concerning the social character of resentment that entails that it cannot be self-applied. The interpersonal and the personal are two aspects of the same process. Negative emotions do not function without the "self-regarding" first-person attitude according to Strawson; they are accordingly formed through our own personal application of other-oriented attitudes and social norms to ourselves.

3 | *Freedom and Resentment*, pp. 14–15.

4 | Ibid., pp. 24–25.

5 | Ibid., p. 9.

In his 1962 essay, Strawson did not examine questions of whether resentment is actually an elemental truth of human life, whether it is indeed normal or pathological, and whether and how resentment should be confronted within the interpersonal first and second-person perspective of agents. These issues concerning the psycho-social bio-politics of resentment troubled earlier philosophical discourses. To take another step back in time, the German phenomenologist Max Scheler contended in the early twentieth century that resentment is a basic problem of factical ethical life, although it should not be construed as a fundamental dimension of genuine ethical life.

Scheler rejected Kantian ethical formalism for the sake of a material and content-centered value-ethics, grounded in an anti-naturalistic philosophical anthropology and in the notion of a material *a priori*. Scheler modified a typical Neo-Kantian argumentative strategy in opposition to the hermeneutical life-philosophical emphasis on the immanent self-articulation and interpretation of life unfolded in the writings of Wilhelm Dilthey and Friedrich Nietzsche. Scheler concludes that facticity threatens and overthrows (*Umsturz*) the ideal values with which it should be contrasted and contested.

In *Ressentiment in the Formation of Morals* [*Das Ressentiment im Aufbau der Moralen*], first published in 1912, Scheler portrayed *ressentiment* as a pathological state of resentment, the potentiality for which varies according to the level of social-political equality and the stability of classes in society. In genuinely egalitarian societies or in stable class societies, i.e., in any society where persons accept their roles and places, there are fewer opportunities for pathologically resenting others in heightened states of envy, jealousy, vengefulness and spitefulness. *Ressentiment* should not be associated with Christianity, Scheler argued against Nietzsche, but with its negation and the negation of the spiritual in modern bourgeois societies. Such societies are characterised by both a relative—yet still deficient—equality and the relentless competition to be better than others and feel superiority over one's neighbours.

Despite the qualified roots of *ressentiment*, Scheler stressed the potential for broader epidemics: "Through its very origin, *ressentiment* is therefore chiefly confined to those who serve and are dominated at the moment, who fruitlessly resent the sting of authority. When it occurs elsewhere, it is either due to psychological contagion—and the spiritual venom of *ressentiment* is extremely contagious – or to the violent suppression of an impulse which subsequently revolts by 'embittering' and 'poisoning' the personality."[6]

Such a pathological psycho-social condition, which involves the fateful self-poisoning of the wounded mind, defies the basic moral character of humanity. Scheler remarked: "*Ressentiment* helps to subvert this eternal order in man's consciousness, to falsify its recognition, and to deflect its actualization."[7] In Scheler's account, accordingly, the facticity of *ressentiment* is the exception, and

---

6 | Max Scheler, *Ressentiment*, Milwaukee: Marquette University Press 1994, p. 48.

7 | Ibid., pp. 72–73.

the ideal exhibited in solidarity, love and mutual sympathy is normative. Scheler reverses Nietzsche's conclusion in the *Genealogy of Morals*. Approximating Kierkegaard's diagnosis of ordinary life as a spiritual sickness that calls for a transformative awakening to its absolute source in *Sickness unto Death*, Scheler concludes that it is the lack of the ultimate motive and object of action (that is, the divine) that generates the potential for radical *ressentiment*.

Scheler's conceptualisation of *ressentiment* was formulated in response to Nietzsche's earlier diagnosis of resentment as a socio-historically constituted yet basic element of ethical life. In Nietzsche's genealogy of the formation of morals and moral systems, the overcoming of resentment, revenge and the ostensibly negative emotional states taught in religion and morality is not identified with the realisation of a superior spiritual condition in relation to the eternal. The idea that one has overcome resentment, which Nietzsche recurrently attributed to the doctrines of universal Christian love and socialist solidarity, is depicted as the further fulfillment and primary form of destructive *ressentiment*. Christian *ressentiment* runs so deep that it shapes the anti-Christian resentment of Western modernity, as in Nietzsche's portrayal of the English psychologists who remain all too Christian in their enmity and rancour against Christianity.[8]

Nietzsche's conception of *ressentiment* encompasses much more than a deficiency of sympathy for the other and the psychologically morbid departure from the eternal depicted by Scheler. *Ressentiment* is, on the contrary, realised in the non-recognition of resentment, that is, in not recognising oneself as resentful and in perceiving others as motivated by a resentment that is not understood as informing one's own attitudes and actions. The first-person perspective stressed by Strawson and the hermeneutics of trust do not adequately confront the problems and pathologies of self-deception that are crucial to the hermeneutics of distrust at work in the accounts of Scheler and Nietzsche.

Whereas resentment always has a particular resented object and a specific content and reference, *ressentiment* is a condition that has been detached from particular experiences of resentment and definite resented persons, groups, or objects. Paradoxically, at first sight at least, Nietzsche claims that *ressentiment* is most characteristic of individuals and groups who believe they have overcome ordinary resentments. The simmering reactive psychophysical condition of *ressentiment*, according to Nietzsche, belongs to natures that lack the capacity to react and respond with ordinary active and reactive affects. *Ressentiment* is accordingly not the same as ordinary resentment.

Nietzsche scholars can obscure the relation between the two when they overemphasise their distinction, since *ressentiment* is related to resentment; it is a transformation of ordinary feelings of resentment into a complex emotional-cognitive state. Nor is *ressentiment* the same as revenge, which for both Nietzsche and the early-twentieth-century Nietzsche-influenced Chinese author Lǔ Xùn 魯迅

---

8 | Friedrich Nietzsche, *On the Genealogy of Morals*, transl. Walter Kaufmann and R. J. Hollingdale, New York: Vintage Books 1967, I.1. [*KSA* 5, p. 257.]

can be an expression of nobility.[9] In Nietzsche's portrayal, *Ressentiment* is a general state of vengefulness against this world and life itself. Nietzsche accordingly describes in the *Genealogy* how the "slave revolt in morality" reverses the high and low and aims at the negation of the other rather than the affirmation of the self. This revolt against the nobility and against loftiness of character originate in the incapacity for real revenge:

> the *ressentiment* of natures that are denied the true reaction, that of deeds, and compensate themselves with an imaginary revenge. While every noble morality develops from a triumphant affirmation of itself, slave morality from the outset says No to what is "outside," what is "different," what is "not itself"; and this No is its creative deed. [10]

The cultivation of an imaginary otherworldly revenge eventually culminates in real violence against others and, in Nietzsche's analysis, the destruction and annihilation of alterity.

To develop Nietzsche's argumentation in response to Scheler's objection, *ressentiment* remains operative in the consciousness of the eternal that does not recognise that it thinks and acts out of ordinary, all too human motivations. These motives, as Nietzsche shows in the *Genealogy of Morals*, are temporal and transient. Human motives are generated and determined by biological, historical and social forces and only secondarily formed by individual decision, rational agency, and ideal value.

In the *Genealogy of Morals*, Nietzsche diagnosed the *ressentiment* constitutive of conventional religion, morality and the politics of equality. The logic of reciprocal recognition, equal exchange and sacrifice of the one for the many requires and cultivates a reactive fear and envy of the other who must be tamed, disciplined and brought under control or rejected, excluded and eliminated as a hostile foreign power. The *ressentiment* of vengeful priests, their secularised heirs, and the manipulated masses provides the motivational basis for domination. Nietzsche contrasted this reactive yet cunning and skillful resentment with the lordly affirmation of the self in the immanence of its own desires and vitality of life. Nietzsche's ethics of self-affirmation is asymmetrical in prioritising the self of the other even as it undermines the reactive and calculative treatment of others. Noble self-affirmation does not live from negating the other. It affirms the other in an asymmetrical and non-calculative generosity and bounty born of its own excess and of that overflowing sense of self that Nietzsche compares in *Thus Spoke Zarathustra* to the bounteousness of natural phenomena such as the sun and water.[11]

---

9 | Compare Chiu-yee Cheung, Lu Xun, *The Chinese "gentle" Nietzsche*, Frankfurt/Main: Lang 2001 p. 45.

10 | F. Nietzsche, *Genealogy of Morals*, I.10. [*KSA* 5, p. 270.]

11 | On the different senses of naturalism and anti-naturalism in the development of Nietzsche's thought, see my paper Eric S. Nelson, "Naturalism and Anti-Naturalism in

Nietzsche is criticised as a radically anti-egalitarian and hierarchical thinker by proponents of standard conceptions of socio-political equality—for instance, Jürgen Habermas and Axel Honneth—and praised as the postmodern thinker of an alterity and difference which resist the relentless logic of identity and enmity.[12] In this context, it is sensible to question whether Nietzsche's historical analysis presupposes an objectivising stance that misses the internal or immanent character of interpersonal relations as described by Strawson, and whether it overthrows the reciprocity and mutuality of self and other required by Scheler's ethical vision.

2. Nietzsche and the Resentment of "Confucian China"

Nietzsche's argument that moralism and religiosity are the higher achievements of resentment informed his infrequent discussions of Confucius and of Chinese culture more generally. In the passage on the "improvers of humanity" in the *Twilight of the Idols*, Nietzsche interprets Confucius as a law-giver like other law-givers such as Manu, Plato, and the founders of the three monotheistic faiths. Confucius is presented in this context as yet another immoral moralist. He becomes a symbol of priestly power who never doubted his right to lie in order to regulate the masses and bring them to conformity through breeding and taming techniques:

> Neither Manu nor Plato nor Confucius nor the Jewish and Christian teachers have ever doubted their right to lie. They have not doubted that they had very different rights too. Expressed in a formula, one might say: all the means by which one has so far attempted to make mankind moral were through and through immoral.[13]

Confucius is also compared to the founders of political empires in an unpublished note from 1885. Nietzsche insists that "great artists of government" (*Regierungskünstler*) and power from Confucius to Napoleon use noble lies and moralistic deception to pacify the masses through physiological-spiritual programs of "spiritual enlightenment":

> Spiritual enlightenment is an infallible means for making humans unsure, weaker in will, so they are more in need of company and support—in short, for developing the herd animal in humans. Therefore all great artists of

---

Nietzsche." *Archives of the History of Philosophy and of Social Thought*, Volume 58, (2013), pp. 213–227.

12 | I consider alterity and asymmetry in Confucian ethics from a different perspective in Eric S. Nelson, "Levinas and Early Confucian Ethics: Religion, Rituality, and the Sources of Morality", in: *Levinas Studies*, Vol. 4, ed. Jeffrey Bloechl, Pittsburgh: Duquesne University Press 2009, pp. 177–207.

13 | Friedrich Nietzsche, *Twilight of the Idols*, Harmondsworth: Penguin 1990, vii, 5. [Nietzsche, *KSA* 6, p. 102.]

government so far (Confucius in China, the imperium Romanum, Napoleon, the papacy at the time when it took an interest in power and not merely in the world), in the places where the dominant instincts have culminated so far, also employed spiritual enlightenment—at least let it have its way (like the popes of the Renaissance). The self-deception of the masses concerning this point, e.g., in every democracy, is extremely valuable: making humans smaller and more governable is desired as 'progress'![14]

Nietzsche interpreted China, which he described as "a country where large-scale discontentment and the capacity for change became extinct centuries ago," through the prism of a construction of enlightened power that destroys all that is individual and unique in reducing life to a banal equality and happiness.[15]

Akin to Strawson's less dramatic argument about the role of resentment in normal interpersonal life, Nietzsche is arguing that the apparent absence of resentment is in fact more problematic than its active or reactive presence. However, Nietzsche goes further than Strawson to the extent that the objective stance is not a justifiable—if temporary—departure from the participant perspective. He sees it as the self-deceptive illusion of not having a perspective and not being a participant. Such a state is the result of discipline and training and the bundling and redoubling of ordinary resentments.

Further, altruistic attitudes are genealogically interpreted as dispositions that are more deeply motivated by *ressentiment*. In this setting, Nietzsche constructs and construes "Confucius" and "China" as warnings to Europe about the last fruits of resentment, that is to say, of a condition where resentment and the reactive affects appear to have been tamed and trained. But the spiritual and enlightened conquest of these affects has not led to their overcoming. They are intensified and poisoned in becoming the invisible—and hence all the more powerful—motives operating behind the face of tranquility, equanimity and altruism.

Playing with the Chinese expression xiǎoxīn 小心 ("be careful"; taken too literally, "small heart"), Nietzsche depicted "late civilizations"—such as that of the modern European who could only be perceived as distasteful and dwarfish by an ancient Greek—as affecting a "smallness of heart."[16] Nietzsche maintained that the altruistic goodness and spiritual awakening promoted by Confucius and the Buddha had reduced the Chinese to passivity and to an abject equality under an all-powerful despot, arguing that Europe faced a similar fate from its forces of political and spiritual enlightenment that "might easily establish Chinese con-

---

14 | Friedrich Nietzsche, *The Will to Power*, New York: Vintage Books 1968, 129 (1885). Friedrich Nietzsche, [KSA 11, p. 570.]

15 | Friedrich Nietzsche, *The Gay Science: With a Prelude in German Rhymes and an Appendix of Songs*, Cambridge: Cambridge University Press 2001, I. 24, p. 49. [KSA 3, p. 399.]

16 | Friedrich Nietzsche, *Beyond Good and Evil: Prelude to a Philosophy of the Future*, trans. Walter Kaufmann, New York: Vintage Books, 1966 p. 267. [KSA 5, pp. 220–221.]

ditions and a Chinese 'happiness.'"[17] In *Ecce Homo*, the self-denial and self-sacrifice distinctive of altruistic ethics is said to "deprive existence of its great character and would castrate men and reduce them to the level of desiccated Chinese stagnation."[18]

China and the Chinese are peripheral to Nietzsche's concerns, as he usually employs Indian and Buddhist examples in his works. They move closer to the center—if not of course into the center itself—of Nietzsche's geopolitics, which is focused on the Christian-Jewish world, when he branded the Chinese, German, and Jewish peoples as three examples of "priestly peoples" in the *Genealogy of Morals*.[19] In the context of his polemic against "decadence" characterised by *ressentiment*, and despite their difference in ability and rank, Nietzsche described them as "peoples with similar talents." Here Nietzsche is again describing a generalised priestly character or type. They are three different exemplars of "priestly nations" dominated by *ressentiment*. In most of his discussions of China, however, Nietzsche continues to use the language of ahistorical stasis and "Oriental" despotism developed by earlier German thinkers such as Kant and Hegel.

Granting that the validity of Nietzsche's assessment of Confucius is questionable, we should begin to appreciate the ambivalence at work in Nietzsche's dialectic of power and resentment. Nietzsche is commonly thought to be a thinker of power and even at times—although this is noticeably incorrect—an apologetic defender of established powers. In these passages, Nietzsche reveals existing power to be constituted and its constitution to rest in deception, illusion and—in many cases—revenge and resentment. The masses, whose bodies have been shaped by discipline and whose minds have been manipulated by their own fears and feelings of resentment, become passive instruments of this formation and projection of power.

Resentment appears as a complex point of mediation in ethical life in that it constitutes both power and weakness. Resentment grows from impotence and inability and remains operational through *ressentiment* even when it has assumed power. It is a misreading to conclude that power is necessarily noble in Nietzsche. On the contrary, power can be structured by, and an expression of, *ressentiment*. Such power poisons the self which is unable to use it freely and generously, as it takes on pathological forms oppressive to the self as well as to others. Nietzsche repeatedly confronts this type of power that he stylises as priestly power.[20] It is born of real suffering and trauma and poisons the wound

---

17 | F. Nietzsche, *The Gay Science*, I. 24, p. 49. [*KSA* 3, p. 399.]

18 | Friedrich Nietzsche, *Ecce Homo*, trans. Walter Kaufmann, New York: Random House 1967, IV.4. [*KSA* 6, p. 369.]

19 | "By contrast [with the Romans], the Jews were a priestly nation of *ressentiment* par excellence, possessing an unparalleled genius for popular morality: compare peoples with similar talents, such as the Chinese or the Germans, with the Jews, and you will realize who are first rate and who are fifth." *Genealogy of Morals*, I.16. [*KSA* 5, p. 286.]

20 | See Eric S. Nelson, "Priestly Power and Damaged Life in Nietzsche and Adorno",

in order to survive. Nevertheless, despite their being evident in only a few rare historical moments, Nietzsche held on to the hope that freedom and nobility are accomplished in the genuine exercise of power. The genuine feeling of power in the self is contrasted with the myths and idols of the negation of power that signify its hidden and pathological exercise.

3. Resentment, Recognition, and Ethical Life in the Analects

One of the most basic issues of ethical life appears to be the complex feeling of resentment. It has two dimensions: (1) the lack of acknowledgment and recognition from others and (2) how to cope with feelings of resentment in oneself and others. Scheler emphasises transcending these feelings of resentment through positive feelings of empathy and sympathy, even though Nietzsche identifies this kind of emotional transformation as a more deeply entrenched and poisonous form of resentment that he designates with the French word *ressentiment*. The emotional complex designated by *ressentiment* is a kind of character and thus differs from ordinary feelings of resentment. Nietzsche's critique of *ressentiment* could be potentially applied to the *Analects* (Lúnyǔ 論語), a diverse fragmentary compilation that is attributed to Kǒngzǐ (孔子), as Lǔ Xùn suggested in the spirit of Nietzsche. Lǔ Xùn compared the everyday practice of *Confucian* values to cannibalism in "A Madman's Diary" (*Kuángrén Rìjì* 狂人日記), one of his most influential short stories and—like "The True Story of Ah Q" (Ā Q Zhèngzhuàn 阿Q正傳)—a story of a culture dominated by *ressentiment*.[21]

Nietzsche and Lǔ Xùn are certainly correct that a particular understanding and institutionalisation of Confucian morality can lead to weakened and pathological conditions of resentful passivity in which the self is burdened by all the cares and obligations of paternal, familial and communal expectations. However, the story of "Confucian *ressentiment*" told by Nietzsche and Lǔ Xùn becomes more complicated if we turn to the *Analects* and the Confucian classics. Several significant passages propose the necessity of countering various reactive feelings of resentment. In the very first lines of the *Analects*, Confucius is recorded as asserting:

學而時習之, 不亦說乎。有朋自遠方來, 不亦樂乎。人不知而不慍, 不亦君子乎。

To learn something and practice it; is this not a pleasure? To have friends come from afar; is this not a delight? Not to be resentful (yùn 慍) at anoth-

---

in: Nietzsche, *Philosoph der Kultur(en)?/Philosopher of Culture?* Ed. Andreas Urs Sommer, Berlin: Walter de Gruyter 2008, pp. 349–356.

21 | There is a rich and varied literature concerning Lǔ Xùn, Nietzsche, and *ressentiment*; for example, see Cheung: *Lu Xun, The Chinese "gentle" Nietzsche*, p. 59; Kirk A. Denton, *The Problematic of Self in Modern Chinese Literature: Hu Feng and Lu Ling*, Cambridge: Cambridge University Press 1998, p. 58; Peter Button, *Configurations of the Real in Chinese Literary and Aesthetic Modernity*, Leiden: Brill Press 2009, pp. 98–99.

er's failure to recognize (bùzhī 不知) one, is this not to be a gentleman (jūnzǐ 君子)?[22]

In *Analects* 1.1, being noble, or ethically exemplary, is explicitly linked with not being yùn 慍, which has been translated as indignant, feeling hurt, to be bothered, and resentful. This feeling of resentment is linked to bùzhī 不知, which means that the other does not "know" one, implying the other's lack or denial of recognition and appreciation. The conception that ethical exemplarity requires responding to the absence or privation of something significant for oneself from the other without resentment is likewise found in 1.16:

不患人之不己知，患不知人也。

I do not worry (huàn 患) about not being recognized.
I worry (huàn 患) about not recognizing (bùzhī 不知) others.[23]

In this passage, recognition is again the occasion for another type of worry that is not typically directly translatable as resentment. Huàn 患 can mean to suffer from (illness, misfortune, disease), to be troubled by, or—as possible in its first occurrence—something very much like resentment. In this passage, huàn 患 indicates an inappropriate resentment in its first use and an appropriate state of being worried in its second use.

In Mencius 4B28.7, huàn 患 operates as a type of anxiousness contrasted with yōu 憂, which has an overlapping yet divergent range of meanings: anxiety, worry, being bereft, and sorrow. Mencius (*Mèngzǐ* 孟子) distinguishes having anxieties and perturbed emotional states from the exemplary person's moral concern for benevolence and propriety that is a task of a lifetime.[24] Benevolence (rén 仁), as Master Zēng 曾子 stated in the *Analects*, is a heavy burden that ends only with death.[25] The path of virtue is a difficult undertaking that is pursued without anxieties or resentment against heaven and humans.

Resentment is an anxiety-provoking affliction bound up with processes of misrecognition or the perception of a lack of recognition. Early Confucian texts indicate an asymmetrical strategy of dismantling compounds of resentment by minimising what is expected from others while intensifying what one expects of oneself. Instead of focusing on what others ostensibly owe one, and the slights one might have received from this due regard not being given, we are asked to turn our attention to whether and how we are recognising the other.

In *Analects* 1.16, the asymmetrical priority of the other over the self is upheld. This asymmetry is not a pure self-sacrifice or self-negation; nor is it the asymmetry of the self and God that concerns Kierkegaard and Levinas. Asymmetry is

---

22 | *Analects*, 1.1.

23 | *Analects*, 1.16.

24 | Mencius 4B28.7. *Mengzi: with selections from traditional commentaries*, trans. Bryan W. Van Norden, Indianapolis: Hackett 2008, p. 112.

25 | *Analects*, 8.7.

conceived as the extension and broadening of the self in the context of its ethical self-concern and self-cultivation. The give and take, the rituals and spontaneous moments of everyday ethical life are not motivated by pure selflessness and otherness. The vitality and motivation of moral life arises from the self being concerned for itself and its ethical character in its relations with and concern for others. It is not through the "slave-morality" of negating ordinary desires and reactive affects that the ethical is achieved.

As Strawson and the early Confucians each realise in their own way, it is in effect these ordinary non-heroic and mundane motives that shape and encourage one's becoming an ethical self conceived of as a responsible participant in the everyday life of the family and community. But where Strawson emphasised the role of reactive feelings in the first-person participant perspective as necessary to moral life, Confucians prioritise transforming reactive affects within the participant perspective without appealing to notions of a third-person neutrality, a God's-eye transcendent perspective, or a contextless objective point of view from nowhere.

Anglo-American moral philosophers, such as Strawson and Bernard Williams, have rejected the intellectualism of Kantian deontological and consequentialist moral theory. They argue that intellectualist moral theories require inappropriately distancing the agent from her or his emotional life. Owen Flanagan notes in "Destructive Emotions" how self-transformation through structuring one's cognitions and affects, including transfiguring the emotions, is not only a basic characteristic of Eastern ethics but of traditions of moral wisdom.[26] In Flanagan's analysis of Buddhist moral psychology and in Confucianism, working through and eliminating negative emotions in cognitive-affective restructuring is not alienation from unchangeable "natural" states. Receptively working with one's emotions belongs to the dynamic of moral wisdom itself.[27]

A third word associated with sentiments of resentment is evident in passages concerning one's attitude toward one's parents and the virtuous brothers Bóyí (伯夷) and Shūqí (叔齐).[28] 怨 yuàn means to blame, complain, and resent and Confucius is portrayed as associating the absence of the feeling of resentment with benevolence or humaneness (rén 仁) itself. In *Analects* 7.15, it is said that the two brothers did not feel resentment (yuàn 怨) but: "They sought and obtained humaneness, what would they resent?" In 5:23, it is said that they "did not recall old grievances, and so there was little resentment (yuàn 怨) against them." A fourth less commonly used term in the classical literature is fèn 愤. It also shares

---

26 | Owen Flanagan, "Destructive Emotions", in: *Consciousness and Emotions*, 1, (2) 2000, p. 277.

27 | Also compare his discussion of resentment (Sanskrit: *dvesha*, Pali: *dosa*, often translated more generally as "aversion") in the context of the Buddhist account of mental afflictions or negative emotions (Sanskrit: *klesha*, Pali: *kilesa*) in Owen Flanagan, *The Bodhisattva's Brain: Buddhism Naturalized*, Cambridge: MIT Press 2011, pp. 21, 105.

28 | Respectively, *Analects*, 4.18 and 5:23, 7.15.

this sense of not angering others or of not becoming the cause of resentment and enmity in others.

This general concern is interpreted ethically in the distinction between gratitude and resentment in the dàoshù 道術 chapter of the "New Writings" (Xīnshū 新書). This political treatise by the early Han dynasty scholar Jiǎ Yì 賈誼 (200– 168 BC) advocates the regulation of classes in society through the principle of benevolence: "If there is an immanent order to practicing virtue it is deserving gratitude; to reverse deserving gratitude is to cause resentment (yuàn 怨)."²⁹

Confucius describes how lower forms of conduct that cause resentment in others can be avoided by expecting much of oneself and little of others.³⁰ The ethical concern with not producing and furthering resentment in the other is not adequately elucidated in Nietzsche's genealogy of how reactive emotions have structured and deformed ethical life. Passages such as *Analects* 5.23 illustrate how action for the other, done out of what Scheler would have described as sympathy, is a basic strategy for reducing resentfulness against others and within oneself.

The strategy of a self-interestedness oriented towards the other, conceived as conjoined and complementary rather than as irreconcilable contraries in early Confucian ethics, introduces a modification to how resentment should be conceptualised in contrast to the Western either-or between selfishness and selflessness. According to this interpretation, Confucian ethics suggests that reducing resentment in others reduces its being turned against oneself by others. In the image of "selling resentment" as "buying disaster," the ethical is conjoined with pragmatic considerations. Distinguishing these two dimensions, the idea is that engaging in this social interactive process of undermining the causes of resentment would accomplish more than pragmatically decreasing resentment against oneself. It would, furthermore, undo the feverish state of resentment in oneself. Undoing resentment is therefore a shared social project instead of the romantic task of the heroic, isolated, noble individual.

4. Confucius contra Nietzsche?

One could well provide reasons for the positive role of resentment in social life or for an equality of strength that is articulated through the affirmation of the nobility and generosity of the self. Both could be strategies for modifying Nietzsche's genealogical critique of morality. A different strategy is suggested by the analysis of resentment developed in the *Analects*.

Nietzsche distinguishes two different ideals of character: the reactive resentful character and the affirmative lordly one. The early rú 儒 or "Confucian" authors of the *Analects* attributed to Kǒngzǐ likewise interpreted the distinction between the noble person (jūnzǐ 君子) and the petty person (xiǎorén 小人),

---

29 | "施行得理謂之德反德爲怨"; Xingguo Wang: *Jia Yi ping zhuan*, Nanjing: Nanjing da xue chu ban she 1992, p. 228.

30 | *Analects*, 15.15.

the "small person" who is unable to exhibit "smallness of heart," in light of the question of resentment. The petty or ignoble person is portrayed as resenting being kept at a distance. The petty act out of a small-minded self-interest and mean-spirited feelings of resentment towards others in an anxious and insecure self-centered and partisan search for profits, favours, comforts and accolades. As the *Great Learning* (*Dàxué* 大學) reconfirms, contrasting the path of resentment with that of kindness and tolerance, animosity and resentment undermine the capacity to achieve a straightness of mind and wholeness of character.[31]

The authors of the *Analects* recognised the pervasiveness of resentment under certain conditions and the ethical requirement to challenge it both within oneself (e.g., not being resentful) and in relation to others (e.g., not engendering resentment in others in personal life and in government). Nietzsche did not recognise the latter as being part of the noble character, yet this is emphasised in the Confucian understanding of resentment and related affects, some of which are worthy of praise such as indignation against injustice and viciousness, an indignation that is designated by a variety of terms: yùn 慍 (to be indignant, to feel hurt or discontented by), yuàn 怨 (to blame, to complain of), fèn 憤 (to be indignant or angered), and huàn 患 and yōu 憂 (to suffer, be worried or troubled by).

Undoing resentment in oneself as well as in others is a primary element of becoming a gentleman, who, as Mencius notes, does not resent heaven or humans, and genuinely noble in the ethical sense for Kǒngzǐ, in contrast with the petty person fixated on his or her own concerns. This emphasis on the self accordingly should be part of a well-rounded account of undoing resentment. Recognition of the asymmetry necessary for letting go of resentment can be seen in *Analects* 1.1 and 1.16. To this extent, early Confucian literati demonstrate a more nuanced and realistic moral psychology of resentment as well as the ethical self-cultivation and self-rectification necessary for dismantling resentment and achieving a condition of humaneness (rén 仁).

The early Confucian model of self-affirmation through cognitive-affective self-rectification suggests an alternative to Scheler's appeal to the eternal and to Nietzsche's underestimation of the ethics of the other. Self-affirmation does not demand the negation of the other. It leads to a cultivation of the self that involves confronting one's own resentment, which is tied up with a narrow self-concern and egoism that expresses a limited or small conception of the self as well as an exaggerated sense of one's merits, such that one can act for others without necessitating the same in the calculating expectation of exchange.

The Confucian ethical point of view relies on the reciprocity (shù 恕) of seeing the other as being analogous to oneself. This is not, however, the symmetry of a conditional exchange. An ethical claim is perceived as being asymmetrically made upon oneself independent of one's own claim upon the other and thus does not entail the symmetry that reduces the other to oneself and of the self at not

---

31 | See particularly sections 7 and 10, Ta Hsüeh and Chung Yung, *The Highest Order of Cultivation and on the Practice of the Mean*, trans. Andrew Plaks, London: Penguin 2003, pp. 11, 17–18.

being treated equally by the other. Analogy is in this setting not identity, given the importance of making distinctions in moral judgment and given also the asymmetries operative in interpersonal human relations.

The asymmetrical and proportional character of the ethical signifies the impossibility of expecting of others the same as what one expects of oneself and of experiencing this ethical demand without resentment. Thus, to expect and demand more of oneself than of others, such that the other's lack of recognition and appreciation is not perceived as a justification of one's own lack. Indeed, more than this, it brings forth the asymmetrical demand that one recognise the other regardless of whether the other recognises oneself. Even if the logic of reciprocal and equal exchange naturally flows into resentment against others, the asymmetry in the early Confucian articulation of mutuality (shù 恕)—a notion in which sympathy and kindness toward the other come to be accentuated rather than a pragmatic instrumental exchange—turns questions of resentment and responsibility back upon oneself:

不患無位, 患所以立; 不患莫己知, 求爲可知也。

I do not resent being unrecognized; I seek to be fit to be recognized.[32]

The project of self-cultivation in the *Analects* encompasses resisting reactive feelings in the self even as it calls for asymmetrically recognising the difficulty of not having such reactive feelings under challenging life-conditions. We are thus told that: "To be poor without resentment (yuàn 怨) is difficult. To be rich without arrogance is easy."[33] Nonetheless, despite the relative ease and difficulty involved, the wealthy are more likely to be arrogant than the poor resentful in the Confucian understanding. The powerful fail to recognise and show reverence for the weak and destitute, which reveals a pettiness and lack of appropriate ethical self-cultivation.

The "petty person" is small by faulting and blaming others whereas the exemplary person reflectively turns blame into an opportunity for self-examination. "Pettiness" reveals itself to be a moral rather than a class designation in the *Analects* to the extent that it signifies the person who should know and do better and yet does not. In a claim further developed in the *Mencius*, the asymmetry of benevolence implies that the ordinary person's resentment should not be judged and criticised in the same way as the person who acts out of resentment and pettiness despite enjoying more of the advantages of life. Contrary to existing conservative discourses of resentment, early Confucian ethics is more concerned with the resentment of the rich and the powerful than with that of the poor and the weak who deserve benevolence and equity rather than blame, condemnation, and the suffering too often inflicted upon them.

---

32 | *Analects*, 4.14.

33 | *Analects*, 14.10.

5. Is the Ethical the Ultimate Form of Ressentiment?

According to Nietzsche, in the *Genealogy of Morals*, what is conventionally conceived to be moral and the highest good is in fact lowly and only the ultimate
realisation of *ressentiment*. Indeed, impartial and universalised love is the highest fulfillment of *ressentiment*. This objection, despite Nietzsche's own understanding of Confucius, misses the point of early Confucian discourses insofar
as they reject Mohist doctrines of an impartial universal love as insufficient
for caring for others and for oneself. The universal ethical point of view or a
completely altruistic moral perspective is an impossible ideal that is detrimental to ethical life that begins with family, friends, and neighbours rather than
universally equal persons. We see in the *Mencius* examples of how it is a moral
ideal that cannot be performatively put into practice without falling into either
contradictions or moralistic fanaticism. Early Confucian ethics offers a robust
rationale for the cultivation of an asymmetrical and graded humaneness in contrast with an undifferentiating objective stance or an equalising global feeling of
love or sympathy. Impartiality need not entail neutrality, since it requires being
partial towards those for whom one has greater responsibility.

Ethical agency presupposes affectively grounded yet reflective processes of
discernment and judgement. The ethical agent cultivates her or his abilities to
make distinctions about merit, character and the significance of relative bonds
of friendship, filiality, family and familiarity. Confucian texts such as the *Classic
of Familial Reverence* (*Xiàojīng* 孝經) stress the asymmetrical responsibilities of
parents to children, the old to the young, the powerful to the weak, and the
wealthy to the poor. In its opening chapter, familial reverence is described as
the root of education and remembrance of others as orientating self-cultivation
(xiūshēn 修身).[34] Familial reverence, the medium of moral life and its cultivation,
accordingly does not aim at mere control and subordination. Its purpose is to pre-
pare children for becoming autonomous and socially responsible moral agents
who have a sense of their own individual moral life.[35]

Scheler rejected Nietzsche's thesis of the ascetic nature of altruism, distinguishing genuine sacrifice for the other from the domination of the other that
occurs in the name of a higher good that is in reality born of *ressentiment*. Scheler
accordingly claims that in his work on *ressentiment*: "I pointed out that it is precisely this aspect of true sacrifice which distinguishes true asceticism from the
illusory asceticism of *ressentiment*."[36] The distinction between appropriate and
inappropriate self-sacrifice reflects Scheler's strategy of differentiating a genuine

---

34 | Xiaojing, ch. 4; *The Chinese Classic of Family Reverence: A Philosophical Translation
of the Xiaojing*, trans. Henry Rosemont and Roger T. Ames, Honolulu: University of
Hawai'i Press 2009, p. 107.

35 | Compare Paul R. Goldin, *Confucianism*, Durham: Acumen 2011, p. 35.

36 | Max Scheler. *Formalism in Ethics and non-formal Ethics of Values*, Evanston: North-
western University Press 1985, p. 231.

form of ideal values that would evade Nietzsche's critical suspicions. This escape, however, presupposes that which Nietzsche has placed in doubt: a transcendent realm of ideal spiritual values and the eternal.

A different strategy to those of Scheler and Nietzsche is indicated in the early Confucian discourse of resentment. This involves cultivating the self in the context of the real psychological motives of action. The lack of magnanimity associated with resentment, for instance, is not overcome by being negated and transcended in order to realise a superior state of being. It is rather recognised and confronted within the very workings of the self. In early Confucian philosophy, ethical reflection and judgement have need of a realistic yet ethically oriented sense of human psychology and anthropology in order for the ethical to be enacted and practiced. Observing, listening and learning from others becomes central to ethically interacting with others and cultivating one's own disposition. The late Eastern Han dynasty philosopher Xú Gàn 徐幹 articulated in his *Balanced Discourses* (Zhònglùn 中論) how sociability—listening to others and attuning one's feelings in relation to others—furthers and constitutes wisdom.[37]

It is better to cause resentment in others than to do wrong, such as—in an example in the biaoji 表記 chapter of the *Book of Rites* (Lǐjì 禮記)—causing resentment by refusing to make a promise that cannot be fulfilled. Wisdom includes not being an unnecessary cause of the other's resentment. This wisdom extends to the art of government that needs action while minimising "animosity and resentment."[38] It encompasses even the king's ability to govern. Mencius, as we have seen, and Xúnzǐ 荀子 portray how the king's rule is destabilised by permitting the resentments of the people and other kings to flourish. The festering of resentment eats away at, and dissolves, ethical life. The destruction of the ethical brings disaster upon families, communities and society.

The Confucian concern with counteracting and lessening reactive feelings in others, and with not provoking such feelings, is utilised in Confucian arguments for the necessity of ritual, music and poetry for moral life. The purpose of this is to maintain the fabric of everyday life and stable government. These practices of ritual, music and poetry are not secondary ornamental considerations, as they instruct and orient agents, helping them to regulate their emotions appropriately. The rituals of everyday interactions and ritual propriety (lǐ 禮) accomplish much more than a regulation of the emotions. They emancipate the self from its narrowness and place it into the fullness of life in all of its dimensions.

The repeatedly stated esteem of Confucius for the *Book of Odes* (Shī Jīng 詩經) is centered in an appeal to their function in promoting ethical self-cultivation and balancing nature and nurture. The classic songs of Zhōu 周 do not serve to conservatively reinforce the conformity of traditional tastes. Poetry and music join one with others and with the self, allowing for the creative appropriation of contextual relationships. The odes teach sociality and the art of sociability; they

---

37 | Xu Gan, *Balanced Discourses: A Bilingual Edition*, trans. John Makeham, Beijing and New Haven: Foreign Language Press and Yale University Press 2002, p. 7.

38 | *Xiaojing*, ch. 1; p. 105.

promote self-contemplation and reveal how to regulate feelings of resentment (yuàn 怨).[39]

Confucian ethics requires confronting self-deception and false consciousness with honesty and straightforwardness of mind. It calls for honesty with oneself and others and for a recognition of one's own resentment rather than its concealment, something which also concerned Nietzsche. The emphasis is on not feigning a moral condition one does not understand. In *Analects* 5.25, Confucius is said to explain:

巧言, 令色, 足恭, 左丘明恥之, 丘亦恥之。匿怨而友其人, 左丘明恥之, 丘亦恥之。

Clever words, a pretentious appearance, and excessive courtesy: Zuǒ Qiūmíng found them shameful, and I also find them shameful. Concealing resentment (yuàn 怨) and befriending the person resented (yuàn 怨): Zuǒ Qiūmíng found them shameful, and I also find them shameful.[40]

The Confucian critique of flattery and obsequiousness, as in *Analects* 1:15 and 2:24, and the promotion of a genuineness of feeling, straightforwardness of mind, and individual constancy in the face of social pressures point toward a resonance between the ethics of nobleness in the texts of Nietzsche and early Confucianism. James S. Hans has argued that both appreciate the reality and mechanisms of resentment in ordinary moral life. Neither employs guilt—the resentment against resentment—in a futile and toxic attempt to cure it and to better humanity through external discipline and internal self-negation.[41] Both rely on their own variety of individual and personal self-cultivation, a project that encompasses emotion and reason. There is good reason not to go as far as Hans' assertion that each practice of individuation occurs in an "aesthetic context without ground", since there is no existential abyss in Confucian thought and self-cultivation is more than aesthetic. Rather, cultivation occurs in, and responds to, a web of aesthetic, ethical and psychological conditions and claims.[42]

Nietzsche and early Confucian thought both highlight the self-cultivation of genuineness and generosity stemming from self-affirmation and both reject motivations formed by the negation of the other. They diverge insofar as Nietzsche performatively and evocatively focuses our concern on our own individuality in opposition to social conventions and pragmatic accommodations, whereas Confucians demonstrate how social rituals and conventions are a principal vehicle of ethical individuation rather than being mere conformity or a prudential self-betrayal.

---

39 | *Analects*, 17.8.

40 | *Analects*, 5.25.

41 | James S. Hans, *Contextual Authority and Aesthetic Truth*, Albany: State University of New York Press 1992, p. 337.

42 | Ibid., p. 337.

It might be argued in response to such a Confucian critique of Nietzsche that Nietzsche highlights the non-calculative generosity of the cultivated noble self. For example, Nietzsche's Zarathustra is an exemplar of the practice of self-cultivation (*Bildung*) that develops the highest bestowing virtue, which naturally and generously pours forth its gifts like the sun, without any expectation of return or exchange. There are of course many passages in praise of self-overflowing virtue in Nietzsche's works, and such virtue is a key element of Nietzschean self-cultivation.[43] Nonetheless, Nietzschean virtues always proceed from the self to the other without the Confucian concern with, or recognition of, the asymmetrical mutuality (shù 恕) of self and other in which ethics also proceeds from the other to the self.

Nietzschean virtues of friendship and generosity are arguably akin to Confucian shù 恕 in sharing with others without calculation or an instrumental expectation of receiving something in return. They diverge from a Confucian perspective insofar as Nietzsche does not consider as adequately articulate the "push" or extension (tuī 推) that requires seeing and interpreting oneself from the other's perspective and extending one's responsiveness to widening circles of beings from the family to humanity and to the universe itself in the Neo-Confucian interpretation of Mèngzǐ's heart-mind. The non-calculating and incalculable reciprocity (shù 恕) between self and other is a basic feature of Confucian ethics that makes it a significant alternative to Western ethical models.

We can still find traces of the early Confucian discourse of recognition and resentment in later Neo-Confucian texts that reconfirm the affinity and difference between the asymmetrical sociality of Confucian ethics and the asymmetrical individualism of Nietzschean ethics. Wáng Yángmíng 王陽明, for instance, elucidates the idea of reciprocal reproof without causing resentment in oneself or others in his "Encouraging Goodness through Reproof." The "way of friends" is the social realisation of the good. It signifies both accepting reproof from others without feeling resentment towards them, since they are our best teachers, and moving others to improve themselves without fault-finding and without making them feel shame and resentment.[44]

6. Confucian Ethics and the Politics of Resentment

In the early Confucian tradition of moral reflection, resentment is overcome through recognition. To know the self undermines negative affects against others and the course of "heaven" (tiān 天, which should be understood as signifying something closer to "nature" than to a spiritual realm). Xúnzǐ accordingly stated:

---

43 | See, for instance, Friedrich Nietzsche, *Human, All Too Human: A Book for Free Spirits,* trans. R. J. Hollingdale, Cambridge: Cambridge University Press 1996, sections 376 and 587.

44 | Philip J. Ivanhoe, *Readings from the Lu-Wang School of Neo-Confucianism,* Indianapolis: Hackett 2009, p. 176.

自知者不怨人，知命者不怨天；怨人者窮，怨天者無志。失之己，反之人，
豈不迂乎哉！

Those who recognize (zhī) themselves do not resent (yuàn) others; those
who recognize fate do not resent heaven. Those who resent others are bound
to fail; those who resent heaven do not learn from experience.[45]

In contrast to standard interpretations of Nietzsche's philosophy, early Confucian
thinking overcomes resentment through the ethical perspective of acting for
the sake of others while examining oneself in order to achieve self-recognition.
There are appeals to "heaven" (tiān 天) in early Confucian writings, such as
Xúnzǐ's quoted above. Such addresses do not appeal to an otherworldly transcendence or eternity but rely on the immanent course and order of the world.

Scheler amended his philosophical anthropology with its emergent levels of
the organic with a transcendent appeal to metaphysics and religion in order to
introduce and justify his vision of personalism. Confucian ethics accomplishes
in an earthy, immanent and more modest manner what Western religious thinkers, such as Scheler, in his appeal to the eternal, require of the transcendent and
eternal.[46] Confucian ethics offers a philosophical framework for an immanent
ethics of the other, for an altruism that is rooted in the moral feelings of the self
and in the reformation rather than the rejection of the natural and social-histor-
ical forces that condition and shape ethical reality.

Historically, the *rú* tradition has been predominantly anti-egalitarian, hierarchical and traditionalist. Nonetheless, there are also morally-oriented reformist
tendencies that prioritise the well-being of others and the people. Such tendencies are apparent in the *Analects*. For instance, prioritising the ethical while still
connecting it with the pragmatic and instrumental, Confucius is said to remark:
"If there is equality, there will be no poverty; where there is peace, there is no
lack of population."[47]

These tendencies are voiced in particular in the book associated with Mèngzǐ.
Asymmetrical ethics appears there in the context of the self's natural responsiveness and cultivated responsibility toward others. For Mèngzǐ, the cognitive-affective economy of humans is predisposed toward ethics without the appeal to the
transcendent that Scheler wielded against Nietzsche's skepticism. It is, to adopt
a phrase from Owen Flanagan, "naturally structured for morality."[48]

The genuine ethically exemplary person, and the genuine king whose legitimate power is based in the people and serves their well-being, not only acts for

---

45 | Xunzi: 4.5. *Xunzi: A Translation and Study of the Complete Works*, vol. 1, trans. John
Knoblock, Stanford: Stanford University Press 1988, p. 188.

46 | I examine the affinities (more evident in Levinas's Jewish writings) and tensions
(more visible in his philosophical writings) between immanence and transcendence in
Confucian and Levinasian ethics in "Levinas and Early Confucian Ethics", pp. 177–207.

47 | *Analects* 16:2.

48 | "Destructive Emotions," p. 269.

the sake of the people's well-being but hears, listens and responds to their voices rather than resenting their desires, demands and perceived imperfections.

In the opening passages of the book of *Mencius*, it is not the people but the flawed King Huì of Liáng (梁惠王) who is filled with narrow desires, limiting self-interest, and resentment against his people and neighbouring kings. King Huì suffers from his incapacity to recognise that others are suffering and to extend his heart-mind toward others. However, despite his excuses, this king is not naturally or constitutionally unable to do these things. As Mèngzǐ reveals to the king's discomfort in their conversation, King Huì is affectively and reflectively unwilling to be responsive to, and take responsibility for, those affected by his misuse of his position, power and wealth.

7. Conclusion

The line of argumentation from the *Mencius* discussed above remains critically and politically significant. Ideological uses of the "politics of resentment" and even Nietzsche's conception of the smouldering condition of *ressentiment* fail to analyse sufficiently the dialectic of *ressentiment*. The early Confucians maintain that when either coercion and force or power and wealth are abused, the people will be naturally resentful. Confucian thinkers concluded that the resentment of non-elites against elites is ethically less blameworthy and politically less problematic than the arrogance, enmity and resentment of elites against non-elites. Such resentment is evident, I think, in contemporary conservative discourses concerning the distribution of wealth and power that tend to blame the poor, the weak and the voiceless for their condition.

On the basis of these alternate "critical" and transformative tendencies articulated in the classical *rú* tradition itself, particularly in the text associated with Mencius, a contemporary Confucian interpretation of asymmetrical responsibility can well be argued to provide a number of compelling reasons for promoting social-political equality, challenging asymmetrical claims of privilege that serve as an illegitimate justification or excuse for opposing greater fairness and equity among the people. Early Confucian ethics can accomplish this task and be a "critical ethics" by contesting and deconstructing, instead of furthering, resentment and the condition of *ressentiment* that it promotes.

Ressentiment as Moral Imperative: Jean Améry's Nietzschean Revaluation of Victim Morality

Victoria Fareld

> "[I]n the midst of the world's silence,
> our *ressentiment* holds its finger raised"
>
> Améry, *At the Mind's Limits*

In a polemical argument directed against Nietzsche, the Austrian-born writer and Auschwitz survivor Jean Améry (1912–1978) claims that *ressentiment* can provide the emotional basis of a new morality for his time. While he does allude to the ideas of passivity and inferiority associated with *ressentiment*, he re-evaluates the concept by giving it a critical and even revolutionary meaning. Through a Nietzschean *Umwertung*, Améry presents *ressentiment* as the starting point for a re-thinking of morality based on victim experience. For him, to move *beyond guilt and atonement*, which is the title of his first book (*Jenseits von Schuld und Sühne*), means – as it did for Nietzsche in *Beyond Good and Evil* (*Jenseits von Gut und Böse*) – to criticise and to redefine radically the meaning and value of the dominant conception of morality. Améry's revaluation is partly directed against Nietzsche himself, but also against a society that is intent on pathologising *ressentiment* as the symptom of an inner conflict requiring medical treatment. In what follows, the critical potential of Améry's ideas on *ressentiment* will be studied in relation to the notion of an extra-temporal or anachronistic moral responsibility.

Beyond Guilt and Atonement

In 1964 and 1965, while the Frankfurt Auschwitz trials were in progress, a series of five talks about the intellectual in Auschwitz were broadcast on West German radio. The author of these talks, Jean Améry, spoke of his experience of torture and of the collapse of the intellect in its encounter with the Nazi reality. In 1966, the broadcasts were published as *Jenseits von Schuld und Sühne* (*Beyond Guilt and Atonement*), a publication that was Améry's literary breakthrough.[1]

---

1 | Jean Améry, *Jenseits von Schuld und Sühne: Bewältigungsversuche eines Überwältigten.*

The title of the English translation, which appeared in 1980, is *At the Mind's Limits: Contemplations by a Survivor on Auschwitz and Its Realities*.[2] This rendering obliterates, of course, the unmistakable allusiveness of Améry's own title: its reference to Nietzsche's famous work primarily, but also to Dostoyevksy's novel *Crime and Punishment*.[3] Also lost in translation, and maybe untranslatable, is the play on words in the German subtitle: *Bewältigungsversuche eines Überwältigten*, which might be rephrased as "attempts to master [something] by one who has been overpowered [by that thing]". In his use of the word *Versuche* (attempts), Améry modulates or undermines the twofold meaning of *Bewältigung*: to settle something once and for all and to get rid of it. For Améry, as we shall see, the past will never be settled, nor will victims ever be able to put their victimhood fully behind them.[4] In his "phenomenological description of the existence of the victim",[5] Améry refuses uncompromisingly to be reconciled with the past or to accept what happened to him. He thus describes himself as "a vehemently protesting" Jew; his identity is the site of an irresolvable conflict where the "impossibility of being a Jew becomes the necessity to be one".[6]

Werke in neun Bände, ed. Irene Heidelberger-Leonard, vol. 2. ed. Gerhard Scheit, (Stuttgart: Klett-Cotta 2002). Hereafter referred to as *JSS*.

2 | Jean Améry, *At the Mind's Limits: Contemplations by a Survivor on Auschwitz and its Realities*, trans. Sidney Rosenfeld and Stella P. Rosenfeld, Bloomington: Indiana University Press 1980. Hereafter referred to as *AML*. In order to avoid further losses in translation, the original German text is given in the footnotes.

3 | Friedrich Nietzsche's *Jenseits von Gut und Böse: Vorspiel einer Philosophie der Zukunft* was first published in 1886. The most recent translation is by Judith Norman in: Rolf-Peter Horstmann/Judith Norman (eds), *Beyond Good and Evil: Prelude to a Philosophy of the Future*, Cambridge: Cambridge University Press 2002. The title of Fyodor Dostoyevsky's novel, translated into English as *Crime and Punishment*, is most commonly rendered in German as *Schuld und Sühne* (the terms of Améry's title). A more recent German translation of the novel, however, and one that is considered to be truer to the Russian original, is *Verbrechen und Strafe* (like the English *Crime and Punishment* instead of *Guilt and Atonement* which would be the direct English translation of '*Schuld und Sühne*'). For a discussion of this translation, see Ulrich Busch, "Übertretung und Zurechtweisung" in: *Die Zeit* 07.01.94, p. 40.

4 | In contrast to *überwältigen* (overpower, overwhelm), which signals a play of forces that can take new forms and whose outcome ultimately remains open, the word *bewältigen* (master, overcome) expresses a movement towards closure or completion in which the act of successful overcoming also implies that something has been definitively dealt with or settled (as in the complex notion of *Vergangenheitsbewältigung*, or mastery of the past). See Victoria Fareld, "History and Mourning" in: Hans Ruin/Andrus Ers (eds), *Rethinking Time: Essays on History, Memory, and Representation*, Stockholm: Södertörn University Press 2011, p. 241.

5 | Améry, "Preface to the First Edition, 1966" in: *AML*, p. xiii; "Vorwort zur ersten Ausgabe 1966", in: *JSS*, p. 21: "Wesensbeschreibung der Opfer-Existenz".

6 | Améry, "Preface to the Reissue, 1977", in: *AML*, p. x; "Vorwort zur Neuausgabe 1977",

Améry was born as Hans Mayer in Vienna 1912 to a Roman Catholic mother and a Jewish father. When he was five years old, his father died on the battlefield. "The picture of my father – whom I hardly knew", Améry writes, "did not show me a bearded Jewish sage, but rather a Tyrolean Imperial Rifleman in the uniform of the First World War."[7] His Jewish origins had no particular significance for him until 1935, when the Nuremberg Laws were implemented in Germany. Only at that point did it occur to him that the anti-Semitic legislation which had turned him at the stroke of a pen into a *"nicht nicht Jude"*, or a "a Non-non-Jew", concerned himself.[8] After Austria's *Anschluss* to Nazi Germany three years later, the double alienation became a reality. Not only had he become the stateless Hans Israel Mayer, a Jew without citizenship and an intellectual without *Heimat*, but he had also been expelled from the German language and *Bildungskultur* which had been his natural abode: "I was no longer an I and did not live within a We".[9]

Mayer, as he still was, fled Vienna in 1938 and ended up in Brussels, where he earned his living as an independent journalist and writer. His hopes of a safer existence in exile were not realised, however. Following Germany's attack on Belgium in 1940, he was sent – as a foreigner and potential enemy – to a detention camp in southern France. A year later he managed to escape and returned to Brussels, where his stay would be, once again, of brief duration. In 1943, he was imprisoned and tortured by the Nazis for his activities in the Belgian Resistance, and subsequently, when his Jewish origins were revealed, he was deported to Auschwitz, and thence, at the end of the war, to Bergen-Belsen.[10] Following the Liberation in 1945, Mayer returned to Brussels as one of approximately six hundred Jews who had survived, from roughly twenty-five thousand deported from Belgium. It was at this point that he changed his name (and the language – German – with which it was associated), retaining, however, some traces of the old name in the new one: Hans becomes the French name "Jean", and Mayer becomes, anagrammatically, the Frenchified Améry. Although he resumed his literary work, it would be more than two decades before he would write about his experiences of war, torture and the camps.

---

in: *JSS*, p. 16: "Die Unmöglichkeit, Jude zu sein, wird zum Zwang, es zu sein: und zwar zu einem vehement Protestierenden".

7 | Améry, "On the Necessity and Impossibility of Being a Jew", in: *AML*, p. 83; "Über Zwang und Unmöglichkeit Jude zu sein", in: *JSS*, p. 150: "Das Bild des Vaters – den ich kaum gekannt habe [...] zeigte mir keinen bärtigen jüdischen Weisen, sondern einen Tiroler Kaiserjäger in der Uniform des ersten Weltkriegs".

8 | Améry, "Über Zwang ...", p. 167; "On the Necessity...", p. 94.

9 | Améry, "How Much Home Does a Person Need?", in: *AML*, p. 44; "Wieviel Heimat braucht der Mensch?", in: *JSS*, 90: "Ich war kein Ich mehr und lebte nicht in einem Wir".

10 | All biographical information concerning Améry is, unless otherwise indicated, taken from Irene Heidelberger-Leonard, *Jean Améry: Revolte in der Resignation*, Stuttgart: Klett-Cotta 2004.

Temporal Disorder

In the preface to the first edition of *Jenseits von Schuld und Sühne*, Améry raises a number of questions: "[h]ow had I gotten to Auschwitz? What had taken place before that? What was to happen afterwards? What is my situation today?"[11] These questions, which relate to the experience of sequence, of a beforehand and an afterwards, reveal Améry's difficulty in defining for himself a "now". In fact, *Jenseits von Schuld und Sühne* revolves around the experience of time. Thus, when the author apologises to his readers for his lack of "tact", he is referring not only to a lack of discretion or measure, a certain outspokenness which, he claims, often characterises the stories told by victims in an effort to translate their experience of victimhood into words.[12] This "tactlessness" also refers to his being out of touch or out of sync with the world, with the present or even with time itself. And indeed, Améry is, in a sense, out of step with time. Thus, throughout the two full decades that separated his war-time experience from the publication of his book, he had observed a near-complete silence about the crimes committed in the name of National Socialism. This long time-lapse corresponded to the protracted process through which Germany was transformed into an international exemplum of the confrontation with guilt on a national scale.

In 1950, Theodor Adorno claimed that "the mention of Auschwitz already provokes bored resentment. Nobody is concerned with the past anymore".[13] This lack of public debate about what had happened in the concentration camps aroused Améry's indignation. Indeed, the more society tried to suppress its past, the harder he tried to hold on to it. Society's amnesia was for him a summons to remember. And crucially, he placed at the centre of that moral imperative the feeling of resentment, a feeling welcomed, however, by nobody: "I speak as a victim and examine my resentments. That is no amusing enterprise, either for the reader or for me".[14]

Améry often returns to this expectation of a certain tension in the relation to his readers, from whom he anticipates reticence or even rejection: "You don't want to listen? Listen anyhow", he urges.[15] He underestimated his readers, however, in this respect: not only did they read his work, but they read it in a spirit

---

11 | Améry, "Preface to the First Edition, 1966", p. xiii; "Vorwort zur ersten Ausgabe 1966", p. 20: "Auschwitz. Doch wie war ich dahin gelangt? Was war vorher geschehen, was sollte nachher kommen, wie stehe ich heute da?".

12 | Améry, "Resentments" in *AML*, p. 63.

13 | Theodor W. Adorno, "Spengler after the Decline" in: *Prisms*, Cambridge, Mass.: MIT Press 1981, p. 58.

14 | Améry, "Resentments", p. 63; "Ressentiments" in: *JJS*, pp. 119–120: "Ich spreche als Opfer und untersuche meine Ressentiments. Das ist keine vergnügliche Unternehmung, weder für ihn [den Leser] noch für mich".

15 | Améry, "On the Necessity...", p. 96; "Über den Zwang...", p. 170: "Ihr wollt nicht hören? Höret."

of acceptance. In fact, the success of *Jenseits von Schuld und Sühne* meant that he was a much-invited guest on the German literary stage of the 1960s and 70s. The book's publication could hardly have been more timely, marking as it did the dawning of a transition period in German public life. Coinciding with Améry's radio talks, the Frankfurt Auschwitz trials, which received massive media coverage and made public hundreds of detailed testimonies about life in the camps, had boosted the growth in public awareness and discussion of the Nazi genocide. Germans were thus being forced to begin to confront the reality and scale of the crimes committed under National Socialism. Yet, although his work was widely hailed as a "spectacular triumph",[16] Améry himself was ambivalent about his own success and his reservations are clearly expressed in one of the essays of his book:

> There I am with my resents, in Frankfurt, Stuttgart, Cologne, and Munich. If you wish, I bear my grudge for reasons of personal salvation. Certainly. On the other hand, however, it is also for the good of the German people. But no one wants to relieve me of it, except the organs of public opinion-making, which buy it. What dehumanised me has become a commodity, which I offer for sale.[17]

The author's concern to remain focused on the past is based on a feeling of anger and bitterness that he calls *ressentiment* (and that the translators of his book have unfortunately chosen to render as "resentment"). For him, remaining a victim – by not letting go of his *ressentiment* – means not only adopting an attitude of non-reconciliation with the past, but also revolting against the very notion of linear time and demanding the impossible: namely "that the irreversible be turned around, that the event be undone".[18] His claim that "[t]he moral person demands an annulment of time" entails an ethical imperative: it requires that society's chronological time be disrupted in favour of a dis-ordered or non-linear, moral temporality in which the past is inseparable from the present.[19] By holding onto this disjointed sense of time, Améry develops a temporally extended and radical notion of moral responsibility, which not only turns *ressentiment* into a moral imperative, but which also makes us all – in the present as well as in the future – potentially guilty of crimes committed in the past. This guilt is exclusively, however, a function of our relationship with time, and especially with what we want

---

16 | Gerhard Scheit, "Anhang zu *Jenseits von Schuld und Sühne*. Nachwort", in *JSS*, p. 669.

17 | Améry, "Resentments", p. 80; "Ressentiments", p. 147: "Da stehe ich in Frankfurt, Stuttgart, Köln und München mit meinen Ressentiments. Was ich nachtrage, meinetwillen, aus Gründe persönlichen Heilsvorhabens, gewiss, aber doch auch wieder dem deutschen Volk zugute – niemand will es mir abnehmen ausser den Organen der öffentlichen Meinungsbildung, die es kaufen. Was mich entmenscht hatte, ist Ware geworden, die ich feilhalte".

18 | Améry, "Resentments", p. 68; "Ressentiments", p. 128: "[D]as Irreversible solle umgekehrt, das Ereignis unereignet gemacht werden".

19 | Améry, "Resentments", p. 72; "Ressentiments", p. 133: "Der sittliche Mensch fordert Aufhebung der Zeit".

to call, or want to relegate to, "the past". In other words, it is through the desire of later generations to leave the past behind that they too incur moral guilt.

The temporal distortion associated with *ressentiment* is made explicit in Améry's text: "[t]he time-sense of the person trapped in resentment is twisted around, dis-ordered, if you wish, for it desires two impossible things: regression into the past and nullification of what happened".[20] To have a disordered time-sense means that the chronological separation of history's past, present and future tenses has imploded. Thus Améry is eternally bound to what happened to him in the past, forever chained to a defining event experienced as an eternal now: "Whoever was tortured, stays tortured", he writes.[21] The passage of time cannot bridge the widening gap between himself and the world: "Twenty-two years later I am still dangling over the ground by dislocated arms".[22] Améry's tortured and distorted body – he was beaten while hanging from a hook in the ceiling so that his arms were dislocated – leads to a twisted sense of time and a disrupted narrative.[23] Disrupted time cannot, however, be reduced to a shattered temporality or to the persistence of the past in a frozen "now", located beyond time. Instead, through the ambiguous ever-presence of the past, time has lost its directionality: "[f]or two decades I had been in search of the time that was impossible to lose", he writes in the preface to his book.[24] His is a time which is both present and absent, which can neither be fully forgotten nor entirely remembered, hence the enduring need to bring it to mind and keep it there.

In an effort to explain his (dis)position, Améry writes that "[r]esentments [sic] as the existential dominant of people like myself are the result of a long personal and historical development.[25] His *ressentiment* is a belated but endless reaction

---

20 | Améry, "Resentments", p. 68; "Ressentiments", p. 127: "[D]as Zeitgefühl des im Ressentiment Gefangenen ist verdreht, ver-rückt, wenn man will. Denn es verlangt nach dem zweifach unmöglichen, dem Rückgang ins Abgelebte und der Aufhebung dessen, was geschah".

21 | Améry, "Torture", in: *AML*, p. 34; "Die Tortur", in: *JSS*, p. 75: "Wer gefoltert wurde, bleibt gefoltert".

22 | Améry, "Torture", p. 36; "Die Tortur", p. 79: "Ich baumele noch immer, zweiundzwanzig Jahre danach, an ausgerenkten Armen über dem Boden".

23 | Torture "mark(s) the limit of the capacity of language to communicate. If someone wanted to impart his physical pain, he would be forced to inflict it and thereby become a torturer himself", Améry, "Torture", p. 74. W. G. Sebald writes, with an infallible sureness of pitch, about Améry's language as being on the verge of breakdown. See W.G Sebald, "Against the Irreversible: on Jean Amery", in: *On the Natural History of Destruction: With Essays on Alfred Andersch, Jean Améry and Peter Weiss*, Anthea Bell (trans.), London: Penguin 2004, pp. 143–67.

24 | Améry, "Preface to the First Edition, 1966", p. xiii; "Vorwort zur ersten Ausgabe 1966", p. 20: "Ich hatte mich zwei Jahrzehnte lang auf der Suche nach der unverlierbaren Zeit befunden".

25 | Améry, "Resentments", p. 64; "Ressentiments", p. 121: "Die Ressentiments als

which continuously pulls the past back into the present. It is also associated with temporal displacement in the sense of *Nachträglichkeit*, a notion that has a clear bearing on the literal meaning of the word *ressentiment*. After all, the French verb *re-sentir* means "to feel anew" and thus refers both to the compulsive quest for "lost time" and to its involuntary resurgence, as when one suffers from the after-effects of something that took place in the past, or when one understands retrospectively the consequences of a past event.

Améry's disordered time could, of course, be seen as a response to a state of trauma.[26] The author himself, however, rejects a medical classification of his situation and insists: "I [...] am not 'traumatised', but rather my spiritual and psychic condition corresponds completely to reality."[27] Part of Améry's revolt is indeed directed against a society in which the survivors were neither spoken nor listened to; it is also directed against medical science which gave survivors a diagnosis but no voice of their own: "[A]fter observing us victims, objective scientific method, in its lovely detachment, has already come up with the concept of the 'concentration camp syndrome'", he points out ironically and continues: "The character traits that make up our personality are distorted [...] It is said that we are 'warped'. That causes me to recall fleetingly the way my arms were twisted high behind my back when they tortured me".[28] Améry uses here the German prefix *ver-* (*verdreht, verrückt, verbogen*) in order to describe the consequences of a movement or torsion that has gone too far; it evokes something that has been pulled or bent out of shape. What is crucial, however, is that in depicting this movement, he himself imposes even more torsion on his position by placing deformation at the centre of his mission: he refers, after all, to tackling the "task of defining anew our warped state" and identifies that state as a "form of the human condition that, morally as well as historically, is of a higher order than that of healthy straightness".[29] In this way, as a victim of persecution

---

existentielle Dominante von meinesgleichen sind das Ergebnis einer langen persönlichen und historischen Entwicklung."

26 | Cf. Fred Ankersmit, "Trauma and Suffering" in Jörn Rüsen (ed.), *Western Historical Thinking: An Intercultural Debate*, New York: Berghahn Books 2002, p. 78. "The paradox of trauma", Ankersmit points out, "is that it gives us a past that is neither forgotten nor remembered". On the relation between trauma, memory and history, see also Cathy Caruth, *Trauma: Explorations in Memory*, Baltimore: John Hopkins University Press 1995.

27 | Améry, "On the Necessity...", p. 99; "Über den Zwang...", p. 175: "bin nicht 'traumatisiert', sondern stehe in voller geistiger und psychischer Entsprechung zur Realität da".

28 | Améry, "Resentments", p. 68; "Ressentiments", p. 127: "objektive Wissenschaftlichkeit hat aus der Beobachtung von uns Opfern in schöner Detachiertheit bereits den Begriff des 'KZ-Syndroms' gewonnen [...] Die Charakterzüge, die unsere Persönlichkeit ausmachen, seien verzerrt [...] Wir sind, so heisst es, 'verbogen'. Das lässt mich flüchtig an meine unter der Folter hinterm Rücken hochgedrehten Arme denken".

29 | Améry, "Resentments", p. 68; "Ressentiments", p. 127: "Das stellt mir aber auch

and torture with a consequentially disordered sense of time, Améry consciously keeps himself out of phase with his own time in order to claim a new point of departure for morality. It is the feeling of *ressentiment* that lies at the heart of this moral outlook and that lends an ethical dimension to temporality. *Ressentiment* thus makes "history become moral".[30]

Ressentiment

It is no coincidence that Améry uses the French word *ressentiment,* which is also mobilised by Nietzsche in *On the Genealogy of Morals* (1887).[31] Although, like Nietzsche, Améry uses the French term in his original German text, the English translators have, as already noted, chosen to translate it into English. Not only is there no adequate English or German translation of the spectrum of meanings corresponding to the French term, but the Nietzschean connotations are lost in the English translation.[32] Readers of the English version thus miss out on Améry's allusions to the Nietzschean concept; even more regrettably, they lose out on Améry's attempt to re-write or even re-evaluate the Nietzschean notion by inverting its meaning.

Nietzsche used the word *ressentiment* to describe the morality of the weak, whom he characterises as "natures that are denied the true reaction, that of deeds, and [thus] compensate themselves with an imaginary revenge".[33] For Nietzsche, the person driven by *ressentiment* is obsessed with past wrongs but lacks the strength required to act and change the course of events. Hence the revenge only occurs in the person's imagination, which leads to a lingering bitterness and an internalised feeling of hatred. The "man of *ressentiment*" never really deals with his enemies, but rather clings to them parasitically in order to uphold his identity as good or moral, in contrast to his enemies whom he represents as being evil or amoral.[34] In Nietzsche's account, *ressentiment* expresses a passive, reactive stance; it does not promote action or lead to real change. Instead,

---

die Aufgabe, unsere Verbogenheit neu zu definieren: und zwar als eine sowohl moralisch als auch geschichtlich der gesunden Geradheit gegenüber ranghöhere Form des Menschlichen".

30 | Améry, "Resentments", p. 78; "Ressentiments", p. 143: "Moralisierung der Geschichte".

31 | For a discussion of the importance of not translating Nietzsche's *ressentiment* by resentment see Walter Kaufmann, "Editor's Introduction", in: *Friedrich Nietzsche,* ed. Walter Kaufmann, trans. Walter Kaufmann & R.J. Hollingdale, *On the Genealogy of Morals; Ecce Homo,* New York: Vintage Books 1989, pp. 5–10.

32 | For a discussion of the difference between the two words, see Bernard N. Meltzer/ Gil Richard Musolf, "Resentment and Ressentiment", *Sociological Inquiry,* 72:2 (2002), pp. 240–55.

33 | F. Nietzsche, *On the Genealogy,* p. 36.

34 | Ibid., pp. 36–56.

the memory of the past becomes a "festering wound", which never heals and gradually embitters the victim: "one cannot get rid of anything, one cannot get over anything, one cannot repel anything – everything hurts".[35]

Nietzsche's claim that *ressentiment* involves a desire for revenge and a failure to express the revenge in real action is repeated in Max Scheler's 1912 treatment of the feeling. *Ressentiment*, Scheler points out, "can never emerge without the mediation of a particular form of impotence".[36] It is, he claims, fueled by "the tormenting desire of an impossible revenge".[37] Both Nietzsche's and Scheler's accounts of *ressentiment* as a low and misguided, self-defensive feeling are echoed in contemporary definitions of the term. In Jeffrie Murphy's typology, bitterness and self-absorption are the dominant traits of *ressentiment*, which is "by definition, an irrational and base passion. It means, roughly, 'spiteful and malicious envy'. It thus makes no sense to speak of rational or justified or honorable *ressentiment*".[38] Envy, revenge and self-preoccupation are at the core of the complex as theorised by the two German thinkers. For them, Ressentiment is a response to a feeling of injury to oneself, to one's self-esteem or sense of self-worth. It does not concern injuries to others, and does not have any moral, social or political content.[39] As we shall see, however, Améry inverts this understanding of *ressentiment* by transforming it into a call for responsibility, and into a critical tool aimed at bringing about socio-political change.[40]

In Nietzsche's *Beyond Good and Evil* the word *Umwertung* appears as an explicit theme.[41] It is a notoriously difficult notion to translate. The most common English translations are "transvaluation" and "revaluation", but neither one fully conveys the meaning of the German word.[42] Neither "trans-" nor "re-"

---

35 | F. Nietzsche, "Ecce Homo" in *On the Genealogy*, p. 230.

36 | Max Scheler, *Ressentiment*, Lewis A. Coser/William W. Holdheim (eds), Milwaukee, Wis.: Marquette University Press 1994 [1915], p. 42.

37 | Scheler, *Ressentiment*, p. 57.

38 | Jeffrie Murphy, "Moral Epistemology, the Retributive Emotions, and the 'Clumsy Moral Philosophy of Jesus Christ", in: *The Passion of Law*, ed. S. Bandes, New York: University Press 1999, p. 152.

39 | See for instance Jean Hampton and Jeffrie Murphy, *Forgiveness and Mercy*, Cambridge: Cambridge University Press 1988, pp. 14–87.

40 | For a lucid critique of the dominant modern understanding of resentment in relation to Améry, see Thomas Brudholm, *Resentment's Virtue: Jean Améry and the Refusal to Forgive*, Philadelphia P.A.: Temple University Press 2008.

41 | For a discussion about whether to translate Nietzsche's *Umwertung* as *transvaluation* or *revaluation*, see Duncan Large, "A Note on the Term "Umwerthung", *Journal of Nietzsche Studies* 39 (2010): 5–11. "Whereas 'transvaluation' was initially used, the modern consensus favors 'revaluation,' which is preferred in almost all postwar English translations", p. 5.

42 | "In English, the choice between 'transvaluation' and 'revaluation' has become a

captures the ambiguous sense of the German prefix "um-". The latter connotes change and transformation in a broad and value-neutral sense and can thus accommodate both the negative and the positive significations of Nietzsche's use of it; that is, both the Judeo-Christian revaluation of values which is the primary target of Nietzsche's criticism, and his own radically new approach to the values that had come to define morality in his time. Nietzsche deplores the "revaluation of all values" ("Umwertung aller Werte"), which is how he describes the historical process whereby the life-denying values of the Judeo-Christian slave morality got the upper hand over the life-affirming values of a master morality.[43] A major theme in his work is also, however, that of the individual standing in opposition to a solid majority and cultivating an independence of mind or judgment. It is in this sense that Nietzsche seeks to move beyond good and evil, thereby leaving behind the conventional morality of the majority and affirming a new moral outlook, indeed a radical overturning of the values dominating traditional morality.[44]

Nietzsche uses the same term, *Umwertung*, to refer to both changes of values, judging the first one negative and the second positive. The German word connotes inversion and has both a spatial and a temporal dimension. The problem is that neither English translation captures this dual dimensionality. The Nietzsche translator, Duncan Large, points out that both "revaluation" and "transvaluation" "denote operations performed on a (preexisting) value": thus both suffixes register the inherent temporal dimension of change. Large notes that the word "revalue" places additional emphasis on temporality: it means valuing again, anew, for a second (or subsequent) time; whereas "transvalue" suggests the more spatial notion of "valuing across".[45] Given that "transvaluation" has a spatial meaning in English, whereas "revaluation" has a heightened temporal sense, the two words suggest a different relation to time. The choice of "revaluation" in this essay is in line with most postwar translations;[46] but it also

---

shibboleth for Nietzsche interpreters [they are both, however,] more or less equally good and equally bad", Ibid., p. 7.

43 | F. Nietzsche, *Beyond Good and Evil*, p. 44 (2nd edn, p. 46).

44 | For the two meanings of revaluation, see F. Nietzsche, *Beyond Good and Evil*, for instance, p. 44 (2nd edition, p. 46): "Nowhere to date has there been such a bold inversion or anything quite as horrible, questioning and questionable as this formula [the Christian 'God on the cross', my comment VF]. It promised a revaluation of all the values of antiquity". See also ibid, p. 91 (2nd edn, p. 203): "where do *we* need to reach with our hopes? – Towards *new philosophers*, there is no alternative; towards spirits who are strong and original enough to give impetus to opposed valuations and initiate a revaluation and reversal of 'eternal values'". For Nietzsche's distinction between slave morality and master morality, see Ibid. pp. 153–56 (2nd edn, p. 260).

45 | D. Large, "A Note", p. 7.

46 | Whereas "transvaluation" was the standard English translation for a long time, "revaluation" became the agreed term after the two influential postwar translations by

recognises the importance of temporality in the notion of *ressentiment* and its heightened significance in Améry's thinking.

Nietzsche's overturning of deeply entrenched moral values, which entails a rejection of the key norms of his time, is clearly echoed in Améry's own inversion of the Nietzschean evaluation of *ressentiment*.[47] Although Améry does not himself use the word *Umwertung* to refer to this move, he does use the synonyms that Nietzsche used for it, namely *Umkehrung* (reversal, turning back) and *Umdrehung* (turning over (or overturning), turning around, rotation, revolution).[48] For Améry, moving *beyond guilt and atonement* means – as it did for Nietzsche in *Beyond Good and Evil* – criticising the meaning and value of the dominant conception of morality and radically redefining it. However, this revaluation is to a large extent directed against Nietzsche himself, more specifically against Nietzsche's outright condemnation of *ressentiment* as a low and unworthy feeling. Through a Nietzschean revaluation, Améry thus launches *ressentiment* as the starting point for a new moral thinking based on victims' experiences. This revaluation implies a temporal revolt or revolution; it twists chronology into a disordered, but more moral temporality.

A Morality for the Powerless: *Ressentiment* Revaluated

Améry's point of departure is the dominant, derogatory understanding of *ressentiment* with its pejorative connotations of weakness, passivity, bitterness and self-indulgence. Whereas *ressentiment* for Nietzsche is an inferior feeling which must be overcome, it constitutes for Améry the "emotional source of every genuine morality, which was always a morality for the losers".[49] The losers, or better said the subordinated or *die Unterlegenen*, which is Améry's word, lack agency. In other words, they do not possess the ability to change their situation. In Améry's account, however, this lack of agency is not caused by personal or individual weakness, as it is in Nietzsche's version of strength and vitality, but is due rather to particular political or socio-historical circumstances. This is

---

Walter Kaufmann and R.J. Hollingdale (see D. Large, *op.cit.*, p. 7). "Revaluation" is also used in the most recent translation by Judith Norman. See above, n. 3.

47 | F. Nietzsche, *Beyond Good and Evil*, pp. 86–92 (2nd edn, pp. 199–203).

48 | See for instance Améry, "Ressentiments", p. 128: "Absurd fordert es [das Ressentiment], das Irreversible solle umgekehrt". The synonyms of *Umwertung* in Nietzsche's work are discussed in Thomas H. Brobier, *Nietzsche's Ethics of Character: A Study of Nietzsche's Ethics and Its Place in the History of Moral Thinking*, Uppsala: Uppsala University, Department of History of Science and Ideas 1995), p. 296, n. 10. In the light of these synomyms, Brobier opts for the term "revaluation" rather than "transvaluation": see D. Large, "A Note on the Term 'Umwertung", pp. 8–9.

49 | Améry, "Resentments", p. 81; "Ressentiments", p. 148: "Die Ressentiments, Emotionsquelle jeder echten Moral, die immer eine Moral für die Unterlegenen war".

why Améry claims that his *ressentiments* are of a "special kind", "of which neither Nietzsche nor Max Scheler [...] was able to have any notion".[50] To harbour feelings of *ressentiment* is not at all the same thing after 1945 as it was at the beginning of the century; postwar *ressentiment* is grounded in a lived experience of persecution, torture and extermination, an experience of which Nietzsche and Scheler could know nothing. Améry politicises *ressentiment* by connecting the weakness and impotence involved in the Nietzschean concept to social and historical circumstances rather than to individual human character. In order to do so, he has to situate *ressentiment* in relation to two different explanations: "[t]hat of Nietzsche, who morally condemned resentment, and that of modern psychology, which is able to picture it only as a disturbing conflict".[51]

Although Améry's *ressentiment* is political, it cannot be instrumentalised as part of a political ideology. As a political force, it can only be appropriated or wielded directly by the losers, the victims or the powerless themselves: by the *Unterlegenen*.[52] In this account of *ressentiment*, personal weakness or subordination is re-interpreted as historical and political powerlessness and is seen, paradoxically, as conferring moral strength. For Nietzsche, the man of *ressentiment* lacks the strength to revolt against the oppressive situation under which he suffers. For Améry, however, the harbouring of *ressentiment* is an expression of precisely this strength; moreover, even if it signifies the ability to resist actively and to defy widely shared norms, the moral strength of *ressentiment* is not contingent on individual character, but is rather a strength that emerges from and within the historical situation that has been experienced or suffered.

This view of *ressentiment* is made perfectly clear in what Améry writes about himself: "I am one of those who [...] escaped that giant dragnet only by chance. A survivor. Not a moral authority, to be sure".[53] His insistence upon his own privileged moral position as victim is based on a sociological or structural definition of victimhood which stands in complete contradiction to the definition proposed by Nietzsche. Independently not only of his own volition, but also of his personal qualities or character traits, historical circumstances have made him "the captive of the *moral truth* of the conflict".[54] In the opening page of *At the Mind's Limits*,

---

50 | Améry, "Resentments", p. 71; "Ressentiments", p. 132: "[D]ie Ressentiments besonderer Art, von denen weder Nietzsche noch Max Scheler [...] hatten ahnen können".

51 | Améry, "Resentments", p. 68; "Ressentiments", p. 127: "So habe ich denn die Ressentiments nach zwei Seiten hin abzugrenzen, vor zwei Begriffsbestimmungen zu schirmen: gegen Nietzsche, der das Ressentiment moralisch verdammte, und gegen moderne Psychologie, die es nur als einen störenden Konflikt denken kann".

52 | Cf. Arne Vetlesen, "A Case for Resentment: Jean Améry versus Primo Levi" in: *Journal of Human Rights*, 5 (2006), pp. 27–44.

53 | "Jean Améry", in: Simon Wiesenthal, *The Sunflower: On the Possibilities and Limits of Forgiveness*, New York: Schocken Books 1998, p. 106.

54 | Améry, "Resentments", p. 70; "Ressentiments", p. 130: "so weiss ich doch, dass ich der Gefangene bin der *moralishen Wahrheit* des Konflikts".

he states bluntly: "My subject is: At the Mind's Limits. That these limits happen to run alongside the so unpopular horrors is not my fault".[55]

It is because of his lived experiences, Améry argues, that the victim is in a position to break with society's consensus. "Only I possessed, and still possess", he states, "the moral truth of the blows that even today roar in my skull, and for that reason I am more entitled to judge, not only more than the culprit but also *more than society* – which thinks only about its continued existence".[56] Améry thus remains true to Nietzsche's plea for the strong individual standing in opposition to the dominant morality of his time. Yet he does so paradoxically by performing a revaluation of Nietzsche's *ressentiment*, transforming it into a morality based on victimhood. Crucially, Améry's *ressentiment* relates to his individual, existential reaction to own his lived experience, but it also serves a political and historical function. As moral criticism directed at redefining the dominant ethical parameters of society, it transcends the personal realm.[57]

The Critical Function of Améry's *Ressentiment*

Contrary to what Nietzsche attacked as the prevailing "slave morality" of his time, Améry's victim morality is an expression of individuality and non-conformity. It is articulated as a moral call directed toward contemporary society; far from representing a herd mentality, it entails a fundamental critique directed against the latter. Persons of *ressentiment*, Améry argues, refuse to go with the flow; they do not compromise their personal responsibility by letting themselves be "deindividualised", or reduced to a function of the social body:

> Whoever submerges his individuality in society and is able to comprehend himself only as a function of the social, that is, the insensitive and indifferent person, really does forgive. He calmly allows what happened to remain what it was. As the popular saying goes, he lets time heal his wounds. His time-sense is not dis-ordered, that is to say, it has not moved out of the biological and social sphere into the moral sphere. As a deindividualised, interchangeable part of the social mechanism he lives with it consentingly.[58]

---

55 | Améry, "At the Mind's Limits", in: *AML*, pp. 1–2; Améry, "An den Grenzen des Geistes" in: *JSS*, p. 24: "Mein Thema heisst: An den Grenzen des Geistes; dass diese Grenzen gerade längs der unbeliebten Greuel verlaufen, ist nicht meine Schuld".

56 | Améry, "Resentments", p. 70; "Ressentiments", pp.130–31: "Die moralische Wahrheit der mir noch heute im Schädel dröhnenden Hiebe besass und besitze ich nur selber und bin darum in höherem Masse urteilsbefugt, nicht nur als der Täter, sondern auch als die nur an ihren Bestand denkende Gesellschaft".

57 | Cf. Thomas Brudholm, "Revisiting Resentments: Jean Améry and the Dark Side of Forgiveness and Reconciliation", in: *Journal of Human Rights*, 5 (2006), p. 15.

58 | Améry, "Resentments", p. 71; "Ressentiments", p. 132: "Wer seine Individualität aufgehen lässt in der Gesellschaft und sich nur als eine Funktion des Sozialen ver-

And he continues:

> In two decades of contemplating what happened to me, I believe [I] have recognised that a forgiving and forgetting induced by social pressure is immoral. Whoever lazily and cheaply forgives, subjugates himself to the social and biological time-sense, which is also called the "natural" one. Natural consciousness of time actually is rooted in the psychological process of wound-healing and became part of the social conception of reality. But precisely for this reason it is not only extramoral, but also *anti*moral in character. Man has the right and the privilege to declare himself to be in disagreement with every natural occurrence, including the biological healing that time brings about. What happened, happened. This sentence is just as true as it is hostile to morals and intellect. The moral power to resist contains the protest, the revolt against reality, which is rational only as long as it is moral.[59]

Ressentiment is here described as an act of resistance and even revolt; more specifically, it is represented as a moral revolt against both linear time and an amoral or immoral social pragmatism. For *ressentiment* to be an active passion, rather than a passive stance or an impediment to concrete action, Améry insists that it should be externalised and socialised, moralised and politicised, rather than envisaged as the purely individualised personal experience of victims. For him, *ressentiment* can only fullfil its historico-political task "by actively settling [Austragung] the unresolved conflict in the field of historical practice".[60] In other words, the historical function which he ascribes to *ressentiment* involves refusing to allow past events to become history: "I rebel", he writes, "against my past, against history, and against a present that places the incomprehensible in

---

stehen kann, der Stumpffühlige und Indifferente also, vergibt in der Tat. Er lässt das Geschehene gelassen sein, was es war. Er lässt, wie das Volk sagt, die Zeit seine Wunden heilen. Sein Zeitgefühl ist nicht verrückt, will sagen: nicht herausgerückt aus dem biologisch-sozialen Bereich in den moralischen. Entindividualisierter, austauchbarer Teil des Gesellschaftsmechanismus, lebt er mit diesem im Einverständnis".

59 | Améry, "Resentments", p. 72; "Ressentiments", p. 133: "In zwei Jahrzehnten Nachdenkens dessen, was mir widerfuhr, glaube ich erkannt zu haben, dass ein durch sozialen Druck bewirktes Vergeben und Vergessen unmoralisch ist. Der faul und wohlfeil Vergebende unterwirft sich dem sozialen und biologischen Zeitgefühl, dass man auch das 'natürliche' nennt. Natürliches Zeitbewusstsein wurzelt tatsächlich im physiologischen Prozess der Wundheilung und ging ein in die gesellschaftliche Realitätsvorstellung. Es hat aber gerade aus diesem Grunde nicht nur ausser-, sondern *wider*moralischen Charakter. Recht und Vorrecht des Menschen ist es, dass er sich nicht einverstanden erklärt mit jedem natürlichen Geschehen, also auch nicht mit dem biologischen Zuwachsen der Zeit. Was geschah, geschah: der Satz ist ebenso wahr wie er moral- und geistfeindlich ist. Sittliche Wiederstandskraft enthält den Protest, die Revolte gegen das Wirkliche, das nun vernünftig ist, solange es moralisch ist".

60 | Améry, "Resentments", p. 69; "Ressentiments", p. 129: "durch Austragung des ungelösten Konflikts im Wirkungsfeld der geschichtlichen Praxis".

the cold storage of history".[61] Letting what has happened become history means for Améry transforming the events of the past into a story that makes it possible to mourn what no longer is, and then to move on. In this way, history ultimately helps us to remember only in order that we may then forget. Viewed against this backdrop, Améry's *ressentiment* can be seen as a protest, not only against the desire for social amnesia but also against the desire for an imaginary closure to historical events. His *ressentiment* shows how the the relationship of the present with the past and the future can be reconfigured and how, when it persists into the present, the past can remain open and unfinished and the conflict unresolved.[62] In the preface to the second edition of *Jenseits von Schuld und Sühne* in 1977, he writes:

> I do not have [clarity] today, and I hope that I never will. Clarification would also amount to disposal, settlement of the case, which can then be placed in the files of history. My book is meant to aid in preventing precisely this. For nothing is resolved, no conflict is settled, no remembering has become a mere memory.[63]

Clearly, Améry opposes the verbal value of *remembering* as an activity or on-going process to *memory* as a fait accompli; the latter, he warns us, is ultimately aimed at forgetting. His refusal to *work through* the conflict in Freudian terms should also be seen in this light. In other words, it is related to the "historical function" that he ascribes to *ressentiment*.[64] Not only does he want to *act out* or to *enact* the fundamentally and permanently unresolved conflict "in the field of historical practice", but he calls for a societal space where conflicts of this kind are treated as social phenomena and as public matters, rather than as individual states of mind or inner mental conditions to be treated or resolved in the private sphere: on the psychoanalyst's couch, for instance, or at the psychiatric clinic.[65] His vehement rejection of the medicalisation of *ressentiment* as an object of medical science is based on the fact that medical discourse would de-politicise

---

61 | Améry, "Preface to the Reissue, 1977", p. xi; "Vorwort zur Neuausgabe 1977", p. 18: "Ich rebelliere: gegen meine Vergangenheit, gegen die Geschichte, gegen eine Gegenwart, die das Unbegreifliche geschichtlich einfrieren lässt".

62 | Cf. Brudholm, *Resentment's Virtue*, p. 109.

63 | Améry, "Preface to the Reissue, 1977", p. xi; "Vorwort zur Neuausgabe 1977", p. 18: "ich bin es heute nicht [abgeklärt] und hoffe, dass ich es niemals sein werde. Abklärung, das wäre ja auch Erledigung, Abmachung von Tatbeständen, die man zu den geschichtlichen Akten legen kann. Gerade dies zu verhindern, will mein Buch beitragen. Nichts ist ja aufgelöst, kein Konflikt ist beigelegt, kein Er-innern zur blossen Erinnerung geworden".

64 | Améry, "Resentments", p. 77; "Ressentiments", p. 141: "eine geschichtliche Funktion".

65 | Améry, "Resentments", p. 69; "Ressentiments", p. 129: "im Wirkungsfeld der geschichtlichen Praxis".

ressentiment and thus undermine it as precisely the moral and social force that Améry wants it to be.

Améry's *ressentiment* is clearly directed, not at the perpetrators of his oppression, but at the world that abandoned him: at the indifference of his fellow human beings, which made the Nazi perpetrations possible; at the revolt that didn't happen; at the personal responsibility not assumed; at the moral action not taken. However, it is not primarily a question of individual affect or responsibility. Moreover, it lies and it acts *beyond* guilt and atonement *per se*, which is exactly what the title of his book suggests. Persistently raising the question as to how a society should relate ethically to the past, it signifies less a bitter and self-absorped obsession with past wrongs and wrongdoings, than an enduring critique of what is going on in the present, and of the ways in which contemporary society relates to, and deals with, its own civilisational failures. Améry's version of *ressentiment* involves first and foremost an effort to force the past into the present in order that society might recognise and address the fact that *present wrongs* echo and perpetuate past failures in a historical continuum. "You don't want to listen? Listen anyhow. You don't want to know to where your indifference can again lead you and me at any time?"[66] Not only is his *ressentiment* primarily concerned with the way that the present deals with its debt to the past, but it also entails a plea directed at us, his current, belated readers, more precisely at our willingness and ability to assume responsibility by responding adequately to his call. The responsibility that Améry requires us to accept transcends linear, progressive time; for morality cannot be a function of biological time alone. It is thus temporal in the sense that it is *a*temporal: progressive time has no hold on it. This means that we (of/in the present) have an infinite responsibility vis-à-vis the past, for we are all, potentially, the perpetrators – in the sense of perpetuators – of wrongs committed in the past. It also means that the key to rejecting or realising our own potential implication in wrongdoing lies in the way that we choose to relate to the past.

Turning Weakness into Merit: From *Victima* to *Sacrificium*

The experience of persecution and torture was for Améry one of radical alienation; it was an experience of a "foreignness in the world that cannot be compensated by any sort of subsequent human communication".[67] The feeling of alienation is therefore irreversible and non-erasable, forever part of his damaged self. It is also, however, a moral position that he consciously accepts as perpetual. In persistently affirming his historically determined identity as a victim,

---

66 | Améry, "On the Necessity ...", p. 96; "Über Zwang ...", p. 170: "Ihr wollt nicht hören? Höret. Ihr wollt nicht wissen, wohin eure Gleichgültigkeit euch selber und mich zu jeder Stunde wieder hinführen kann?".

67 | Améry, "Torture", p. 39; "Die Tortur", p. 84: "einer durch keinerlei spätere menschliche Kommunikation auszugleichenden Fremdheit in der Welt".

and in pushing it to its socio-political extreme on his own terms, he transforms the feeling of alienation into a moral argument directed at the society that had abandoned him. The victim, Améry seems to claim, who has lost trust in the world and who can no longer be at one with it, has a duty to turn the experience of alienation into a position from which he can act morally and politically.

Nietzsche described the historical revaluation of slave morality as a process in which "[w]eakness is being lied into something *meritorious*".[68] Nietzsche's critical discussion of this reversal of the values of weakness and strength resonates in Améry's thinking. Améry, however, inverts this reversal in turn, transforming the self-deception and falsity that Nietzsche places at the core of slave morality into authenticity and duty. He thus transmutes weakness into merit in his own revaluation of *ressentiment* as the emotional source of victim morality – a morality for the subordinated and disempowered of history.

In affirming his victimhood, in valuing what had been forced upon him, Améry radically rewrites the meaning of the historical revaluation ascribed by Nietzsche to *ressentiment*: "As a Non-non Jew, I am a Jew", he writes, "I must be one and must want to be one. I must accept this and affirm it in my daily existence", and he continues: "Thus, I too am precisely what I am not because I did not exist until I became it above all: a Jew".[69] Being a Jew is for Améry tantamount to being a victim: "Antisemitism", he writes, "made a Jew of me".[70] By affirming his identity, both as a Jew and as such as a victim, he reclaims a position of self-definition. Moroever, in insisting upon his victimhood – in appropriating his alienation – he can negate negation and thereby transform a position of resignation into an affirmative strategy of revolt.

The German word *Opfer* has two meanings: victim and sacrifice. Forced into exile, tortured and deported, Améry is undoubtedly a victim in the first sense of the word, from the Latin *victima*: namely, a person who has innocently suffered from the destructive wrongdoing of others. The word *Opfer* can be used in this passive sense to refer to someone who is subjected to the actions of others without acting or being able to act. *Opfern*, however, can also be used in a more active, voluntary or intentional sense, to mean *sacrificium*, as when one denies oneself something or offers something up in order to gain something else or to achieve a certain purpose.

It is *ressentiment* that allows Améry to transform victimhood into a moral assignment, turning victimhood into action "for the good of the German people". *Victima* thus becomes *sacrificium* as Améry endeavours both to save

---

68 | Nietzsche, *On the Genealogy*, p. 47.

69 | Améry, "On the Necessity...", pp. 94–95; "Über Zwang...", pp. 167, 169: "Als Nicht-Nichtjude bin ich Jude, muss es sein und muss es sein wollen. Ich habe es anzunehmen und in meiner täglichen Existenz zu bekräftigen [---] So bin auch ich gerade, was ich nicht bin, weil ich nicht war, ehe ich es wurde, vor allem anderen: Jude".

70 | Améry, "On the Necessity...", p. 98; "Über Zwang...", p. 174: "Der Antisemitismus, der mich als einen Juden erzeugt hat...".

German society from itself and from moral amnesia and also to save or release himself "from the abandonment that has persisted from that time until today".[71] Paradoxically, however, this salvation relies upon the recognition that "[w]hoever was tortured, stays tortured". If one wishes one's sacrifice to have a purpose, then one cannot forget, transcend or erase one's victimhood. Thus, Améry clings to his *ressentiments*. He refuses to recover in, through or from history, and urges us, his readers, to follow him in rescuing the past from history in order to save it for the future.

---

71 | Améry, "Resentments", p. 70; "Ressentiments", p. 131: "Um die Erlösung aus dem noch immer andauernden Verlassensein von damals geht es mir".

Ressentiment beyond Nietzsche and Améry

H. G. Adler between Literary *Ressentiment* and Divine Grace

Helen Finch

Ressentiment and the Consequences

How can a victim of injustice at once reintegrate into a society eager to forget, while at the same time maintaining their anger at injustice done? What occasions the greater *ressentiment*: the original injustice perpetrated on the victim, or a society that refuses to listen to the testimony of the victim, thereby confirming them in their bitter isolation? In this article, I consider the contribution of two German victims of National Socialist persecution, Jean Améry and H. G. Adler, to this question, and suggest that the largely unknown works of Adler hold a solution to the scandal posed by *ressentiment*. When we consider the history of *ressentiment* from Nietzsche to Max Scheler to the present, it appears that, with very few exceptions, the "man of *ressentiment*" is always someone else. *Ressentiment* is an affect of spiteful individualism, directed against the roots of society, those of forgiveness and commonality; it refuses the consensual time-sense of society which allows time to be linear, move on and heal all wounds.[1] Klaus Scherpe, in 2008, remarks that *ressentiment* eludes criticism; it is an illegitimate position between an affect and a theoretical concept.[2] This anti-social, untimely affect provokes a counter-*ressentiment* in response, shown by an edition of *Merkur* in 2004, dedicated to *ressentiment*, where the majority of the essays evaluated the sentiment negatively. *Ressentiment*, Scherpe notes, is the property of the do-gooder, the avant-gardist, the constant insurgent, the notorious 68-er.[3] Nobody likes the *Ressentimentmensch*, the "man of ressentiment", who

---

1 | Jean Améry, *At the Mind's Limits. Contemplations by a Survivor on Auschwitz and its Realities*, trans. Sidney Rosenfeld and Stella P. Rosenfeld, Bloomington & Indianapolis: Indiana University Press 1980, p. 71.

2 | Klaus R. Scherpe, "Ressentiment: Eine Gefühlstatsache", in: *Weimarer Beiträge: Zeitschrift für Literaturwissenschaft, Ästhetik und Kulturwissenschaften* 54.2 (2008), pp. 165–181, p. 166.

3 | Scherpe, "Ressentiment", p. 164.

is neither honest nor upright, as Nietzsche tells us, whose soul squints, who remains silent, refuses to forget, humiliates himself.[4] Their resistance to theory notwithstanding, victims of history continue to remember their injuries, to feel wronged by their abusers, and to refuse the joyful forgetting and straightforward action demanded by Nietzsche and the critics of *ressentiment* ever since. The people of *ressentiment* therefore pose a scandal, not only to theorists, but to proponents of transitional justice who search for a way to create social healing based on forgiveness. Derrida has named this problem as an aporia: "forgiveness only forgives the unforgivable", and Lawrence Langer has gone far further, for instance accusing the South African Truth and Reconciliation commission of being informed by a flawed Christian paradigm that privileges forgiveness over the realities of victim suffering, calling it the "dream of an inflexible optimist".[5] Langer's critique of the Truth and Reconciliation commission is grounded in his insistence on the right of the Holocaust victim to justice, and is thus related to Derrida's insight that "the roots of transitional justice, with its baggage of human forgiveness, stretch back to the paradigm case of modern massacres: the Holocaust during WWII".[6] Speaking about the wrongs done to him during the Holocaust, *ressentiment* has its most clear and most radical voice in that of the survivor Jean Améry, who embraces the unloved role of the man of *ressentiment*:

> Only I possessed, and still possess, the moral truth of the blows that even today roar in my skull, and for that reason I am more entitled to judge, not only more than the culprit but also more than society – which thinks only about its continued existence. The social body is occupied merely with safeguarding itself and could not care less about a life that has been damaged. [...] But my resentments are there in order that the crime become a moral reality for the criminal, in order that he be swept in to the truth of his atrocity.[7]

Améry's *ressentiment* takes on a moral and redemptive charge, far both from Nietzsche's dismissal of *ressentiment* as a sentiment of habitual lying, and from the recommendations of such thinkers as Sloterdijk, who demand a joyful *kynicism* in response to modernity.[8] Améry rehabilitates *ressentiment* as an intransigent, backward-looking and profoundly moral sentiment. As such, it has a fam-

---

4 | Friedrich Nietzsche, *On the Genealogy of Morals*, trans. Douglas Smith, Oxford: Oxford University Press 1996, p. 624.

5 | Jacques Derrida, *On Cosmopolitanism and Forgiveness*, trans. Mark Dooley and Michael Hughes, New York: Routledge 2010, p. 32. Lawrence Langer, *Using and Abusing the Holocaust*, Bloomington: Indiana U.P. 2006, p. 87.

6 | Giovanna Borradori, "Living with the Irreparable: A Critique of Derrida's Theory of Forgiveness", in: *Parallax*, 17, (2011), pp. 78–88, 81.

7 | Améry, *At the Mind's Limits*, p. 70.

8 | Sjoerd van Tuinen, "A Thymotic Left? Peter Sloterdijk and the Psychopolitics of Ressentiment", in: *Symploke*, 18, 1/2, (2011), pp. 47–64.

ily resemblance to melancholy, and it is thus unsurprising that W. G. Sebald, the anatomist of melancholy,[9] admired Améry's work on *ressentiment*. Sebald finds that Améry's essay contains perhaps an even more unbearable aporia than Derrida's; an aporia between Améry's Utopian imagination of "the restitution of the lost homeland",[10] and the revolutionary fantasy of "fire, the perfect medium of the force of divine retribution".[11] Caught in this aporia, Sebald suggests, it is no wonder that Améry's life ended in suicide – suicide, Sebald adds, not as resignation to his fate, but as a protest in itself.[12] Sebald's essay is full of admiration for Améry's uncompromising stance, but still offers no hope of bridging the gap between the suffering victim, and the society which refuses the Utopian transformation that might allow for reconciliation with its victims. Moreover, as Primo Levi points out in a thoughtful response to Améry, there is a high price to be paid for such utopian recalcitrance and truculent adherence to dignity; they lead to "positions of such severity and intransigence as to make him incapable of finding joy in life, indeed of living".[13] Levi attributes Améry's eventual suicide to his recalcitrant stance. That Levi himself most probably committed suicide shortly after writing these words, in 1988, despite claiming that he held no such resents, only highlights the dangers presented by *ressentiment* and its cousin, trauma. In both cases, that of Améry the self-proclaimed man of *ressentiment* and Levi the survivor who claims that he is satisfied by the workings of justice at the Nuremberg trials and since, the recursive action of resenting can destroy the individual at the same time that it asserts individual dignity against the demands of society. *Ressentiment* may not be theorizable, but it appears threatening both for the individual and for the society it troubles.

The scholarly and literary work of the Prague German writer, historian, sociologist and theologian H. G. Adler (1910–1988) may point to one path through the seemingly intractable aporia of unbearable *ressentiment* and unjust forgiveness after the crimes of the Holocaust. Adler's multifaceted scholarly work worked out a programme that combined a commitment to political justice with a possibility of theological redemption through a return to piety and morality (*Sittlichkeit*). His pioneering scholarly works on Theresienstadt (*Theresienstadt 1941–1945. Das Antlitz einer Zwangsgemeinschaft. Geschichte Soziologie Psychologie*, 1955) and on the deportations of European Jews by the National Socialists (*Der verwaltete Mensch*, 1974) rely scrupulously on documentary evidence and on effacing Adler's subjective voice. They therefore contributed significantly to public knowl-

---

9 | Rüdiger Görner, (ed.), *The Anatomist of Melancholy. Essays in Memory of W. G. Sebald*, Munich: Iudicium 2003.

10 | W. G Sebald, *On the Natural History of Destruction*, trans. Anthea Bell, London: Penguin, 2004, p. 162.

11 | Sebald, *Natural History*, p. 172.

12 | Ibid., p. 169.

13 | Primo Levi, *The Drowned and the Saved*, trans. Raymond Rosenthal, London: Abacus 1988, p. 110.

edge about Nazi crimes and also formed the basis for several expert witness statements at the trials of National Socialists.[14] However, at the same time as Adler was working on these magisterial historical works which made him an authoritative figure in early Holocaust studies, he was also producing a series of novels bearing literary testimony to his experiences in the Shoah, only two of which were published during his lifetime. The last of these novels, *The Invisible Wall* [*Die unsichtbare Wand*], (posthumously published in 1989) archives traces of a *ressentiment* that is distinct from Améry's, but nonetheless a sentiment that asserts the right of the individual to record, satirise and retain their outrage at the injustices done to them not only by their Nazi tormentors, but also by the post-war world in general and their own community in particular. In the rest of this study, I will trace some steps of the intellectual journey that Adler made towards this seeming overcoming of *ressentiment* in his scientific and sociological work, while analysing the archive of *ressentiment* held in *The Invisible Wall*. In doing so, I demonstrate the extent to which Adler's double move can represent one strategy for achieving the socially desirable goal of forgiveness between victim and perpetrator, while allowing untimely, anti-social and righteous *ressentiment* its own, intransigent voice.

Adler, born in 1910, was an aspiring poet and intellectual when he was sent to Theresienstadt in 1942. From here, he was deported to Auschwitz in 1944, where his wife was immediately murdered. Adler suffered in a series of camps, including Theresienstadt, Auschwitz and Langenstein, connected to the infamous Dora works, until the end of the war. Determined never again to live in a country where the Nazis had been in control, and persecuted as a German-speaker by the post-1945 Czechoslovak Republic, Adler went into exile in England in 1947, where he lived until his death in 1988. This brief biographical sketch indicates the similarity of his history to that of Améry, his fellow Austrian Jewish victim of Nazi crimes. Indeed, soon after the German-language publication of Améry's *At the Mind's Limits* [*Jenseits von Schuld und Sühne*], (1966), Adler wrote to Améry to express his admiration for the book:

> I have never read anything like this about this subject matter, and I am not entirely unversed in this area. Your radical uprightness, which brings a pious attitude to life, humanity and justice into perfect harmony, deserves the highest recognition. I am thankful to you.[15]

Adler's archive contains no response from Améry. Although Adler's enthusiastic endorsement of Améry's essays on *ressentiment* might suggest that their philosophical positions were similar, Adler's theology sees an answer to human sin and wrongdoing in divine grace; hence, at the end of his long and in many ways extremely difficult life, Adler was able to state, "As a survivor I say: There

---

14 | Marcel Atze, (ed.), "Ortlose Botschaft". Der Freundeskreis H. G. Adler, Elias Canetti und Franz Baermann Steiner im englischen Exil, *Marbacher Magazin*, 84, (1998), Marbach: Deutsche Schillergesellschaft 1998, p. 145.

15 | *H.G. Adler to Jean Améry*, 27.5.68, DLA Marbach A I 10. Translation is mine.

was mercy upon me".[16] If Améry attacks Nietzsche for his moral condemnation of *ressentiment*, Adler, in an essay entitled "The Transvaluer of Values, Nietzsche and the Consequences", acquits Nietzsche of the charge of anti-Semitism but condemns him for his attacks on Christianity, and for his contribution to dismantling the distinction between good and evil.[17] Indeed, Adler reverses Nietzsche's own attack on the man of *ressentiment* by accusing Nietzsche himself of 'irrational hatred' against Christianity[18] and 'bitterness' in his discussions of compassion.[19] Adler does not use the term *ressentiment* in his evaluation of Nietzsche, but in attacking Nietzsche's bitterness and boundless individualism, he comes close to performing precisely that condemnation of *ressentiment* that Améry himself resents. Although Adler underwent similarly harrowing experiences to Améry, and like Améry chose to spend the rest of his life in exile from German-speaking countries, Adler maintained a philosophy based on piety, individualism and a faith in democracy. His humanist philosophy was constructed in an opposition to what he named "mechanical materialism". For Adler, the latter is a stiffly rationalist form of thinking that reduces the human being to an object, rather than respecting its autonomy as a being with a soul, personality and dignity.[20] In his understanding, the crimes of National Socialism were caused by the fall of the modern world into "mechanical materialism", which is ultimately a result of sin, the universal condition of man. Only through confronting one's own sin can the refusal of guilt be broken through, and the grace of conscience can become the guide of one's own actions.[21] Adler's scholarly publicisation of the crimes of National Socialism seeks, not to achieve the gesture of Christian forgiveness reviled by Améry and Langer, but rather to make the German people aware of their own particular guilt in order that they can turn away from their denial of that guilt to become ethically autonomous human beings.[22] This philosophy underlies Adler's acts of intellectual rapprochement and reconciliation with Germany, by undertaking an extensive programme of public education, via journalism, radio broadcasts and lecture tours, about not only the murder of the European Jews but also about German culture. Moreover, unlike Améry, who

---

16 | Jürgen Serke, *Böhmische Dörfer. Wanderungen durch eine verlassene literarische Landschaft*, Vienna: Tsolnay 1987, p. 334. Translation H. Finch.

17 | H.G. Adler, *Die Erfahrung der Ohnmacht. Beiträge zur Soziologie unserer Zeit*, Frankfurt a. M.: Europäische Verlagsanstalt 1964, p. 88.

18 | Ibid., p. 50.

19 | Ibid., p. 56.

20 | H.G Adler, Theresienstadt 1941- 1945. *Antlitz einer Zwangsgemeinschaft*, Göttingen: Wallstein, 2004, p. 643. (¹1948, Erstdruck 1955, 2. verbesserte Auflage 1960). Trans. H. Finch.

21 | Thomas Krämer, *Die Poetik des Gedenkens. Zu den autobiographischen Romanen H. G. Adlers*, Würzburg: Königshausen & Neumann 2012, p. 74.

22 | Ibid., p. 67.

wrote his essay "Resentments" in response to the oppressive cultural climate urging forgiveness in the wake of the Auschwitz trials, Adler was able to participate in the process of justice. He made a direct contribution to the legal process of prosecuting those responsible for the murder of European Jews; a "genuine reaction", in Nietzsche's terms.[23] As a leading scholar of the deportations, Adler provided key evidence in the trial of Adolf Eichmann, thereby materially contributing to the legal process of retribution against Nazi criminals, although his initial request to be allowed directly to question Eichmann in the dock was quickly dismissed.[24] This active participation allowed him to achieve a position, if not of forgiveness, then of justice towards Eichmann. Adler's ethical commitment to humanism meant that, although he believed that the trial was likely to have a "positive influence" on the Federal Republic of Germany, he was unhappy with the sentence imposed on Eichmann and wanted to sign a Martin Buber-led petition of Jewish intellectuals protesting against the death sentence.[25] For Adler, the significance of the trial lay less in its act of retribution against an individual and more in its educational value in opening the world's eyes to the tragedy of the murder of European Jewry. This position, combining justice with mercy, was in keeping with Adler's overall theological position.

Reconciliation and *Rapprochement*: Adler's Journeys to Germany

At the beginning of Améry's essay "Resentments", he undertakes a journey to an idyllic modern Germany, "this peaceful, lovely land, inhabited by hard-working, efficient, and modern people".[26] The seeming paean to contemporary Germany swiftly switches to Améry's radical analysis of his *ressentiment*; despite all the intellectual, economic and doubtless moral virtues that he discerns in the modern Germany, Améry clings to his "retrospective grudge", his untimely resentment against the German people and the German nation. By contrast, two unpublished essays by Adler, "Political Fate and German Politics" (Das Politische Verhängnis und Deutsche Politik), dated 22–26.1.1953, and "My Experiences with Germany" (Meine Erfahrungen mit Deutschland), 19–20.1.1967, trace precisely that generous journey away from mistrust and fear of the new West German nation towards forgiveness and acceptance that Améry refuses to make, despite the pressures upon him to do so.[27]

---

23 | Nancy Wood, "The Victims's Resentments", in: Bryan Cheyette/Laura Marcus (eds and introd.), Homi K Bhabha, (foreword), Paul Gilroy, (afterword): *Modernity, Culture and 'the Jew'*, Stanford, CA: Stanford UP 1998, pp. 257–67, p. 259.

24 | Atze: *Ortlose Botschaft*, 145.

25 | Ibid., 148.

26 | Améry: *At the Mind's Limits*, p. 63.

27 | In: *Adler Nachlaß*, DLA Marbach, A II 3. All translations by H. Finch.

The earlier essay was written before the publication of Adler's *magnum opus Theresienstadt*, that was to win him recognition in the German-speaking world. "Political Fate and German Politics" expresses disquiet about the future of West German politics, questioning whether the current moral condition of Germany is sufficient "to place Germany on a democratic basis in the sense of Western European or North American orders". Like Améry, he is not convinced that the German people and the West German State truly realise their perpetrator guilt. Instead, he quotes the "war anthem" of the eighteenth-century German poet Matthias Claudius, "I long not to have been guilty of it!", and suggests that this supposedly "apolitical" desire never to have been guilty is still a motive force of contemporary German identity.[28] Adler fears that this desire to be unpolitical and guiltless may lead, not to the resurgence of the National Socialists, which he believes to be unlikely, but rather to the rehabilitation of former war criminals and a refusal to carry out justice. In particular, he is concerned at the reaction of the German political establishment to the Naumann affair of January 1953, when English agents arrested six former Nazis in the territory of West Germany, and all sides of the German political establishment, including Interior Minister Lehr (CDU), expressed outrage.[29] For Adler, in this essay, the challenge facing West Germans is to take on political responsibility for their state; an action which looks forward to a just and participatory democracy, as well as backwards to punishing the sins of the past.

Even in this essay written only eight years after his liberation from the camps, Adler's vocabulary is not that of personal *ressentiment*, but of theological categories of sin and grace. The political substance of the essay comes only after an introductory passage stating that "every real social condition is to be viewed in the fate of the Fall into sin", and that righteous political action is therefore to be viewed as a "constantly outdated and always contemporary messianic action", working in conjunction with a metaphysical grace, to overcome the Fall. The theological framing of this essay allows Adler to move his questions of justice, guilt and retribution away from the personal and physical locus of the tortured body, where Améry sites his own *ressentiment*. Adler's belief in a divine grace also contrasts with Améry's statements throughout *At the Mind's Limits* that he is an atheist, and one who cannot find meaning in Marxist critiques of society either. Nonetheless, the essay's disquiet means that Adler's conception of grace does not serve the Nietzschean function of facilitating forgetting – grace as the privilege of the powerful alone and not accessible to the man of *ressentiment* – but instead sets out the social conditions under which a divine grace could come to fruition.

The essay is headed with a handwritten note in Adler's capitals: "Germany <Not to be printed in the work, unless in an appendix, but keep on file [*aufbewahren*]>". In the event, the essay was not printed in *Theresienstadt* or any other work, but the content of its disquiet archived. By contrast, "My Experiences with

---

28 | Matthias Claudius, 'Kriegslied', 1774.

29 | Norbert Frei, *Adenauer's Germany and the Nazi Past: The Politics of Amnesty and Integration*, trans. Joel Golb, New York: Columbia U.P. 2002, p. 284.

Germany", written fourteen years later, formed the basis for several public talks. Instead of the dispassionate tone of the earlier essay, it takes an autobiographical approach, although even this is qualified with the remark that Adler would like to "leave everything out which is entirely or mostly linked only with my private fate". In contrast to the warning function of the earlier unpublished essay, "My Experiences with Germany" contains emollient elements, gesturing towards that supposedly "antimoral natural process of healing" with post-war Germany that Améry condemns.[30] Adler insists that he "was not actually resentful towards the German people after the liberation" in 1945, and mirrors Améry's friendly depiction of the new Federal Republic without the savagely ironic undertone: Adler claims that he has in general found "much friendliness and human understanding" in Germany and avers that he has been "well treated" by officials, even when he is putting in a claim for reparations. Nonetheless, Adler severely criticises German justice, in particular when he was called as an expert witness in "a large trial against people who were accused of national socialist crimes of violence" (we may assume that this refers to the Frankfurt Auschwitz trials).

> I regarded the accused without prejudice and without passion, my feelings towards the court and above all towards the defence could not remain so cool. During this trial I felt as though I were transposed to the time before 1945. (Ibid.)

Here, Adler imputes untimeliness not to himself, but to the inhumane mechanisms of German justice. His sentiments towards the Nazi criminals remain dispassionately grounded in the post-war present, rather than returning to pre-war injury, but the court reprises the "mechanical materialism" that Adler feels led to the rise of the National Socialist regime. Adler's personal time sense, in this essay, is not *ressentiment*, which, as Scherpe points out, must repeat something (such as a traumatic experience) and which is linked to revanchism and repetition.[31] Instead, it is the German court that is at once untimely and out of time; this is linked to Adler's belief, one not shared by Améry, that Nazism was a particular expression of a generally fallen condition of modern society, and that therefore even in 1967 it has not been consigned to the past. As he writes in *Theresienstadt*, "mechanical materialism with its ideological grimaces still grows rampant, Theresienstadt has remained possible", and the inhumane and adversarial workings of the German court reflect this continuing existence of "mechanical materialism".[32] Adler does not wish the moral "annulment of time" advocated by Améry, indeed he has no desire to perform any operations on the past at all: "The past, the word says it, is past. It cannot be changed, so it also cannot be "mastered". The present is the only effective moment of social action, and it is in the present, not the past, that the battle against "mechanical materialism" is to be fought.

---

30 | Améry, *At the Mind's Limits*, p. 77.

31 | Scherpe, "Ressentiment", p. 168.

32 | H.G. Adler, *Theresienstadt*, p. 684.

"My Experiences in Germany" demonstrates the kind of forward-directed thinking, facilitated by a legal process of retribution, that transitional justice scenarios would seem to require. Adler concludes by saying that his good relationships with Germans allow him to hope that all evils can be overcome,

> as long as we only have grace [...]. At least two people, who stand on opposite sides, must reach out their hands. This is not to speak of any weak and bloodless brotherliness, which only covers up conflicts, without resolving them. Forgetting helps nothing.[33]

Nonetheless, alongside this active message of reconciliation lies the same peculiarly Adlerian *ressentiment* which we will later discuss in relation to *The Wall*. Adler's resentment is directed not against the torturers who abused him, but instead against post-war societies which *misrecognise* him as a victim. He describes how (unlike Améry) he wishes to be dissociated from his suffering at the hand of the Nazis, but instead finds himself constantly recognised for his experiences in the camps, rather than for his scholarly and literary achievements. After the publication of *Theresienstadt* in 1955, however, he writes, 'now I was labelled, my past could no longer be turned off *[ausschalten]*.[34] This misrecognition and victim identity contributes far more significantly to his feeling of alienation from Germany than does his experience at the hands of National Socialism. A more intimate *ressentiment* is therefore generated by the feeling that not only was his reputation as 'Theresienstadt-Adler' cemented in the public eye – the German public in general – but his old friends in particular had turned against him:

> Unlike Jews who came from Germany, also unlike those German speakers who moved to the Federal Republic in the immediate post-war years, I was and remained a stranger there, at least a foreigner. I had no envoys in the country, no friends, no acquaintances from the pre-war years (my old German friends from Prague were in part dead, in part missing, and also most of them had given me the cold shoulder since 1938). I was lacking every kind of personal connection to people in Germany.[35]

The direct accusation levelled at his faithless friends contrasts markedly with the impersonal language in which he describes his persecution by the National Socialists: "In 1939 I was caught up into the whirlwind of the Jewish persecution, which devoured eighteen of my close kin, including my wife, parents and step-parents".[36] The impersonal nature of this description is clearly not connected to any squeamishness about naming those who tormented him directly, as his active role in the Eichmann trial shows, but rather to his desire not to "embarrass" his German partners, and to relieve them from the "constraints"

---

33 | H.G. Adler, "My Experiences in Germany", MS. p. 12, trans. Helen Finch.

34 | Ibid., p. 4.

35 | Ibid., p. 2.

36 | Ibid., p. 1.

that arise in conversation with them when the details of Adler's past emerge.[37] Adler prefers not to identify as the victim of suffering in order that an intersubjective healing process can take place, and so that a genuine trust and moral relationship may build between himself and the German people. By contrast, the reference to his old friends who gave him the "cold shoulder" suggests that Adler feels that they also carry a burden of guilt for their abandonment of him, one that he is not so quick to put aside for fear of embarrassing them, and that he clings to a victim identity created by such slights. Nancy Wood suggests that Améry's identity as a victim was cemented, not by the injuries inflicted by the perpetrator as such, but by his abandonment by a society which had failed to protect him against such persecution.[38] If Améry emphasises his essential loneliness in the face of his persecutors, Adler emphasises his loneliness at having been abandoned by friends.[39] This victim identity, as a victim of a breakdown of trust between friends as much as of a victim of violence and murder, finds much deeper expression in *The Wall*.

The Fiction of *Ressentiment*

In the atmosphere in Germany of the 1950s, when Adler commenced publishing his scholarly and literary work, Jewish *ressentiment* was most certainly unwelcome. A culture of philosemitism, advocating German-Jewish reconciliation, dominated against a strong undercurrent of anti-Semitism, and German citizens in general wished to leave the past in peace.[40] If, as the essays discussed above suggest, Adler was profoundly troubled by this desire to forget, his literary writing – poetry, novels and short prose – also continues, to a large extent, the project of witness contained in his scholarly work.[41] It is informed by a similar mode of impersonal witness, as Adler says: "As a historian, sociologist and creative writer I was only allowed to bring to bear whatever belongs to my own past insofar as it had also affected other people".[42] His first two novels are in keep-

---

37 | Ibid., p. 4.

38 | Wood: "The Victim's Resentments", p. 258.

39 | Améry, *At the Mind's Limits*, p. 260.

40 | Wolfgang Benz, "Jewish Existence in Germany from the Perspective of the non-Jewish Majority: Daily Life between Anti-Semitism and Philo-Semitism", in: Leslie Morris/ Jack Zipes (eds), *Unlikely History. The Changing German-Jewish Symbiosis*, 1945–2000, New York: Palgrave 2002, pp. 101–118, p. 113; Katja Behrens, "The Rift and Not the Symbiosis", in ibid, pp. 31–48, 33f.

41 | See Thomas Krämer, "Two Modes of Remembrance – One Autobiographical Project. On the Relationship between Scholarship and Literature in H.G. Adler's Work", in Helen Finch/Lynn Wolff (eds), *H. G. Adler/W. G. Sebald. Witnessing, Memory, Poetics*, forthcoming.

42 | H.G. Adler, "My Experiences in Germany", p. 4.

ing both with this project of impersonal witness and with the project of moral catharsis outlined above. His first published novel about the Holocaust, *Eine Reise (The Journey*, 1962) met with a relieved reception from German reviewers, who, although they were often baffled by its complex poetics, were certain that the novel avoided all taint of *ressentiment*. Despite its harrowing depictions of the murder of a family in the *univers concentrationnaire*, it was described as a "great and in the final analysis also a positive book",[43] Josef Michels in the *Rheinische Post* was certain that Adler had not written the book "because he wanted to accuse",[44] and the *Neue Bücherschau* wrote categorically, "The book is not an accusation".[45] This reading is presumably supported by the fact that the sole survivor of the novel, Paul Lustig, ends his journey through the camps in a state of grace, confident that he will not feel ashamed before the dead any more and that "the hand of life has been extended to him".[46] This affirmative ending comes, however, after a narrative that depicts physical and psychic horrors, and which contains several bitterly satirical depictions of perpetrators as well as of the general German population and of the occupying German troops; the reviewers who refused to detect any *ressentiment* in the text are under the suspicion of operating under precisely those systems of denial that Adler's work sought to demolish.

The Wall, however, which was only published in 1989, after Adler's death, contains an archive of accusations and *ressentiments*, not against the torturers of the protagonist – the camps and persecution are never described – but against the German friends and acquaintances who give him the cold shoulder after his return to society from the camps. Unlike Améry's *ressentiments*, directed against individual tormentors and against the German collective as a whole, these *ressentiments* are directed at friends who have failed and continue to fail the survivor, as well as against callous bureaucracies. The survivor-protagonist, Arthur Landau, is struggling to maintain faith in his own existence, to hear the words 'I am'. Deeply traumatised, his sense of self destroyed, his wife and family murdered in the camps, Landau moves to Prague and then to London in an attempt to put the past behind him and build a career as a scholar. However, in a movement that demonstrates the recoiling, redoubling nature of *ressentiment*, Landau finds himself accused by the German exile community of being untimely, anti-social, devious and excessively attached to a traumatic and worthless past. In London, he gains the reputation of "a morbid person, an anti-social, corrosive type; my terrible past, about which people could only weep, had ruined me; someone like that remains forever useless for a positive life."[47] Landau wishes to create a positive

---

43 | Anonymous review, in: Bücherei-Nachrichten, October 1963, in *Adler- Nachlaß*, A II 51.

44 | Josef Michels, in: *Rheinische Post* 08.06.1963, in: *Adler-Nachlaß*, A II 51.

45 | Anonymous review, in: *Neue Bücherschau* 02.01.1963, in *Adler-Nachlaß*, A II 51.

46 | H.G. Adler, *The Journey*, trans. Peter Filkins, New York: Random House 2008, p. 283.

47 | H.G.: Adler, *Die unsichtbare Wand*, Berlin: Aufbau, 2005, p. 687. [*The Invisible Wall*] All translations by H. Finch.

work out of his terrible camp experiences, by pursuing a study on the concentration camps – the "Sociology of the Repressed Man" – that combines sociology with a moral critique. However, he is told by an influential intellectual that the work is a "too violent reproof", and that a person who was actually in the camps is rarely suited for such work, because "subjective material is dangerous".[48] A would-be benefactor tells him that he is childish, immature, and will have to let go of his academic aspirations if he is to integrate in society.[49] These accusations – of morbidity, anti-sociality, untimeliness, excessive reproof and excessive subjectivity – are precisely those that make up the persona of *ressentiment*. Landau struggles to re-create a sense of self in the face of these accusations, and clings to the moral truth of his witness. More, he embraces his untimeliness: "The confusion of history and present is my property, it belongs forever to my being."[50] As friend after friend deserts and betrays him, he builds a new, recalcitrant sense of self around his love for his second wife and the intention to move forward: this new self "turns its wheels forwards as hope; it was thus a farewell to remembering. As it drew me on towards a goal, it demanded that I realize myself, and thus memory was only allowed as help along the way, not valid in itself [...] the way itself was the memory",[51] Nonetheless, the fragmented temporal structure of the novel, which constantly moves to and fro within the protagonist's life, confounds this forward-oriented synthesis of memory and action, self and other. His hopes for re-integration in society are destroyed by the abuse he receives, and instead, he decides no longer to hope to achieve self-respect from people who do not love him. Instead, he sets a modest goal: "Endure and await grace".[52]

The *ressentiment* archived in Adler's text lies not in an articulated philosophy of resentment like Améry's, nor in the meticulous evidence against named perpetrators that he provided in his scholarly work, but in the angry, satirical and unforgiving portraits of the friends who turn against him. Franz Hocheneder has provided a reading of the novel as a *roman à clef*;[53] although the novel is clearly distinct from autobiography, the very fact that a knowledge of Adler's biography allows a quick identification of Oswald Birch with Elias Canetti, Professor Kratzenstein with Theodor W. Adorno, demonstrates the personal and interpersonal nature of the hostile portraits that *The Wall* contains. A comparison of the literary representation of Landau's first tentative letters to his one surviving school friend, Soundso, with Adler's surviving correspondence with his close friend Franz Baermann Steiner demonstrate the *ressentiment*-laden reinscription of Adler's own personal experiences into Landau's metafiction. In the novel, Landau spends days

---

48 | Ibid., p. 125.

49 | Ibid., p. 469

50 | Ibid., p. 487.

51 | Ibid., p. 479.

52 | Ibid., p. 621.

53 | Franz Hocheneder, *H.G. Adler (1910–1988): Privatgelehrter und freier Schriftsteller: eine Monographie*, Vienna, Cologne, Weimar: Böhlau 2009, p. 239

painstakingly writing a letter to Soundso that tries its very hardest to spare him the worst horrors of his experience, and to strike a cheerful note. The grotesque nature of this enterprise is self-evident: "Franziska, [Landau's first wife] has gone too. But now really no more of these sad things. I have myself well in hand, I'm not giving up and haven't reckoned up with life yet [...] You would admit: That's Artur, as I've always known him".[54] The extravagant attempts to make lights of unspeakable traumas lay bare the chasm between past self and present social mores. Soundso writes back an ebullient and shameless letter, deliberately misrecognising both the evidently traumatised textuality of Landau's letter itself, in a move that Landau says is typical of the subsequent responses he received from post-war friends, whom he characterises in their letters as "wriggling worms with very small hearts". Landau writes to them in an attempt to reintegrate his sense of self, motivated by the wish "to recognize myself in them, to be in them", but in response his friends demand his pity and his recognition of their suffering: "They fished for my applause, I was supposed to understand them, hold nothing against them, understand their need, advise them, pass on messages, run errands for them, but at most the worms yearned for my consolation".[55]

That this fictional representation of the content of Landau's letters does not tally with the content of Adler's actual post-war correspondence, is clear. Soundso's reply begins with expressing relief that the camps weren't really as bad as reports made out, continues with complaining about the trials of life in exile, and includes an onerous errand that he would like Landau to run for him while he is in their home town; could Landau meet his lawyer about his mother's expropriated house? Soundso continues by telling him that he is untimely – "to be honest, I must doubt if you are *up to date* with your methods, as we say here."[56] Advising him, as Kratzenstein will later, to stick to an objective rather than an ethical theme, he warns him that "although I admit that the horrors were in fashion for a moment, but especially in serious circles interest is already waning significantly".[57] Soundso's assumption that Landau will forget easily reminds us that Améry identified Jewish exiles, among them Victor Gollancz and Martin Buber, as those who "were already trembling with the pathos of forgiveness and reconciliation" immediately following the war.[58] Soundso's letter is at once cruel, unthinking, selfish and smug, but Landau allows that it is clever: "The letter does not offer any surface to grip on to. Superficially everything is nice and smooth. He contorts himself deftly".[59] Such "deft contortions" are not to be found in the documentary letters of Steiner to Adler. In the published correspondence, it is unclear which of the first letters Steiner in fact received from Adler, owing to the

---

54 | H.G. Adler, *Die unsichtbare Wand* [*The Invisible Wall*], p. 255. See notes 61 and 64.

55 | Ibid., p. 275.

56 | Ibid., p. 270.

57 | Ibid. p. 271.

58 | Améry, *At the Mind's Limits*, p. 65.

59 | Ibid., p. 274.

difficulties of the post in the immediate post-war period. There was certainly a two-month delay in Steiner's first response, but the very first paragraph of his letter performs exactly that act of recognition of Adler's trauma and desire to have that trauma communicated to a wider community that Landau craves: "Certainly the memory of the horror must be your most valuable possession. But somehow it must happen that all of this is shared by a community".[60] Steiner's letter is far from the smooth smugness of Soundso's, darting distractedly as it does between difficult and disparate topics – the death of Steiner's parents in Theresienstadt, his literary and academic work, the possibilities for Adler's academic career in the US or Denmark, and whether mutual friends have survived. The unpolished, fragmented textuality of the letters is due in part to the necessity to evade the censor, but also demonstrates the traumatised nature of the communication and of Steiner's text. Steiner's concern about the whereabouts of mutual friends and his attempts to send Adler a package, contrast strongly with Soundso's bland suggestion that Landau and he should go skiing together in the Bohemian mountains, and with his immediate demand that Landau busy himself with restoring Soundso's Czech property.[61] As Carol Tully comments in her introduction to the letters, Steiner's immediate understanding of the value that Adler's "memory of the horror" has for him shows an unusual sensitivity: it might seem an inappropriate sentiment, and yet these memories would be decisive for Adler's future work.[62] The distraught tone of Steiner's letters is far from the supercilious one of Soundso's, and crucially, Steiner affords his friend exactly the recognition of his witness and existence that Landau craves.

Soundso's demand that Landau contact Soundso's lawyer and involve himself in the onerous task of restoring his property is, in fact, mirrored in Steiner's correspondence. Steiner's third letter, dated 19 August 1945, includes in the last paragraph a request that Adler contact Steiner's uncle about some property, and also that he buy books for Steiner. These requests come, nonetheless, after a lengthy and intensely personal discussion of Steiner's discoveries in poetics and poetry in the war years. As we know from the Steiner correspondence, far from the friendship ending like Landau's and Soundso's, Adler and Steiner continued to be intimate friends. They were in constant contact involving visits, mutual advice and discussions about poetry and philosophy until the month of Steiner's death in 1952. After Steiner's death, Adler took on the role of his literary executor and tirelessly sought the publication and promotion of his friend's work in the decades that followed.[63] It thus seems highly unlikely that the novel was intended in any way as a posthumous attack on Steiner's person or reputation.

---

60 | Carol Tully (ed.), *Zeugen der Vergangenheit. H. G. Adler – Franz Baermann Steiner. Briefwechsel 1936–1952*, Munich: iudicium 2011, p. 73.

61 | H.G. Adler, *Die Unsichtbare Wand [The Invisible Wall]*, p. 268.

62 | Carol Tully, "Einführung", in: C. Tully (ed.), *Zeugen der Vergangenheit*, p. 12.

63 | See Jeremy Adler/Carol Tully (eds): *Über Franz Baermann Steiner: Brief an Chaim Rabin. By H. G. Adler* (Gottinger Sudelblätter), Gottingen: Wallstein 2006.

Rather, a clue as to the poetic process that is at work between Steiner's letters and the fictional Soundso's correspondence is provided in *Die unsichtbare Wand* when a young friend of Landau's performs a silly lampoon of Soundso's letter. Peter makes faces as he reads it out, distorting some places that provoke him to "boundless mockery," swapping Soundso's words and syllables around in a meaningless but pompous parody. Landau judges the performance to be "not exactly brilliant", but acknowledges that it had managed to brighten his "inconsolably annoyed mood".[64] Peter's parody works not on the level of intellectual engagement, but of emotional restoration. In the same way, the fictional correspondence between Landau and Soundso may archive subjective feelings of *ressentiment*, abandonment and annihilation occasioned by the very first interactions between survivor and exiled friends. This archive is not intended to serve as a direct accusation of named people. Rather, as a traumatised, non-linear text, *The Wall* annuls the difference between present and past, demonstrating the persistence of untimely feelings of *ressentiment*. Like Améry, Adler requires the reader to interpret what "superficially reads as symptom – a private time out of joint – in terms that are morally and politically more urgent and protesting".[65] Here, it is also important to remember that for Adler, emotional language (the 'lexicon of emotion', in Ludwig Jäger's phrase) has in itself a moral function, placing itself in opposition to the cold, mechanistic operations of National Socialist and culture industry bureaucracies that deny individual subjectivity.[66] If the text is the unstable and hesitant account of a fragile subjective healing, the uncharitable portrayal of Soundso and his friends may in itself, like Peter's parody, have a therapeutic function. This parody is continued in the implausible accusations hurled at him by Soundso's friends and connections, who call him a deserter, a seducer, tell him he should never have survived, and offer him violence at his recalcitrant insistence on bearing scholarly witness rather than meekly integrating into post-war society as an unskilled labourer. Landau's narrative, caught between an angry *ressentiment* and a commitment to grace, contains a precarious compromise that allows him to retain both individual dignity and the memory of violence of the camps. Unlike Jean Améry's philosophy, which contains a retroactive utopianism akin to Benjamin's historical messianism – the wish to make the offence undone – Landau creates a credo which neither wishes to make the past undone, nor rests its hopes in a future utopia of religious or political revolution. Instead, Landau continues with his intellectual project despite his financially precarious situation, while also committing to a conservative philosophy. "Every

---

64 | H.G. Adler, *Die Unsichtbare Wand* [*The Invisible Wall*], p. 273.

65 | Marina McKay, "'Resentments': The Politics and Pathologies of War Writing", in: Petra Rau (ed.), *Conflict, Nationhood and Corporeality in Modern Literature: Bodies-at-War*, Basingstoke: Palgrave 2010, pp. 164–184, p. 177.

66 | Ruth Vogel-Klein, "History, Emotions, Literature: The Representation of Theresienstadt in H.G. Adler's *Theresienstadt 1941–1945: Antlitz einer Zwangsgemeinschaft* and Sebald's *Austerlitz*", in: H. Finch/L. Wolff (eds), *Witnessing, Memory, Poetics. H.G. Adler and W.G. Sebald*, Rochester: Camden House 2014, pp. 180–200.

really original inheritance, the most inner being of the same existence, however it may transform itself, is holy to me."[67] This conservative philosophy allows a retrospective movement, but the pious one of *Gedenken* [remembrance], rather than the anger-laden one of *ressentiment*. Remembrance, Landau declares, is "the holy inheritance that I also honour". Through conserving inherited spiritual values, a new beginning is possible, a new beginning that is at once repetition and movement towards the future. Through the traumatic ruptures of the text, Landau's archive of *ressentiment* accords to his persisting anger and hurt against the breakdown in the social bonds, equal status with this more socially palatable doctrine of conservation and renewal. What binds *ressentiment* to these other moments is the constant insistence on *Gedenken*, remembrance of suffering and of the dead, and on the dignity of the individual.

Adler's archival novel is doubly untimely; written in 1954–1956, it was only published after his death, in 1989. Yet his work, taken as a whole, may provide a rich resource to integrate the otherness of *ressentiment*, mentioned at the beginning of this paper, with a philosophy of social responsibility and the possibility of reconciliation. Adler's complex narrative moves between a sociological work that enabled the workings of justice, a theology that points towards grace and reconciliation and literature that archives *ressentiments* and traumas. Through his multidisciplinary project, Adler allows the subjective moral truth of a victim to speak and accuse a society who is deaf to victims. In the urgent questions of reconciliation and social healing that Derrida and Langer raise anew, Adler shows that literature can perform an important function in archiving the victim's voice in a way that allows for reconciliation without falling into the unjust traps of sentimental humanism.

---

67 | *Die unsichtbare Wand*, p. 702.

Contagion

Jeanne Riou

1. From Asceticism to Compliance: Contagious Origins of *Ressentiment*

Contagion, a familiar term in empathy theory around 1900, has had a chimeric quality in the history of ideas. Nietzsche, for instance, bases his critique of culture and of Christian morality on a notion of contagious fear; rather than empowering human beings to self-realisation, the morality of the Christian world had had a homogenising, debilitating effect (*Beyond Good and Evil* [*Jenseits von Gut und Böse*]; *On the Genealogy of Morals* [*Zur Genealogie der Moral*]). Tertullian, in the 2nd and 3rd centuries AD, was one of the founding Church fathers whose writings advanced the ascetic morality castigated by Nietzsche for its basis in Ressentiment and hypocrisy: "While thus, then, we spread ourselves before God, let the hooks pierce us, the crosses suspend us, the fires play upon us, the swords gash our throats, the beasts leap on us. The very posture of the Christian at prayer is readiness for any torture."[1] By implication, Christian ascetic morality holds the promise that whatever horrors are endured on earth will be transcended in the afterlife. The sinners, by contrast, will be condemned to eternal mortification. In this sense, asceticism – in the light of such fear of eternal damnation – spreads contagiously. For Nietzsche, the Ressentiment at the heart of this, the relishing of the thoughts of the suffering of the "damned", belies fear of the stronger "other", the one who stands alone, the "sinner".

Later, the phenomenologist Max Scheler varies Nietzsche's notion of Ressentiment somewhat. Scheler tries to rehabilitate a Christian version of "giving" (mercy), re-framing this as an act of intentionality.[2] Here, the intentionality of the giver takes precedence over the demand, i.e. the "plea" (such as for polit-

---

1 | Tertullian, *Apology. De Spectaculis*, ed./trans. T.R. Glover, London: Heinemann, Cambridge, MA: Harvard University Press 1966, XXX, p. 153. (Orig.: Apologeticus, 30)

2 | Max Scheler, *Studienausgabe. Gesammelte Werke*, ed. Manfred S. Frings, Bern/Munich: Francke 1973, Vol. 7. Wesen und Formen der Sympathie ('1913), p. 51. Scheler does not refer to this explicitly as intentionality. However, his rejection of a rationalist notion of

ical equality). Therefore "honour" is associated with a merciful giving, itself construed as a phenomenological act. Ressentiment, by contrast, characterises the political demand for change. In both Nietzsche and Scheler, there is a link between contagion and Ressentiment. In each case, the contagious effects are imputed to social and political opposition. To demand equality in Nietzsche's terms is flawed – as is the Christian concept of mercy – because neither stems from the centre of a person who *feels* strong, and whose honour is therefore unbroken.[3] In the following, I will examine these origins of Ressentiment discourse, in particular the association of contagion with morality in both Nietzsche and Scheler. In a second step, I will argue that echoes of Ressentiment-critique in contemporary political discourse tend to align dissent with the "contagious" position of the moral in much the same way that Nietzsche held morality to be intrinsically a corruption of human nature.

Friedrich Nietzsche's thinking on Ressentiment in *On the Geneaology of Morals* [*Zur Genealogie der Moral*] is premised on a contrast between an individual who is strong and free and one whose individuality has failed to develop.[4] 'Nobility', an openness of spirit, coincides with an assumption of nobility of

---

mercy that lacks an existential direction of thought towards the other as a phenomenon is in keeping with phenomenological understandings of intentionality.

3 | For a fuller account of this and of Max Scheler's nuanced distinction between sympathy and imitation – key terms in early empathy theory – see Jeanne Riou, *Anthropology of Connection. Perception and its Emotional Undertones in German Philosophical Discourse 1870–1930*, Würzburg: Königshausen & Neumann 2014. Chapters two and three of this study examine different stages of empathy theory around 1900, including the efforts of both Max Scheler and Henri Bergson to describe the relationship of instinct and intelligence based on observations of empathy as a form of intelligence not just in the human, but in the insect world. Within the present article, an abridged version of this account of empathy, instinct and identification extending to debates on contagion will be presented.

4 | Friedrich Nietzsche, *On the Genealogy of Morals*, trans. Douglas Smith, Oxford, New York: Oxford World's Classics 1996, here p. 24: "While the noble man lives for himself in trust and openness (*gennaios* 'of noble birth' underlines the nuance of 'honest' and also 'naïve'), the man of *ressentiment* is neither upright nor naïve in his dealings with others, nor is he honest and open with himself. His soul *squints*; his mind loves bolt-holes, secret paths, back doors, he regards all hidden things as *his* world, *his* security, *his* refreshment; he has a perfect understanding of how to keep silent, how not to forget, how to wait, how to make himself provisionally small and submissive. A race of such men of *ressentiment* is bound in the end to become *cleverer* than any noble race, and it will respect cleverness to a completely different degree: this is, as a first condition of existence." [Friedrich Nietzsche, *Sämtliche Werke. Kritische Studienausgabe in 15 Bänden*, eds Giorgio Colli/Mazzino Montinari, DTV de Gruyter: Munich 2007 (=¹1980), Vol. 5: *Jenseits von Gut und Böse. Zur Genealogie der Moral.* (=²1988), Vol. 5, p. 272–73: "Während der vornehme Mensch vor sich selbst mit Vertrauen und Offenheit lebt (griechisch 'edelbürtig' unterstreicht die nuance 'aufrichtig' und auch wohl 'naiv'), so ist der Mensch des Ressentiment weder aufrichtig, noch naif, noch mit

class, and the social world in question is probably Ancient Greece. The idea of authenticity, a combination of honesty and naïvety, fits the person who does not have to alter (him)self to encounter others. Not having to make damaging adjustments to his personality and social bearing, the individual is free to develop in an authentic way. Movements based on social protest, on the other hand, fall under suspicion of contagious weakness because, inauthentic in nature, they rest on banding together on the basis of under-development rather than maximisation of human potential. Nietzsche denigrates what he sees as any diminution of spirit, the results of a falseness engendered by the social world. Lacking the openness and untroubled authenticity of the celebrated nobleman, the person driven by Ressentiment "squints", and vies for advantage with others by whatever means rather than honestly facing their odds in the world.

Tertullian, quoted at the outset from the *Apologeticus*, dramatically proclaims the higher purpose of a Christian preparing to be tortured for his or her belief. This would be a good example of what Nietzsche sees as moral weakness. Tertullian's Christian vows to make himself small. He can be expected to offer no resistance to the wild beasts, if they are set on him, and a sense of vicarious pleasure is palpable in the text. If he is prepared to suffer, the Christian does so to become small enough to be forgiven by God, an asceticism intended as atonement. The embracing of suffering, and, potentially of martyrdom, are at the heart of Nietzsche's objections to Christian morality. Aesthetic renditions of selfhood along the lines of those in Tertullian's narrative as someone tiny who is prostrated before a powerful God are examples of what Nietzsche sees as intellectual dishonesty. It is not the act of proclamation, the aesthetic self-referentiality within such Christian writings that is suspect, but rather the sensibility underlying them, which engenders a morally and spiritually diminished sense of personhood. Revelling in smallness rather than squaring up to face the uncertainty of a universe of mythological gods, the aesthetic subjectivity within such narratives of early Christianity established a precedent, for Nietzsche, of impoverishing human experience through self-denial.

Indeed, Tertullian adds a political dimension to this text in exhorting early Christians to accept the rule of Emperors. Referring to Timothy, 2, he invokes the logic of offsetting the ravages of political disorder by praying for the Empire to continue:

'Pray,' he says 'for kings, and for princes and powers, that all things may be tranquil for you.' For when the empire is shaken, when the rest of its mem-

---

sich selber ehrlich und geradezu. Seine Seele *schielt*; sein Geist liebt Schlupfwinkel, Schleichwege und Hinterthüren, alles Versteckte muthet ihn an als *seine* Welt, *seine* Sicherheit, *sein* Labsal; er versteht sich auf das Schweigen, das Nicht-Vergessen, das Warten, das vorläufige Sich-verkleinern, Sich-demüthigen. Eine Rasse solcher Menschen des Ressentiment wird nothwendig endlich klüger sein als irgend eine vornehme Rasse, sie wird die Klugheit auch in ganz andrem Maasse ehren: nämlich als eine Existenzbedingung ersten Ranges [...]."] References to the German edition will be abbreviated in the following to *KSA*.

bers are shaken, we, too, of course, though we are supposed not to have anything to do with the disorder, are found in some corner of the disaster.[5]

There is no suggestion that the rule of the Empire is just. Equally, it is not implied that Christians should pray for its continuation out of any sense of conviction. On the contrary, in what would qualify in Nietzschean terms as Ressentiment, the weaker individual, sensing his or her own powerlessness, aligns him- or herself with the existing power, in this case the Roman Empire. Expediency, therefore, can contribute to Ressentiment. Values and political judgement are thus linked to the perception of what is in the individual's best interests. Rather than withdraw support for an Empire, if, for instance, this were what the individual considered to be the right thing to do, he or she is encouraged to opt for safety. In this way, a political choice is described in terms of the common good. Writing in the late nineteenth century, Nietzsche's objections to morality centre on a belief that from Early Christianity onwards, the notion of the common good disguised forms of crude self-interest in which fear and resentment of more talented others flourished. Ressentiment is thus aligned, for Nietzsche, with strategic thinking. It is precisely this type of intelligence, as distinct from one that favours principled choices, that Nietzsche has in mind (see above) with what he terms the "cleverness" of Ressentiment.[6]

Ressentiment is, obviously, not about conviction: it is about pragmatism with a claim to moral superiority. The veiled reference in Tertullian's *Apologeticus* is to Timothy 2, and the context less the pacifist stance of Christ than the pragmatic recognition in early Christianity that the Roman Empire represented the best chance of spreading Christianity and protecting it from sects, from dissidents, and from general dissolution. In the background is the idea that any weakness will infect the vulnerable people with whom it comes into contact, and so it is better to aspire to (political) strength. Ressentiment is the assumption that such strength achieved out of fear of infection by adopting a stance of moral rectitude is, in fact, real strength. For Nietzsche, it is, of course, the opposite of real strength, since it is a surrendering of vitality to expedience. In this spirit, Ressentiment allows a set of beliefs and moral values to go unchallenged. Based on something which has been sanctioned by a form of collaborative morality beyond the self, something which the individual has not scrutinised and would not have the courage to reject, the supposed humility of the Christian stance as described in the above example by Tertullian is, from a Nietzschean viewpoint, a facade. The unquestioning believer is not really humble, but simply too frightened to face a hostile world and leans instead on the identity gained through a shared set of values. Depending on this, he or she is too pragmatic to risk causing offence.[7] Applying this to the nineteenth century, Ressentiment, the

---

5 | Tertullian, *Apology*, XXX, p. 155.

6 | Friedrich Nietzsche, *On the Genealogy of Morals*, p. 24. [KSA, Vol. 5, pp. 272–273.]

7 | Indeed, as Yovel observes, for Nietzsche, western culture from Socrates, Moses and Jesus to Enlightenment rationalism are all caught up in a similarly cowardly tradi-

opposite of individuality, appears to Nietzsche to be at the heart of a culture that pays homage, in name at least, to the sovereign individual of the Enlightenment. It does so, for Nietzsche, in a way that misses the point. From a Nietzschean perspective, the critique of tradition stemming from the Enlightenment falls intolerably short of the rupture that would be needed to eliminate the link between epistemology and theology. Any shared set of values, irrespective, we can conclude, of Enlightenment corrections to the concept of tradition, nevertheless remains under suspicion of the "cleverness" and cowardice associated with Ressentiment.[8] Therefore the very notion of morality cannot be reformed, and Nietzsche's linking of morality with contagion is a critical element in the conceptual history of Ressentiment.

In his insightful study of Ressentiment and the phenomenon of guilt, Abou El Magd interprets this critique of "cleverness" from a slightly different perspective, that of a flight from reality.[9] Linking it to Nietzsche's claim that the weak individual shuns reality and is unable to face its consequences, he points out that in the place of an honest engagement, Nietzsche sees outright untruth at work in Ressentiment. Unable to face his or her own inadequacy, the person driven by Ressentiment constantly revises their own past failings. They blame others rather than themselves for ongoing disappointment and frustration.[10] Cleverness in this sense is not a pure intelligence, rather a devious, misdirected and misused one.

There is a dual strand to Early Christian morality that should be mentioned here, because both are central to the critique of morality in Nietzsche and in subsequent Ressentiment discourse. The first is asceticism, an example of which we have just seen in Tertullian. The second is the privileging of compassion. Examples of this include Heb. 10, 34: "For ye had compassion of me in my bonds, and took joyfully the spoiling of your goods, knowing in yourselves that ye have in heaven a better and an enduring substance,[11] Matt. 9.35, "And Jesus went about

---

tion. See Yirmiyahu Yovel, "Nietzsche und die Juden. Die Struktur einer Ambivalenz", in: Jacob Colomb (ed.), *Nietzsche und die jüdische Kultur*, Vienna: WUV Universitätsverlag 1998 (trans. Helmut Dahmer), pp. 126–142, cf. 127.

8 | See footnote 4.

9 | Esam Abou El Magd, *Nietzsche. Ressentiment und schlechtem Gewissen auf der Spur*, Würzburg: Königshausen & Neumann 1996, p. 21: "Der Mensch des Ressentiment kann nicht adäquat auf seine Umwelt reagieren. Statt auf die Gegenwart durch re-aktives Handeln einzugehen, sieht er sich durch sie beständig zurückgeworfen auf seine erlittenen schmerzhaften Verletzungen in der Vergangenheit." [The person driven by Ressentiment cannot respond adequately to their environment. Instead of engaging with the present through reactive action, he finds himself constantly thrown back on painful disappointments and hurt endured in the past.] (Trans. Jeanne Riou).

10 | Ibid. El Magd is referring in particular to *On the Genealogy of Morals* [*Zur Genealogie der Moral*].

11 | Hebrews, 10.76, in: *The Bible. Authorized King James Version with Apocrypha*, Oxford: Oxford World Classics 2008 (=¹1997), p. 268.

all the cities and villages, teaching in their synagogues, and preaching the gospel of the kingdom, and healing every sickness and every disease among the people", Matt. 9.36, "But when he saw the multitudes, he was moved with compassion on them, because they fainted, and were scattered abroad, as sheep having no shepherd", Mark 6.34, "And Jesus, when he came out, saw much people, and was moved with compassion toward them, because they were as sheep not having a shepherd: and he began to teach them many things." These biblical examples show compassion as linked to pity, but also to leadership (Matt. 9.36 and Mark 6.34), and encouragement to follow. In Heb. 10.34, being merciful and suffering wrongdoing without seeking revenge are linked to transcendence – a just reward in eternal life. But for Nietzsche, "Mitleids-Moral" – morality based on sympathy or compassion – far from being virtuous, is an entirely negative phenomenon, having engendered a philosophy in which life itself cannot flourish. To thrive, an individual must be life-embracing, which puts him or her at odds with a morality which is hostile to life. By life-embracing, he means self-regarding rather than being ethically bound to show compassion. The biblical examples, on the other hand, place no emphasis on the self – the good deed is done for the sake of the other, and all life holds the promise of transcendence (eg. Heb. 10.34).

To show compassion is enshrined in Christian morality (Mark 12.31 [...] "Thou shalt love thy neighbour as thyself. There is none other commandment greater than these") and is echoed in the burgeoning social democratic and communist movements of the nineteenth century. But for Nietzsche, it is mistaken to equate compassion with paradigms of equality or duty. To do so involves reducing the strong to the level of the weak:

> The sick represent the greatest danger for the healthy; it is *not* the strongest but the weakest who spell disaster for the strong. Do we appreciate this?... Broadly speaking, it is not fear of man which one would wish to reduce: for this fear compels the strong to be strong and on occasion fearful – it *maintains* the well-constituted type of man.[12]

Paying attention to the suffering of the sick and the weak takes away from the vitality of the strong. In this metaphor, the strong, since they must possess the capacity for empathy or for being altered by what they experience, are best kept in isolation from the weak. Were they to lack the capacity to be transformed by the prospect of suffering, there would, after all, be no danger. In this view, as sentient beings, the healthy are vulnerable to the weakening effects of the sick. It is not difficult to detect the nineteenth-century preoccupation with infection and disease in this line of thinking – suffering as a potentially transferable infestation that threatens the species. Therefore a morality that aspires to

---

12 | Friedrich Nietzsche, *On the Genealogy of Morals*, 3(14), p. 100–101. [KSA 5, p. 368: "Die Krankhaften sind des Menschen grossen Gefahr: nicht die Bösen, nicht die 'Raubthiere'. Die von vornherein Verunglückten, Niedergeworfnen, Zerbrochnen – sie sind es, die Schwächsten sind es, welche am Meisten das Leben unter Menschen unterminiren [sic], welche unser Vertrauen zum Leben, zum Menschen, zu uns am gefährlichsten vergiften und in Frage stellen."]

supporting the weak at the expense of the strong is at odds with nature. Those termed "immoral" or, as he puts it here, predatory ("Raubthiere") are not the source of danger at all. On the contrary, danger comes from the Christian prerogative of showing compassion for the unfortunates, those who are broken in body and spirit, because Nietzsche believes compassion to be a product of fear.

If fear is infectious, this is because human beings are inherently malleable. One of the reasons for a conclusion like this is disillusionment with an anthropocentric tradition of Enlightenment, a tradition that rests, to some degree, on the autonomy of the subject at the heart of Idealism. With disdain for all abstract, intellectualised philosophy, Nietzsche's writings suggest instead a porous, aesthetic subjectivity. Malleability is an intrinsic risk of a self that is open to its environment, a risk that has to be faced if the individual is to develop. Compliance and contagion are the by-products, both in individual and group terms, if the person, rather than face risk and exude vitality, shelters behind pre-formed ideas such as those of religion and morality.

In *Beyond Good and Evil*, *[Jenseits von Gut und Böse]*, a rejection of mediocrity is linked once again to the false moral preoccupation with social circumstances. Nietzsche refers contemptuously to social need ("Noth") and to those who lie broken and discarded at the bottom of 'society' ("Gesellschaft"). Directing sympathy towards these is the same as idealising the slave classes in ancient societies who can be valorised for fighting for freedom only if our understanding of freedom is a blind, brutish struggle to overcome a particular situation:

> Pity for *you*! That is certainly not pity as you understand it: it is not pity for social "distress", for "society" with its sick and injured, for people depraved from the beginning as they lie around us on the ground; even less is it pity for the grumbling, dejected, rebellious slave strata who strive for dominance – they call it "freedom". *Our* pity is a higher, more far-sighted pity: – we see how humanity is becoming smaller, how *you* are making it smaller![13]

"Real" pity, what is really worthy of sympathy, is the plight of humanity that has given in to the temptation of group-belonging. Human beings are diminished by the contagion of weakness. Sympathy or indeed empathy with the broken and the weak is ill-conceived. We can extrapolate from this Nietzschean view of the contagious effects of Ressentiment that political support for people in a weaker position in society is ill-founded. Within the same paradigm, the determination of any group of people to fight oppression immediately falls under suspicion of

---

13 | F. Nietzsche, *Beyond Good and Evil*, Rolf-Peter Horstmann/Judith Norman (eds), Cambridge, New York: C.U.P.: 2002, p. 116. [*KSA* 5, p. 160: "Mitleiden mit *euch*! das ist freilich nicht das Mitleiden, wie ihr es meint: das ist nicht Mitleiden mit der socialen ‚Noth', mit der ‚Gesellschaft' und ihren Kranken und Verunglückten, mit Lasterhaften und Zerbrochnen von Anbeginn, wie sie rings um uns zu Boden liegen; das ist noch weniger Mitleiden mit murrenden gefrückten aufrührerischen Sklaven-Schichten, welche nach Herrschaft – sie nennen's ‚Freiheit' – trachten. *Unser* Mitleid ist ein höheres fernsichtigeres Mitleiden: – wir sehen, wie der Mensch sich verkleinert, wie ihr ihn verkleinert!"]

being a strategy for camouflaging weak individual spirit. Effectively, Nietzsche's thinking allows for no such thing as oppression, only the oppressive effects of Christian morality and their metaphysical origins. It also allows for the abuse of power by authoritarian nation states. Political oppression does not feature in a detailed way, even if Nietzsche expresses concern at the growth of nationalism and a distaste for anti-Semitism.[14] On occasion, he does offer a more differentiated, if brief, explanation, for instance, for his dispute with socialism. In *Human, All Too Human*, [*Menschliches, Allzumenschliches*] I, aphorism 452, he explains that the fundamental mistake in socialist logic is that re-distribution of wealth provides no guard against the likelihood that those who would benefit from redistribution would be no different in their greed and injustice than those whom they replace.[15] In other words, the cycle would be repeated once the existing propertied classes were replaced by members of lower classes who differ from them only in that they are jealous and resentful of what is denied to them. Nietzsche calls, instead of socialist re-distribution or violent revolution, for a more peaceful and gradual re-thinking.[16]

Suffering, therefore, can be a form of bond in the political sense, but this is held to be problematic. Any marginalised group that bands together to seek "justice" is regarded as weak rather than strong. Examples of political bonds engendered by contagious weakness include Judeo-Christian morality, political nationalism, the suffering of factory workers who had begun to find a voice in social groups such as Chartism in England, then socialism and communism, women, who had begun to make feminist demands – all of these nineteenth-century and earlier or parallel groupings are summarily dismissed by Nietzsche, sometimes implicitly, on other occasions more explicitly. Responding to them would be akin to contagion, a form of spiritual breakdown. Instead, Nietzsche would prefer injustice to disappear from the inside out.

In relation to Ressentiment, his writings provide a critique, therefore, both of the Christian concept of mercy, and of nineteenth-century movements that sought to oppose inequality. Is there a logical link between the notion of mercy and the critique of capitalism? In summary, looking at the legacy of Nietzschean thought, does the desire to protect the weak (and to contribute to what might be called an equality paradigm) involve an intrinsic notion of compassion? For Nietzsche, compassion is, as such, inseparable from Ressentiment. It is on this point that the second major theorist of Ressentiment, Scheler, differs from Nietzsche.

---

14 | See Christian Emden on Nietzsche's critique of authoritarianism in the late nineteenth century, in: Christian Emden, *Friedrich Nietzsche and the Politics of History*, Cambridge: CUP 2008, p. 11. Duffy and Mittelmann also offer an interesting interpretation of Nietzsche's thinking on nationalism and anti-semitism, pointing to the Menschliches, Allzumenschliches aphorism 475, in: Michael Duffy/Willard Mittelman, "Nietzsche's Attitudes towards the Jews," in: *Journal of the History of Ideas* 49, (1988), pp. 301–317.

15 | F. Nietzsche, *KSA* Vol. 2, *Menschliches Allzumenschliches* I und II, p. 293.

16 | Ibid., p. 294.

2. Scheler on Emotional Contagion

Max Scheler, in his 1915 essay on Ressentiment, concurs with Nietzsche on one major point – that aspects of Early Christian asceticism had yielded a problematic, indeed corrupted, morality. For Scheler, however, this is not intrinsic to Christianity, rather a perversion of its values.[17] Indeed, he points to Tertullian and certain passages of the Gospel of St. Luke as offering primary examples of a morality based on glee at the downfall of another. Scheler bases this in part on the fact that Luke, more strongly than the other Evangelists, directs criticism at those who accrue wealth.[18] For Scheler, Early Christian asceticism and the ensuing tradition of morality are the products of repressed feelings of fear, and, in Nietzschean terms, of "declining life", rather than of vitality.

However, Scheler only agrees with Nietzsche's account of this to a limited extent. He differs from Nietzsche in his interpretation of the Christian notion of life. Where Nietzsche decried what he saw as the loss of vitality in Christian ascetic practices directed towards transcendence of the material and towards spiritual reward in the afterlife, Scheler, in a more metaphysical vein, argues that the Christian concept of life centres on what one could call "becoming", albeit this is not the term he uses: "(F)or the Christian, life – even in its highest form: human life – is never the 'greatest good.' Life, and therefore human society and history, is only important because it is the *stage* on which the 'kingdom of God' must emerge."[19] The metaphor of the stage echoes Aristotelian potentiality – life as a formal principle at the same time as a physical reality. The emergence of a "kingdom of God" is consistent with the idea of change, or becoming. Ethical behaviour – if this is framed within an intentionality – and here Scheler gives a phenomenological direction to the Christian notion of love – can enable change: "It is the activity and movement of love which embues *(sic)* life with its *highest meaning and value*."[20] This, he claims, runs counter to the Nietzschean emphasis on vitality. Unlike the latter which is self-centred and also, for Scheler, overly biologistic, life can in these terms be thought of as a becoming, rather than as an end in itself. Human acts of positive intention towards the other (love), hold within them the possibility of change. Scheler's reading of Christianity here displays a metaphysical tendency on the one hand, while the interpretation of love reflects notions of intentionality in early phenomenology on the other. The intention of behaving with a certain will to do good towards the other is framed

---

17 | Max Scheler, *Ressentiment*, trans. Lewis A. Coser, William W. Holdheim with an Introduction by Manfred S. Frings, Milwaukee Wisconsin: Marquette University Press ⁵2010 (=⁴2007), p. 53. [Max Scheler, *Das Ressentiment im Aufbau der Moralen*, ed. Manfred S. Frings, Frankfurt/Main: Klostermann 2004 (¹1978).

18 | Max Scheler, *Ressentiment*, p. 67. [*Das Ressentiment im Aufbau der Moralen*], p. 84. See Luke, 12.13–21.

19 | *Ressentiment*, p. 50.

20 | Ibid.

within an understanding of intentionality that moves away from the Aristotelian legacy of ethical thinking, or, at the very least modifies this. It is characterised instead by a belief in the shaping of both thought and deeds as relationality. Doing good and behaving justly towards the other pre-figure in Scheler's reading of Christianity along lines that suggest a combination of attention towards and understanding of the other. Scheler holds that these do not need to come at a cost of self-sacrifice, the mistake made by Tertullian, and one which led to a degree of corruption, since the self-sacrifice was based on something inauthentic on an underlying level.

"False" self-sacrifice, or corruptions of self, are linked to Ressentiment, since these give rise to an ethics that allow the self to flourish only through negative comparison with the other. Ressentiment, as Scheler puts it at the outset, is like a "poisoning" of either personality or spirit. It arises under specific conditions, and can spread contagiously:

> Through its very origin, *ressentiment* is therefore chiefly confined to those who *serve* and are *dominated* at the moment, who fruitlessly resent the sting of authority. When it occurs elsewhere, it is either due to psychological contagion and the spiritual venom of *ressentiment* is extremely contagious— or to the violent suppression of an impulse which subsequently revolts by "embittering" and "poisoning" the personality. If an ill-treated servant can vent his spleen in the antechamber, he will remain free from the inner venom of *ressentiment*, but it will engulf him if he must hide his feelings and keep his negative and hostile emotions to himself.[21]

In this emphasis on contagion, on poisoning and on the suppression of strong feelings that effectively corrupt the self, Scheler concurs with Nietzsche. If fear, envy and resentment are at the heart of a moral sensibility, but are disguised as something else, then this can become transmitted as part of tradition. Both Scheler's and Nietzsche's understandings of Ressentiment are concerned with moral and spiritual failing emanating from the cultural and political dominance of Christianity. For Nietzsche, Ressentiment is an intrinsic feature of Christianity, while for Scheler, as we have seen, it is not. However, the contagious effects of what both thinkers see as false morality are not dissimilar.

---

21 | Ibid., p. 27. [*Das Ressentiment im Aufbau der Moralen*, p. 7: "Das Ressentiment ist also seinem Boden nach vor allem auf die jeweilig *Dienenden, Beherrschten*, auf die vergeblich gegen den Stachel einer Autorität Anlöckenden beschränkt. Wo es sich bei anderen zeigt, da ist entweder eine Übertragung durch psychische Ansteckung gegeben – deren das ungemein kontagiöse seelische Gift des Ressentiment besonders leicht fähig ist -, oder es ist ein in diesem Menschen selbst gewaltsam unterdrückter Trieb, von dem die Ressentimentbildung ihren Ausgang nimmt, und der nun in dieser Form einer 'Verbitterung' und 'Vergiftung' der Persönlichkeit revoltiert. Darf sich ein schlecht behandelter Diener 'in den Vorgemach ausschimpfen', so verfällt er nicht in jene innere 'Giftigkeit', die zum Ressentiment gehört; wohl aber, wenn er noch immer 'gute Miene zum bösen Spiel' (wie die Wendung so plastisch sagt) machen soll und die ablehnenden, feindseligen Affekte in sich eingräbt."]

Both Nietzsche and Scheler observe a self-righteousness in Christianity originating from sublimation and from a moral compass located outside the self.
Ressentiment criticism, therefore, implies a critique of tradition.

Elsewhere, touching on Nietzsche's critique of compassion, Scheler begins
his counter-argument to Nietzsche in *The Nature of Sympathy* (*Wesen und Formen
der Sympathie*) with his own critique of tradition.[22] In tradition, there is a relationship of the herd animal to the leader. The individual subconsciously takes
over the dictates of custom, thus accepting something which has been handed
down without differentiating it from ideas that have been independently arrived
at.[23] Scheler's account of tradition alternates between descriptions of compliance
and of what he seems to see as more subtle instances of manipulation of the
individual through emotional contagion. These may be within a specific environment such as a political party or an ancestral custom, and the effects of tradition here as in certain other strong societal bonds, are read negatively by Scheler.
Psychoanalysis is given credit for bringing some of these "emotional traditions"
["Gefühlstraditionen"] to light, and, indeed, Scheler's description of tradition as
a mixture of inherited psychical dispositions concurs to an extent with Freud's
understanding of tradition.[24] However, we can infer from Scheler's argument
here that bringing the problems associated with tradition to light has not been
enough. On occasion in history, critical intellectual movements have been able
to provide correctives to tradition, but this, too, had its limitations. The instances
Scheler refers to are Renaissance humanism and the Reformation, each of
which, he claims, managed to de-naturalise something of the power of tradition. However, neither was able to entirely overcome it.[25] Moreover, these critical
movements were themselves only possible as an expression of the system's own
internal decline. They are, he contends, more a symptom of already dying traditions than a cause of death.[26]

Regarding the relationship between Christianity and capitalism, or, more specifically, the utilitarian ethos of the Industrial Age, Scheler, in the "Ressentiment"
essay, holds Luther to have brought about a major schism between religion and

---

22 | Max Scheler, *The Nature of Sympathy*, New Brunswick: Transaction 2009, (=ˡ2008),
trans. Peter Heath, with an Introduction by Graham McAleer. [*Wesen und Formen der
Sympathie*, ed. Manfred S. Frings, Berlin/Munich: Francke 1974. This 1922 publication
was a revised and extended version of Scheler's 1913 work, *Zur Phänomenologie und
Theorie der Sympathiegefühle und von Liebe und Haß*.]

23 | Scheler, *The Nature of Sympathy*, p. 37. [*Wesen und Formen der Sympathie*, p. 48.]
As references are being made to both the translation and to the German text in the following, short titles will be repeated in footnote references rather than the term "Ibid"
unless references are to the same page in both texts.

24 | Scheler, *The Nature of Sympathy*, p. 37. [*Wesen und Formen der Sympathie*, p. 49.]

25 | Scheler, *The Nature of Sympathy*, p. 39, [*Wesen und Formen der Sympathie*, p. 50.]

26 | Ibid.

morality.[27] The reason for this, he says, is that Luther excludes Christian love of both self and other from the "path of salvation." Love, therefore, becomes a purely human quality that derives from empathy. For Scheler, this is why Christianity after the Reformation had already prepared the way for the altruistic tendencies of positivism in the nineteenth century.[28] Instead of this, he favours an intentionality of love towards the other as connected to the self's own "path of salvation". He understands "real" empathy as being a phenomenological direction of thought towards the other. This is consistent with Christian "acts" of love – something which emanates from the self's own wish to find salvation. Altruism is therefore rejected as are all ethical precepts that are founded dialectically. Accordingly, Scheler, earlier in the "Ressentiment" essay, accuses Spinoza and Hegel as well as Romantic Idealism of being founded dialectically in oppositional relation to the present. He summarises what he regards as the problem with dialectics and its intrinsic Ressentiment as follows:

> The formal structure of Ressentiment expression is always the same: A" – is affirmed, valued, and praised not for its own intrinsic quality, but with the unverbalized intention of denying, devaluating and denigrating B. A is "played off" against B."[29]

In both ethical and epistemological terms, the inference is that the other ("B") cannot be known in this way – it can only be posited, a speculative, abstract step. Therefore empathy based on a relationality of thought towards the other is a better alternative to an ethical directive with dialectical foundation.

As a result of the problem posed by tradition, and the temptation, along the same lines as the problematic identification within tradition, to identify with the suffering of the other on entirely mistaken terms, Scheler calls for a phenomenologically-grounded theory of Mitgefühl, empathy. "Real" Mitgefühl is something he defines as incorporating the nature and existence of the other into the specific object of the other's pleasure or suffering. This is in contradistinction to the speculative position from which the merciful self gazes at the misfortune of the other and mistakes it for its own because what it is preoccupied with is how it would respond itself, with its own personality and circumstances, to the other's dilemma.[30] Scheler describes mercy as "intensified pity" from an exalted position, containing within itself the connotation of a heightening of the power

---

27 | Ressentiment, p. 91. [Das Ressentiment im Aufbau der Moralen, p. 76.]

28 | See Ibid.

29 | Ibid., p. 42. [Das Ressentiment im Aufbau der Moralen, p. 25: "Die formale Struktur des Ressentimentausdrucks ist hier überall dieselbe: Es wird etwas, ein A, bejaht, geschätzt, gelobt, nicht um seiner inneren Qualität willen, sondern in der – aber ohne sprachlichen Ausdruck bleibenden – Intention, ein anderes, B, zu entwerten, zu tadeln. Das A wird gegen das B "ausgespielt."]

30 | The Nature of Sympathy, p. 42–43. [Wesen und Formen der Sympathie, pp. 50–51.]

and dignity of the merciful person.[31] Given the circumstances mercy needs –
the exaltation of the giver – the type of sympathy present in mercy is only likely
to prevail when the person given the sympathy strongly resembles the giver's
own disposition.[32] Similarly, he claims that this moment of consideration regarding the other's worthiness of sympathy is a product of the psychology of the
Enlightenment in France and is consequentially based on an assumption that
human beings are, by nature, egoistical. "Real" sympathy, on the other hand,
lacks this consideration, since it stems from a phenomenological direction of
thought towards the other. Nietzsche, according to Scheler, failed to distinguish
between the different modalities of pity. He made no distinction between a phe-
nomenologically-directed act towards the other and a somewhat hypocritical gesture of, for instance, a person giving money to a beggar simply to be spared the
sight of the beggar, and not to have to witness human suffering.

For Scheler, what Nietzsche had dismissed as pity being the sign of a weak
sensibility was based on a very narrow definition of pity.[33] *Mitleiden* (compassion)
and *Mitfreude* – being pleased for another's pleasure – are not synonymous with
either the suffering or the pleasure of the other. They have to be thought of as
separate. This is illustrated by the difference between notional pain and the suffering of pain. It is possible for pain to be present, but not felt, thanks to the nar-
cotics used during an anaesthetic.[34] Therefore in real sympathy, the other's situation is construed as part of the his or her experience and within a whole that goes
to making up the other as he or she is. The specific affect does not itself carry over
to the sympathiser. It is distinct from those "infectious" and therefore politically
highly dubious phenomena of *Einfühlung* (empathy) or, perhaps, the over-identification he refers to elsewhere. A further, related problem is the self that is
gradually diminished by viewing itself through the eyes of others. Presumably,
this self-deception takes the form of a series of projections, so that gradually, the
substance of the self's own thoughts and judgements becomes eroded:

> This attitude and assessment are now no more than derivative, being deter-
> mined by the changing *regard* in which the other person holds or might
> hold us, and which he may demonstrate. We think well of ourselves in find-
> ing favour with him, and badly when we do not. Our very acts and decisions
> are determined by the implicit demands inherent *in his conception of us*.[35]

---

31 | Ibid.

32 | See Ibid.

33 | *The Nature of Sympathy*, p. 41, [*Wesen und Formen der Sympathie*, p. 52.]

34 | Ibid.

35 | *The Nature of Sympathy*, p. 42, [*Wesen und Formen der Sympathie*, p. 53: "Dieses Ver-
halten und diese Beurteilung wird nurmehr als abhängig bestimmt und den wechseln-
den *Bildern*, die dieser andere von uns hat, haben mag und kundgibt: wir fühlen
uns gut, wenn wir "vor ihm" es sind, "schlecht", wenn wir "vor ihm" schlecht sind.
Auch unsere Willensakte und Handlungen werden bestimmt von den immanenten
Forderungen, die in *seinem Bilde von uns* liegen."]

This results in a pattern of what Scheler calls "reactive behaviour" that is consequentially of diminished ethical value.[36] It affects extremely vain individuals who are, as he continues, the "slaves" of others' admiration.[37] A related example is the individual who, lacking an inner life, lives vicariously through that of others. By degrees, such an individual's behaviour, originally "sponging" the emotions of an idealised other, proceeds to a more predatory and systematic invasion of the intimate lives of other people, all in the interests of filling the internal vacuum.[38]

Also in *The Nature of Sympathy*, Scheler recalls Adam Smith's eighteenth-century account of a phenomenon that could be called "false conscience".[39] He ponders Smith's historical example of women in the Salem Trials of 1692. Some of the women found guilty of witchcraft, although innocent, revelled in the thoughts of their supposedly just punishment. Instead of protesting their innocence, these women somehow persuaded themselves that it was right that they should be burned at the stake.[40] In *The Theory of Moral Sentiments* (1759) as well as in the passage itself from *The Wealth of Nations* (1776), Smith muses on what would later be termed "emotional contagion". In the opening passage of *The Theory of Moral Sentiments*, he holds sympathy, which depends on imagination and hence can be shared, to be contagious and illustrates this with the example of witnesses of a man being tortured. Although it is not possible to experience the same pain as the victim, the imagination of the sympathetic onlooker seems to "spread" to the stranger's feelings:

> By the imagination we place ourselves in his situation, we conceive ourselves enduring all the same torments, we enter as it were into his body, and become in some measure the same person with him, and thence form some idea of his sensations, and even feel something which, though weaker in degree, is not altogether unlike them.[41]

Commenting on this and on Smith's line of argument on the notion of guilt, Scheler points to the complexity of judging whether a conscience is actually guilty in the sense of culpable, having perpetrated an unjust act, guilty in the sense of internalising a societal behest that is not necessarily just in itself (therefore innocent), or altogether guilt-free in feeling. An absence of a sense of guilt may also arise if the individual is wilfully not cognizant of the effects of his or

---

36 | *The Nature of Sympathy*, p. 44, [*Wesen und Formen der Sympathie*, p. 54.]

37 | Ibid.

38 | Ibid.

39 | Ibid., p. 6. [*Wesen und Formen der Sympathie*, p. 18.]

40 | See Scheler's reading of Smith, *The Nature of Sympathy*, p. 7, [*Wesen und Formen der Sympathie*, p. 18–19.]

41 | Adam Smith, *The Glasgow Edition of the Works and Correspondence of Adam Smith*, Vol. 1, *The Theory of Moral Sentiments*, Clarendon Press: Oxford 1976, p. 9.

her acts on others. However "guilty" he or she may be on the level of having acted harmfully towards other persons or things, this is not consciously accepted.[42] Altogether, Scheler concludes, there are complications in an understanding of ethical behaviour that speak against *Mitgefühl* (sympathy or empathy) as being a necessary component. Some judgements of others or of one's own guilt or complicity circumnavigate what the injured party may or may not experience. Feeling innocent or guilty may not in itself be a reliable measure of subjective states.

According to Scheler, authors (or novelists, as he somewhat disingenuously calls them) including Herbert Spencer, Darwin or Nietzsche confuse empathy (*Mitgefühl*) with emotional infection.[43] They base their understanding of sympathy and empathy on the notion of the survival instinct of the herd. Here, he quotes Nietzsche, who, as we saw, referred to *Mitleid* (sympathy) in terms of an infectious disease. Quoting from the *Antichrist,* he shows Nietzsche castigating a culture based on its elevation and idealisation of the misery and suffering as personified by Christ. Scheler argues that suffering does not become infectious through processes of sympathy or empathy, that precisely in situations where suffering becomes infectious, sympathy is fully ruled-out.[44] At the moment where the suffering becomes personal or immediate, it is the subject's *own,* and the response is to try to escape, or avoid the image. Scheler contends that even in the case of infection with the suffering of another, the identification with the other's suffering has the effect of being a safety valve for the self, perhaps relieving the pressure of experiencing anew some suffering that was felt in the past. He counters Nietzsche by saying that this would only be what Nietzsche terms a "multiplier of misery" ["Multiplikator des Elends"] if what is felt by the self were identical to the image of suffering purveyed, which is not the case.[45] Immediate suffering, for Scheler, is confined to such situations as the two parents at the graveside of their dead child. Since *Mitgefühl* or sympathy can never be one and the same as this, it is never in danger of being what Nietzsche derides as a beacon of falsely-held morality.

Continuing on the relationship between sympathy and empathy, Scheler turns his attention to what he calls *Einsfühlung* (a variation of the German noun "Einfühlung", or empathy), which has been translated as "emotional unity".[46] Scheler describes this particular type of closeness as "bordering on contagion" ("ein Grenzfall der Ansteckung").[47] *Einsfühlung* refers to the total identification of the self with the other, and also takes place on an unconscious level. The loss of

---

42 | Compare Scheler's summary of the different ethical possibilities in: *The Nature of Sympathy,* p. 7, [*Wesen und Formen der Sympathie,* p. 18–19.]

43 | *The Nature of Sympathy,* p. 17, [*Wesen und Formen der Sympathie,* p. 28.]

44 | Ibid.

45 | *The Nature of Sympathy,* p. 18, [*Wesen und Formen der Sympathie,* p. 29.]

46 | Ibid.

47 | Ibid.

identity named here encompasses the phenomena that Freud would describe in terms of totemism and ranges beyond temporary states of "ekstasis".[48] In so-called *primitive* thinking, *Einsfühlung*, a oneness of self and other, is something which guarantees an identity of ancestor with descendent. Later, in the religious practices of antiquity, *ekstasis* – being outside the self – was the aim of techniques of re-enacting the rhythms of life and of fate. Scheler holds that these gradually lost something of their ritualistic nature, giving way to freer patterns of symbolic expression in theatrical form. In this way, he says that *Einsfühlung*, the oneness of self and other, gradually changes into *Einfühling*, in which the self has to try to transport itself to the other in order to understand it, but can never *be* the other.[49]Enduring examples of *Einsfühlung*, he claims, are a protracted state of hypnosis, where the self is entirely at the behest of the other and remains submerged, unconscious that every act it carries out is not of its own volition, but that of the "other" ego.

Drawing on the thinking of Paul Schildner on hypnosis, Scheler cites the hypnotic trance as only one technique among other primitive forms of ritually enacting oneness with the other, and which draw on parts of the brain that date back in evolutionary terms to such times. Hypnosis is therefore an example of a modern trance-technique in which the subject loses the ability to distinguish between perception and imagined idea, so that the boundary of self and other is effectively disabled. This process restores the ecstatic state that primitive peoples practiced ritually in which the self's attention was purged into the other as it reached a heightened affective state and experienced powerful libidinal surges.

Following his account of hypnotic states of *Einsfühlung*, Scheler speculates on similar, weakened instances of self-subjugation in primitive relations of weak and strong. He describes a tendency for the weak to desire their own subservience to the strong, since in this way, they are allowed to participate to some extent in the power-surplus of the stronger party. This, he claims, is a primitive drive, an instinct that serves self-preservation and protects the vulnerable weaker party from the threat of the stronger one. In alliances that come about in this way, the strong use the weak – there is never equality. To show this, he cites Schopenhauer's tale of the squirrel that lands in the mouth of the snake while watching it in a hypnotic gaze – that of the weak towards the strong: "The squirrel identifies in feeling with the snake, and thereupon spontaneously establishes corporeal 'identity' with it, by disappearing down its throat". ["Das Eichhörnchen steht in Einsfühlung zur Schlange und wird spontan dadurch auch körperlich "eins" mit ihr, indem es in ihrem Rachen verschwindet"]. [50] A similar process is at work in masochism, he continues, and it is also is very close to, if not identical to sadism: "Even for the masochist, the object of enjoyment is not pure passivity as such, but his self-identifying participation in the dominance of the

---

48 | Ultimately, however, Scheler fails to deliver an account of the narcissistic processes thought by psychoanalytic theory to be at work here.

49 | *The Nature of Sympathy*, p. 20. [*Wesen und Formen der Sympathie*, p. 31.]

50 | *The Nature of Sympathy*, p. 22, [*Wesen und Formen der Sympathie*, p. 32–33].

partner, i.e. a *sympathetic attainment of power."* ["Denn auch im Masochisten ist
es nicht die pure Passivität als solche, sondern die einfühlende Teilnahme an
der Überaktivität des Partners, d.h. die *sympathetische Machtgewinnung,* die zum
Gegenstand des Genusses wird."][51] Scheler quotes Schildner, commenting on
the phenomenon in erotic relations of the self identifying to such an extent with
the other that it takes on its concerns and carries out actions for the other as
though they were its own.[52] This can, of course, offer a theory of power, a reason
why weaker parties in situations of discrimination do not necessarily respond
by fighting their oppressor, rather on occasion by aligning with the oppressor.

In citing Schopenhauer's analogy of the squirrel and the snake, Scheler deliv-
ers a powerful example of over-identification. On one level, this is something
we can view as part of the theorising of empathy in early phenomenology. On
another, it remains, as it had been for Schopenhauer, a pointed reminder of the
erotic dimension of power.

3. Contagion and Absence of Dissent

Drawn by the fascination with something so much stronger than itself, the
squirrel in Schopenhauer's analogy thinks itself safe in simply watching. But
the more intense its gaze, the more its consciousness of self is diminished. With
this seduction of power, the loss of self is such that the squirrel forgets that it
is a squirrel, staring into the throat of its potential killer. What probably interested Scheler in this image is no less pertinent to today's power dynamics. The
concluding section of this article will be concerned with "contagion" and lack of
dissent in political discourse following the post-2008 economic crisis.

If one considers contemporary political power in Western Europe, it does
not seem exaggerated to say that there is an effective, if not total, absence of
dissent, particularly as far as the phenomenon of "austerity" is concerned. The
fact that from 2008 onwards contagion has become a frequent rhetorical term
may have something to do with the perception that by implying consent to dominant, transnational policies, a community remains strong. The banking crisis
and economic crash of 2008 brought about a politics of "austerity" – severe cut-
backs in public spending – in a number of European states. In 2014, media
commentators suggested a gradual end to the crisis, although pointing to an
ongoing fragile economic situation in France and Italy, and a looming downturn
in Germany. An absence of effective opposition to the remedies proposed by
the EU can be explained as fear of contagion. In other words, in those countries
whose governments have implemented "austerity", this has tended to be identified with a national survival instinct. While debate, indeed dissent, was not pro-
hibited, an overwhelming rhetorical effect of political coverage of the economic

---

51 | Ibid.

52 | Ibid.

crisis was that "austerity" dominated political discussion in a way that seemed to render counter-arguments null and void. However, as Jacques Rancière has pointed out, "The essence of politics is *dissensus*. Dissensus is not a confrontation between interests or opinions."[53] By this, he means that the Habermasian model of communicative action will not work, since it "presupposes partners that are already pre-constituted as such and discursive forms that entail a speech community, the constraint of which is always explicable".[54] In a political climate where whole nations fear economic and political collapse, such partners in a potentially equal framework are absent, as I will argue in the following, leaving a vacuum. Rancière, unlike Habermas, believes in dissent as a type of interruption in politics, an important correction to any concept of the public sphere that rests in the communicative action paradigm on an understanding that interest groups, political identities, oppressed minorities can represent both their reasoned arguments and the identities they hold which give rise to these. Instead of this reasoned argument from a subject-position, however pragmatic and contingent, Rancière emphasises the need for dissent, interruption and demonstration. As he puts this: "A political demonstration is [...] always of the moment and its subjects are always precarious. A political difference is always on the shore of its own disappearance: the people are always close to sinking into the sea of the population or of the race; [...]".[55] It would seem that this "shore of its own disappearance" is the rhetorical force, applied to the current political climate and its fear of contagion, that has engulfed dissenting voices. Rancière later adds that at the heart of politics (and of political philosophy which has somehow served to legitimise it) is that the political "subject" from which an identity position emerges is intrinsically faulty, that "the distinguishing feature of politics is the existence of a subject who 'rules' by the very fact of having no qualifications to rule [...]."[56]

Again, applying such logic to contemporary liberalism, the role of consensus within the European Union as to how to deal with economic contagion could be said to exemplify this. The governments of some of the biggest and seemingly most powerful economies within the EU, notably Germany and France, were at great pains to present a united front as policies were being formulated. Although dissent made itself felt in the shape of demonstrations in Greece, Spain and Portugal in particular, consensus, as this *seemed* to emanate from the Franco-German example, appeared too powerful to argue with, and electoral results as well as economic policies in many states across Europe reflected a public fear of potentially contagious weakness. In the absence of notable dissent, the political line of consensus was that the weak economies must change, and their governments submit to whatever punishments are meted out in the name of austerity.

---

53 | Jacques Rancière, *Dissensus. On Politics and Aesthetics,* trans. Steven Corcoran, London, New Delhi, New York et al: Bloomsbury 2013 (=¹2010), p. 38.

54 | Ibid.

55 | Ibid., p. 39.

56 | Ibid., p. 40.

As this volume prepares to go to press in 2016, it is unclear whether resistance to austerity by the Greek-led Syriza party will lead to Greece's forced departure from the Eurozone and possibly from the EU. Syriza's lone stand sparked renewed fears of contagion in the event of Greece's defaulting on its scheduled repayments to its international creditors. The electoral swing to economically and sometimes socially right-wing parties in Europe in recent years seems to suggest a phenomenological gaze towards the binding power of the strong. On an individual level, it could explain why, in a late stage of capitalism, resistance is so difficult. Trade unions still exist, but they do not represent everyone, and they do not cover all working scenarios of the electronic age. Social solidarity is less likely to come about in groups, and the isolated individual, unless he/she is as naïve as the squirrel, will know who is strong and who is weak. In contemporary liberal society, we could extrapolate from this: it is accordingly quite likely that many people accept the rationalisation of public services, cuts in salaries, reduction of workers' rights, removal of unemployment and sick leave benefits, as well as witnessing a general deterioration of working conditions in a climate where dissent seems futile, because there is a large block of (neoliberal) consensus, however indirectly expressed, that the strong must be followed. And in this way, Schopenhauer's image of erotic fascination seems to transfer to those who say that the only way to be is to conform, and to gaze upon the powerful, not the weak.

In the Ressentiment discourse of Nietzsche and Scheler, as we have seen, to demand justice or equality (rather than to "give" such things freely) was to adopt an intrinsically weak and undesirable position. It requires that one band together within an artificial circle of self-interest with others who also perceive themselves as having been unjustly treated. Contagion, therefore, the spreading of this circle, can be seen in a climate like that of the present-day, to stem from such weakness. Protesters can be dismissed as demanding political change without deserving it. The implications of Ressentiment discourse for a conservative political theory are not difficult to discern. Political opposition and the demand for rights fall under suspicion of contagion. However, the extent and degree to which conservative and liberal policies have combined at EU level in recent years suggests a significant shift in conservatism. Rather than favouring some degree of social democratic protection of the lower paid, the sick and socially weaker members of society, and on maintaining essential public services, conservative-led parties and coalitions within the EU insisted on drastic reductions in public spending in "bailout" countries such as Greece, Portugal, Spain, Cyprus and Ireland regardless of the social cost. That "austerity" would mean large-scale unemployment (Greece, Spain, Portugal, Ireland) and, in the cases of Greece, Spain and Portugal, massive reductions if not cessation of unemployment benefits from the state did not seem to concern the Christian-Democratic led German government or its sister parties and governments elsewhere in Europe where the credit-crash had not decimated the economy. Consensus between France and Germany (and sometimes also Holland and Finland alongside these two) was rhetorically emphasised as essential for the survival of the European community. However, the meaning of this community was irrevocably changed by a new departure within conservatism which would not accord to the countries in which the economy had failed any degree of social protection to its citizens – a situation not replicated in Germany, France, Holland or Finland themselves, where the range of social benefits was largely maintained. In a series of striking images, the German photographer, Eva Leitolf, in September 2012 presented pictures of many beautiful beaches in Greece in the weekend magazine of the influential *Süddeutsche Zeitung* newspaper. What was different about these photographs compared to other holiday supplement images was that, as the text accompanying each photograph explained, on each of these beaches, a Greek person, devastated by the loss of their livelihood, by unemployment, debt or inability to provide for their families, had taken their lives on one of these beaches.[57] The photographs and accompanying text appeared in sharp contrast to the intense criticism of the Greeks in the German press between 2009–2012, and served as an ironic comment on the ongoing popularity of Greece among Germans as a tourist destination.

Greece, of course, was not alone. As many economies of the European continent in addition, to some extent, to the USA have experienced crippling debt crises, and rating agencies rather than political agency determine decision-making, whole countries have fallen in recent years under suspicion of contagion. Weakness, lack of credit-worthiness in the eyes of "nervous" investors has prompted the intervention of previously non-interventionist state and fiscal institutions. Contagion refers to those weak economies which must be saved by the strong, not out of concern for the human consequences of debt, but to offset the predatory actions of "nervous" speculators. Contagion here is understood under the auspices of what might be described as a new financial order, one which began with neoliberal abstentionism and which, by stealth, dismissed all warning voices as the lonely cries of the weak and disenfranchised, an envious oppositionalism born of Ressentiment. Ressentiment, it seems, can be used (and has been used) by both neoconservative and liberal positions alike to discredit political opponents and limit the critical potential of dissident voices. Indeed, the spectacular rise of far-right parties in the European elections of May 2014 suggests that voters in France and Denmark in particular were attracted by the anti-immigration rhetoric of these parties – the idea that migrant workers would be a burden on the state and a source of contagious weakness. Naturally, this point leaves aside the other specific reasons in both France and Denmark, and these countries were not alone – many EU member states showed a significant rise in the far-right share of the vote. Nevertheless, the fact that far-right sentiment is increasingly based on anti-immigration and fear of economic contagion suggests that the austerity consensus of recent years has fostered a belief that the state must strip itself of assets and perceived burdens as much as possible in order to offset contagion.

---

57 | Entitled, "Am Meer, Griechenland, 2012, 7 Postkarten In Kooperation mit dem Süddeutschen Zeitung Magazin", Eva Leitolf's photographic series has been archived and curated in a Munich exhibition. See http://www.grossekunstausstellungmuenchen. de/leitolf.html, accessed on 14.5.14.

Despite the harsh courses of fiscal correction post-2008, little or no dissent has made itself felt, and one reason for this has less to do with economics than with a form of critical vacuum. It seems to be the case that dissenting voices can be dismissed in terms of (economic) naïvety for not accepting a consensually-designated imperative to curb all spending, irrespective of the consequences. Protest can be, and has been, explained away as driven by envy and arguments refuted simply on the basis that protesters, since they are protesting, must be driven by Ressentiment. The construal of "weak" versus "strong" is part of a notional consensus whereby economic stability depends on the containment of weakness. If this seems too simplified, it should be noted that when, after the crisis of 2008 and the economic collapse in several countries that for a while seemed to threaten the European Union, very little protest at a politics of austerity had any impact on political representation. On the contrary, the fact that the balance of power in the EU has swung overridingly to the conservative and, in some instances, further right-wing populist blocks suggests that European voters dismissed protests against capitalist lending and the dire consequences of this for the economies of Spain, Portugal, Ireland, Greece, Cyprus. In France, local elections in March 2014 saw an immense swing to the far right as a response to unemployment, the perceived weakness of the president, Hollande, and as a result of the Ressentiment-based anti-immigration rhetoric of extreme-right parties, most notably Marine Le Pen's "Front National." The emergence of the "Front National" as the outright winner of the European elections in France two months later showed that this tendency was far more than a momentary protest vote. It marked a breakthrough for all those who felt that austerity had either not gone far enough, or had targeted "mainsteam" society rather than eliminating sources of contagious weakness. Hence, this vote was a triumph of Ressentiment-discourse.

The policies of austerity in Europe, above all in the so-called "bailout nations", led to a certain amount of opposition from the left, at least if large-scale public demonstrations in capital cities are a realistic measure of this. However, if lack of impact on critical policy-making at EU level is the yardstick, it would seem that protesters in Spain, Portugal and Greece, although their protests were broadcast across Europe, were not regarded as having something valid to say. In the face of an overriding European political consensus, their actions were easily dismissed as an unwillingness to accept change and failure to accept the fate of their respective collapsed economies. Meanwhile, some of the richer countries of the European Union demanded particularly virulent corrective measures for errant economies. In Finland, for instance, frustration with "contagion" reached the point in 2012 that the Finnish government, with the support of the Dutch government, tried to prevent a permanent "bailout" fund being set-up by the European Union. The approach taken by the Finnish and the Dutch was that even these bailouts with damagingly high interest rates were too lenient towards collapsed states.[58] In a political sub-atmosphere such as this where sentiments

---

58 | See http://www.bbc.com/news/world-europe-18675496. Read 17 March 2014.

similar to those of Finland and Holland were present, what I would call the "main" atmosphere – that which supported bailouts, whatever the terms, became more mainstream. Not to have acceded to Finnish, Dutch or indeed anti-bailout and anti-EU sentiments appeared a triumph of solidarity, and the effects of these crippling economic burdens effectively fell below the political radar. Those who complained that the terms of economic correction were too harsh, that public pay and public services in these countries would collapse, were easily sidelined. The period following the economic crisis can therefore be described on one level as a political vacuum. Corrective economic measures were indeed taken, but no European-wide movement of dissent against multilaterally-sanctioned programmes of fiscal hardship made itself felt. Dissent was easily contained as though it were a matter of Ressentiment, of the weak envying the strong and not wanting to admit to their own abject failure.

4. Critical silence and "postconceptual reality"

In their analysis of power and political agency, Michael Hardt and Antonio Negri refer in *Empire* (2000) to a resurgence of Imperialist tendencies in a contemporary context.[59] Drawing on the writings of Thucydides, Livy, Tacitus and Machiavelli, they argue that Empire has been described historically as something which came about not to promote forceful expansion for its own sake, but to justify (military) intervention with the aim of resolving existing conflicts and bringing about peace.[60] Imperialists, therefore, while expanding their territories, claimed to be increasing the amount of consensus and thus bringing about a peaceful state: "The first task of Empire, then, is to enlarge the realm of the consensuses that support its own power."[61] Empire is thus characterised by expansionism which in turn lays claim to universal juridicial validity. Taking what is variously referred to as postmodern, postindustrial, or, more recently, postconceptual[62] reality, the merit of this particular analysis is that it allows us to consider the present phase of capitalism as one which rests on an implicit view of itself as naturally ordained, inherently just. Consolidating its power base in order to ensure its own preservation is a primary objective of an empire. If war is necessary to protect its borders or, more pertinently, to overcome adver-

---

59 | Michael Hardt/Antonio Negri, *Empire*, Cambridge, MA: Harvard University Press 2000, p. 20.

60 | Ibid., p. 15.

61 | Ibid.

62 | See Peter Osborne, "The postconceptual condition. Or, the cultural logic of high capitalism today", in: *Radical Philosophy*, 184, (2014), pp. 19–27. Osborne suggests that rather than considering the phase of late-capitalism to have passed, possibly succeeded by the postmodern condition referred to by Lyotard, that there is no reason to believe that high-capitalism has indeed been surpassed. This suggests that the postconceptual implies a relational critique both to (late) capitalism and historicity. Cf. pp. 19–21.

sarial threat, then this war within the logic of the empire is a just war, *bellum iustum*. Hardt and Negri quite rightly view the second Gulf war in this tradition. Their now famous book preceded the attacks on US twin towers, the thwarted attack on the Pentagon, and the hijacking and suicidal destruction of a United Airlines jetliner on 11 September 2001. The subsequent US invasion of Iraq and the rhetoric of George W. Bush's "War on terror" indeed corresponds even more closely to what Hardt and Negri had already described as the "banalization of war".[63] Horror and outrage at the events of 11 September 2001 were invoked to justify an image of the "enemy" in a way that made it more difficult to question the extent to which political discourse had become simplified.

Applying Hardt and Negri's analysis, the US response became increasingly imperial. Central to the logic of the empire is that the notion of the adversary is the contrastive pole to a reified understanding of the consensual "us", or "we". This consensual cohesiveness could be regarded as having been present in extreme form in the US war on terror. However, if Hardt and Negri's analysis is correct, the extreme form only points to an underlying propensity across the board to forming such consensus in North American and Western European democracies. In other words, a consensus seems to exist that power is wielded in a just way if it is in the hands of a democratically-elected nation or state. Hardt and Negri's analysis in their 2000 publication sets out that capitalism in the current age, rather than being thought of somewhat vaguely as "globalised", should instead be understood as a form of superstate. It acts, along the lines of an empire, to defend its interests, and these are not those of a nation state or single sovereign power. The state is the capitalist system itself, and therefore an economic order. Here, the enemy is not a geographical or political entity. On the contrary, it comes from within, namely, wherever there is serious opposition to its own claim to being the desirable order of things. Hardt and Negri use the analogy of a machine that produces a constant balance. This consists of sets of systems and processes that are kept in check within one overriding order of totality.[64] The logic of the empire gives rise to a form of legal positivism which assumes an ideational centre. This, although based only on an assumed capability of forming a consensual community representing subjects, acts as an agency and gathers force like a slipstream.[65] Hardt and Negri see an analogy to imperial self-legitimation in today's capitalist order:

> Empire is emerging today as the center that supports the globalization of productive networks and casts its widely inclusive net to try to envelop all power relations within its world order – and yet at the same time it deploys a powerful police function against the new barbarians and the rebellious slaves who threaten its order.[66]

---

63 | Hardt/Negri, *Empire*, p. 13.

64 | Ibid., pp. 29–30.

65 | Ibid.

66 | Ibid., p. 20.

At first sight, the suggestion of a police state seems quite sharply exaggerated, particularly given the ongoing and very real existence of certain police-states which routinely torture and kill dissidents and those deemed, for whatever reason, undesirable, or enemies of the state. If we accept the proposition that a police state within a democracy is a contradiction in terms, then either Negri and Hardt vastly overstate their case, or, in a less literal sense, the democratic rule of law is more gradually eroded by the residual sense of an indeterminate enemy, the *potential* dissident, the voice that might expose the illegitimate expansion of a machine-like order of things. The idea that there may be such a hegemonic tendency within modern power systems is not far removed from Marcuse's analysis of one-dimensionality. Marcuse, following Horkheimer's and Adorno's dialectics of enlightenment, believed that processes of negation of critical opposition were an effect of hegemonic power. They were not just the rationalisation that Horkheimer and Adorno had seen within instrumental rationalism. Instead, elevated to the social, hegemony for Marcuse took on an additional layer in making dissent seem ineffable. As Øjvind Larsen has put it:

> Marcuse links this "rational" hegemony to social hegemony, so that social hegemony is rationalized through technological-instrumental rationality in such a way that even social hegemony comes to appear rationally based (Marcuse 1964: 167ff). Thus, the negation mentioned in Horkheimer and Adorno becomes rationalized away in the general dominance of techno-logical-instrumental rationality in modern society. In this way, modern society becomes, according to Marcuse, "one-dimensional". The repro-duction of modern society is presented through the dominance of tech-nological-instrumental rationality as an impersonal totalitarian hegemony in which every form of negation comes to appear as irrational and thus meaningless.[67]

Effectively, the possibilities for critique are thus diminished, the dissident voice no longer seeming to criticise something substantial, but to bemoan in an irrational way some perceived loss of status. Marcuse thus warns that even the Frankfurt School cannot break the impasse. The nature of the hegemony is such that (progressive) society appears of itself to incorporate any necessary minor adjustments, making it all the more difficult for dissenting positions. Instead of radical change or even vocal opposition, the progressive society appears on its path of improvement to be making such changes along the way as are necessary: "Technical progress, extended to a whole system of domination and coordination, creates forms of life (and of power) which appear to reconcile the forces opposing the system and to defeat or refute all protest in the name of the historical prospects of freedom from toil and domination."[68] Writing in

---

67 | Øjvind Larsen, *Right to Dissent. The Critical Principle in Discourse Ethics and Deliberative Democracy*, Copenhagen: Museum Tusculanum Press 2009, p. 101.

68 | Herbert Marcuse, *One-Dimensional Man: Studies in the Ideology of Advanced Industrial Society*, Boston, MA: Beacon 1964, p. 9.

1964, Marcuse is already describing a post-critical society, one which seems, of itself, to overwhelm all forms of opposition. Given the onset of the electronic age and the changes to the political spectrum in the post-communist world, what is surprising is the extent to which Marcuse's comments could still be said to apply today. The main reason for this is a transition that had occurred earlier, something Marcuse himself alludes to, namely the integration of the different social forces (or class-structures) into what he calls industrial society, and what we might well call its post-industrial continuation.[69] With such a high degree of integration, criticism then, as now, can easily be dismissed as the sole stance of a disgruntled oppositionalist, someone inherently incapable of keeping the pace. His or her dissenting voice is easily misheard as Ressentiment, a protest born of envy and individual discontentment.

Arguably, in Europe and North America since the economic crisis that began in 2008, the concept of weakness has become a marker of economies that threaten to carry over their malheur to healthy, "A-rated" (or triple-A) credit zones. The contact with a weakened economy, to take this metaphor further, would suffice. Irrespective of the cause of supposed weakness, the contagion of damaged economies would infest the moral and fiscal rectitude of the stronger financial regions. With warnings of domino effects, a politics of austerity spread throughout the Euro zone after the bailouts first of Greece, and then of Ireland, then of Portugal and Spain and Cyprus, with the large Italian economy intermittently teetering on the brink. Irrespective of levels of unemployment in these countries, it became commonplace to expect that their public services and social welfare systems would be attacked, if not dismantled. A wave of privatisation of any state assets of the "bailout nation", met with little effective political opposition in Europe, and, in the case of Ireland, surprisingly, hardly any opposition within Ireland itself. That there should be public resentment at such happenings in Ireland, most of which were caused by a banking crisis – Ireland's banks having speculated wildly and encouraged unsustainable borrowing for years on end – was to be expected. However, dissent did not transpire, something which is probably accounted for by subcurrents of thinking along the lines of Nietzsche's charge of Ressentiment. Public anger was directed only to a degree at banking and property speculation, whereas there was little public opposition to the idea that state spending on public services must bear the brunt of fiscal correction.[70]

Not only did no sustained political opposition emerge, it seems fair to say that a strong degree of political opposition which was palpable in 2010 grad-

---

69 | On the dearth of criticism, or paralysis of opposition, Marcuse contends: "Confronted with the total character of the achievements of advanced industrial society, critical theory is left without the rationale for transcending this society", in: Ibid., p. 10.

70 | Despite the strong performance of the left-wing nationalist Sinn Féin Party in the European elections of May 2014, there is little evidence of public appetite for reversing any cuts in funding to the devastated public sectors of health and education. It is likely that the strong showing of support for Sinn Féin, while expressing great public disgruntlement and the very real suffering of many citizens, marks frustration at the perceived control of the IMF and European Union over Irish fiscal policy.

ually subsided. If anything, what we might call "compliance" increased when the social democratic party, "Labour", joined a conservative-led coalition in 2011 and this coalition implemented sustained policies of austerity from 2011 until this volume went to print in 2015. But, one could say, this too, was inevitable, as the Irish government had had little choice other than to channel all energy into economic recovery. In other words, servicing Ireland's colossal national debt incurred by the 2010 bailout and the state guarantee of bank debt which had precipitated it became the only political prerogative. Austerity, therefore, seemed to be about survival. But is such logic not perilously close to an accusation that dissent and, indeed, resistance, are contrary to the "national cause", namely survival? This would have the same effect of Nietzsche's dismissals of such movements as socialism and his belief that being in a weakened position, if one is to avoid acting out of Ressentiment, is no reason to join a political interest-group. This type of argument, even before the 2008 crisis, was already widespread in the EU and North America.

Indeed, the discourse of Ressentiment is by no means solely a European phenomenon. The backlash against Obama-care in the US was not only fuelled by those who had no need of universal health care. Some of those demanding its abolition were also lower-paid or socially vulnerable individuals who adopted an anti-interventionist stance, buying into American conservative and (neo)liberal rhetoric in which everyone is the creator of their own happiness and their own economic fortitude. This would be a case of not wanting to be aligned with others who are perceived as socially disadvantaged, struggling or worse, and held to be inherently undeserving. It is also a short step from a tacit dislike of political alignment to an apolitical stance when those who could defend a common interest choose not to do so because it may, potentially, lower their status even further in the eyes of others. Of course, this is not apolitical, but an indirect affirmation of dominant policies. The dissenting voice grows quieter as a precedent is established along the lines of "only losers complain".

Returning to Europe, one additional reason for the absence of dissent in recent political discourse has been the "reform agendas" in the area of education. One of the stated aims of the reform agenda was widening access to education. A good example of this is how Tony Blair's infamous "third way" for the British Labour party involved a new take on education. As many school-leavers as possible were to be "sent" to university, because this was in line with equality and broadening access.[71] This policy, which seems to have spread to several other European countries, has proven difficult to argue with, because it ostensibly promotes equality. The fact that it went hand-in-hand with pressure to vocationalise education and to turn the university primarily into an affirmative institution that generates economic wealth is often overlooked. Within education, it is fre-

---

71 | The then Prime Minister Tony Blair made a significant speech in 2001, outlining his target of increasing the number of British Schoolleavers who attend Third-Level education to fifty per cent. Cf: *The Guardian*, 23 May 2001, URL: http://www.theguardian.com/politics/2001/may/23/labour.tonyblair.

quently the case that dissent is forfeited by academics who feel that standing up for the university as a place of critical, independent thought will make them appear opposed to equality. They do not want to be seen as opposing the right for most school-leavers to study for a B.A. And those same academics, perhaps fearful of being accused of Ressentiment and disliking change for personal reasons, frequently choose to remain silent. It may well be that this type of subtle manipulation is built in to contemporary discourses of liberalism which cast the dissident in the role of fearful and reactionary "loser".

Remaining with the university, the fashionable rhetoric of "excellence clusters" has camouflaged the fact that it is becoming increasingly easy for university managements to justify staffing cuts and budget cuts for "old-fashioned" disciplines, while investing heavily in elite programmes and elite researchers. One could counter, of course, that there is nothing wrong with innovation and with specialisation, and that little progress can be made without it. What has been disturbing, however, over the last decade of Bologna reform in European education has been the downgrading of independent knowledge and the sustained assault on the university as a place of dissent. Knowledge has been valued and invested in (referring in particular to Germany, the UK, and now Ireland, where this author works) if it is perceived as being compliant with the mission statements of the funding bodies. If it is non-compliant, it easily falls under suspicion of serving "weak" interest groups, those unable to cope with the demands of the economy, or the modern university.[72]

How does this relate to Ressentiment? Friedrich Nietzsche, after all, believed in the growth of the individual through facing adversity, and would not have wanted blind obedience to characterise university life. Neither would Scheler. The problem is that their very critiques of social solidarity make it difficult to dispute such proclamations of excellence versus the perceived mediocrity of the "opponents of excellence". Political opposition for Nietzsche was somehow cast in a similar light to opposition today to (neo)liberal policy. Today's polemics of anti-state intervention throughout the EU and the loud proclamation of elitist individual or team performance in centres of knowledge, in the public sector, the claim that education serves the economy and must become more vocational, are difficult to answer when those who risk disputing them are very easily dismissed as the failed academics, the second-rate doctors, the lazy public servants and, in short, as a person who has not been designated "strong." But who does the designating? If there is a link between Nietzsche's philosophical position, its implications for politics, and present day liberalism, then the legacy of such ideas as the contagion of weakness deserve our ongoing attention, as do their effects on discourses of dissent.

---

72 | See Mary Gallagher's authoritative case study of technocratic reform and managerialism in Irish Third Level Education in: *Academic Armageddon. An Irish Requiem for Higher Education*, Dublin: The Liffey Press 2012, 39f. In this book, the author also relates these developments to international trends in the politics of higher education.

Contemporary media coverage of protest movements in Germany and the charge of *Ressentiment*, with particular focus on "Stuttgart 21"

Caroline Mannweiler

In 2010 the German language society designated the term "Wutbürger" as word of the year, a term that roughly translates as "enraged citizen" or, depending on the interpretation of the word "Bürger", as "enraged bourgeois". The newly-coined word reacted to the phenomenon of several regional protest movements which had sprung up in the country, above all a very active protest against a big infrastructural project in Stuttgart and a protest movement against a school reform in Hamburg, to name only the two which had obtained national, and in the case of Stuttgart, international coverage in the media. This contribution will take a closer look at the reactions that these protests provoked in order to show how the concept of ressentiment is still active today and how it constantly hinders the exchange of arguments. We will focus in particular on the reactions engendered by the protest movement against the infrastructural project "Stuttgart 21".

As the term "Wutbürger" indicates, what was seen as surprising and characteristic of the recent protest movements was the fact that they were apparently driven by "regular", "respectable" citizens – middle-class and even upper middle-class people. The mere fact that people with these social backgrounds participated in the protests was repeatedly pointed out in media commentary and culminated in the creation of the term "Wutbürger". In the case of Stuttgart, the surprise at this type of protest might have been expected to have been greater still, since Stuttgart and the federal state Baden-Württemberg of which it is the capital are known as a region with a disciplined, efficient and rather conservative population which also translates into an over 50-year long political rule of the Christian Democrats (CDU), sometimes in coalition with the Liberals (FDP).

The case of Christine Oberpaur who, in the context of the media coverage of the protests in Stuttgart, appeared in two nationally well-known political talk-shows (on *Maybritt Illner* on 7 October 2010 and on *Beckmann* on 4 October 2010) epitomised this apparent paradox between being a "typical" citizen of Stuttgart and being a protester. Born in 1946, this was someone who had majored in business psychology, whose family owned several businesses in the region and who had voted CDU throughout her life, and who was now being invited to speak as a representative of the protest movement. She explained that she was definitely anything but a "professional protester" but that she was now very disappointed with the government for backing the Stuttgart 21 project which she, like so many others, opposed. At the very height of the protests, on 4 October 2010, more than 50.000 people joined the protest marches in Stuttgart.

With individuals such as Christine Oberpaur being pointed out as representing the new "bourgeois" nature of the protests in Stuttgart, the social background of the protesters became one of the main points of interest that the press focused on. Christian Brommarius from the (somewhat left-wing) *Frankfurter Rundschau* argued that the social background of the protesters was the main reason for the federal government's opting for a mediation process that was intended to reconcile the protesters with the decision-makers in Stuttgart. "The assumption that the protests forced [the government] to take this step, might seem obvious, yet it is inapplicable. There has often been massive resistance against unpopular large-scale projects, but never had politicians seen themselves compelled to look for a discussion with people and to negotiate compromises in a 'mediation process' after the end of the plan-approval and licensing procedures. It is probably less the length and steadfastness of the resistance that have brought about their change of mind than the provenance and self-perception of the protesters against Stuttgart 21. Very predominantly, they are representatives of the middle-classes, representatives of the silent majority much courted by politics. This majority hasn't been keeping silent for quite some time now, and in Stuttgart it came up against the tin-earedness of the politicians it addressed."[1]

The comments of Wolfgang Bosbach, an influential Christian Democrat cited in the *New York Times*, give Bommarius's argument a certain plausibility: "You have all kinds of protest movements springing up all over the place. [...] They consist mostly of educated people who are neither left-wing nor right-wing but somewhere in the middle of the political spectrum. We should be worried. We should be reaching out to them."[2] A parliamentarian in Berlin, Bosbach wasn't directly being addressed by the protests against Stuttgart 21, but his comments nonetheless imply that the social background of the protesters gives their protest a particular relevance. Indeed, the broad social base of the protests not only intrigued politicians and the media but also researchers: Professor Dieter Rucht from the Social Science Research Centre Berlin was on site in October 2010 in order to analyse the motives, political orientations but also the educational and

---

1 | Christian Bommarius, "Die Irrtümer sind verbraucht", in: *Frankfurter Rundschau*, 22 February 2010, URL: www.fr-online.de/stuttgart-21/warum-sich-der-Stuttgart 21-widerstand-lohnt-die-irrtuemer-sind-verbraucht.4767758,4763966.html; [translation, C. Mannweiler])

2 | Quoted in: Judy Dempsey, "'Enraged citizens' movement rattles German politics", in: *New York Times*, 16 May 2011, A7.

social background of the protesters. His findings[3] quickly circulated in the press and underlined the "academic" background of the protesters,[4] while the political orientation emerged as a little less conservative than previously hypothesised by the press. Most of the protesters considered themselves to be in either the centre or left-of-centre of the political spectrum—findings that were later spelled out by Wolfgang Kraushaar from the Hamburg Institute for Social Research. Kraushaar partly revised the new image of the "bourgeois" protesters by tracing back their political background to the 1968 student movements and the anti-nuclear movements growing out of these, movements that now form a major part of the Green party's electorate.[5]

Other researchers, such as Andrea Römmele, professor at the Hertie school of governance, stressed the novelty of the recent protests. As quoted in Judy Dempsey's article in the *New York Times* on 16 May 2011, Römmele distinguishes the "Wutbürger" from the generally left-wing student rebellions: "The Wutburgers [sic] are not ideological as such. [...] They are educated people who are against a certain style of politics in which the political parties have failed to create a platform for citizens' discussions."

Exactly how the ideological background of the protesters might be analysed and interpreted is of no concern for our argument. What needs to be pointed out, though, is the fact that in public discourse on the protests in Stuttgart, the social background of the protesters became a main point of interest, something which apparently merited being mentioned and developed in greater detail than other aspects of the protest.

This shows, *ex negativo*, that protest is usually still attributed to "lower" motives – if not, how could the "academic" background of the protesters have engendered such surprised reactions? – an attribution which forms a central aspect of the ressentiment hypothesis which we find in Nietzsche's *Genealogy of Morals*. When Nietzsche criticises the scientific "elevation" of the values of ressentiment, he distinguishes them precisely from biologically "higher" values such as the active affects of imperiousness and avidity. The reactions to the protests in Stuttgart seem to indicate the underlying presence of the ressentiment argument, insofar as the "middle-class" protests apparently undermined contemporary assumptions concerning protest movements.

Yet, while the ressentiment argument seemed somewhat difficult to apply to the protesters in Stuttgart, forms of negative attribution took place nonetheless, showing how tenacious the tendency to discredit protest by discrediting

---

3 | Rucht gave a summary of his study's findings in the handout for a press conference. See http://www.fjnsb.org/sites/default/files/downloads/handout_stuttgart21_rucht_2010.pdf

4 | See Damir Fras, "Gebildet, links, widerspenstig", in: *Frankfurter Rundschau* 27 October 2010, URL: www.fr-online.de/politik/stuttgart-21-gegner-gebildet--links--widerspenstig, 1472596,4781944.html

5 | See. Wolfgang Kraushaar, "Protest der Privilegierten? Oder: Was ist wirklich neu an den Demonstrationen gegen Stuttgart 21?", in: *Mittelweg*, 36, (2011), pp. 5–22, p.17.

the motives of the protesters appears to be. As soon as the unusual "bourgeois" background of the protesters had become a topic in the press, politicians but also journalists started criticising them. The protesters' "bourgeois" background now became a source of negative attributions. They were identified as spoiled and privileged people, too complacent to be open to progress and therefore as a threat to the economic growth of the region. The minister for justice in Baden-Württemberg, Goll, in an interview with *Financial times Germany* on 4 October 2010, designated the protesters as "wohlstandsverwöhnt", which translates as "spoiled by prosperity". At the time of the protests, German Minister of the Interior, De Maizière, in a morning news tv-show on 19 October 2010, criticised the "well-off parents" who allowed their children to demonstrate. He was referring to the protests of pupils in Stuttgart who had claimed that the money spent on the very expensive infrastructure project should rather be spent on education. As quoted in an article by Peter Unfried in the *taz* on 24 September 2010, the prominent publicist Hajo Schumacher referred to the protesters in Stuttgart as "wellness-protesters" who wanted to recreate Woodstock but merely showed "undemocratic stubbornness".[6] One year after the protests, in October 2011, Gerhard Matzig in the *Süddeutsche Zeitung Magazin* described the "Wutbürger" as complacent people who were above all selfish, unconcerned with the world and primarily looking to conserve their possessions.[7] He also presented his critique in a book called *Einfach nur dagegen: wie wir unseren Kindern die Zukunft verbauen* that translates approximately as *Simply against it: how we damage our children's future.* The question as to whether Germany could remain "future-proof" in the light of the recent protests was also raised by chancellor Angela Merkel. She explained that to proceed with the Stuttgart 21 project would be critical for ensuring the nation's "sustainability". If it did not go ahead, the ability to implement big infrastructural projects would be called into question, and, as a consequence, investors discouraged. This argument was very much in tune with the "threat" expressed by tunneller Martin Herrenknecht whose company was strongly involved in the Stuttgart 21 project which requires many tunnels. In the prominent political talkshow *Maybrit Illner* on 7 October 2010, he mentioned that his company would move to Switzerland if Stuttgart 21 weren't to be built.

In next to no time, the regional protests against a particular infrastructural project had become a question of national relevance and the concrete protests a sign of a general obstacle to economic and technological progress. While the implicit characterisation of the protesters as being motivated by low motives such as envy, frustration and ressentiment had been impossible, their portrayal as reactionary and anti-modern was clearly in evidence. It should be clarified that the pertinence of the criticisms made is not within the scope of this article. What matters in the context of a discussion of ressentiment and its continuous power

---

6 | See Peter Unfried, "Die neuen Revolutionäre", in: *die taz*, 24 September 2010, URL: www.taz.de/!58811/

7 | See Gerhard Matzig, "Schluss mit dem Gemaule!", in: *Süddeutsche Zeitung Magazin*, 2011, 40, URL: http://sz-magazin.sueddeutsche.de/texte/anzeigen/36359/

in discourse is the simple fact that the discourse on Stuttgart 21 reacted to the specific and somewhat unexpected background of the protesters, managing to attribute to them "suitably" negative motives.

These attributions that focused on the personal motives of the protesters instead of addressing the subject matter – namely the pros and cons of Stuttgart 21 – proved to be very successful, since the protesters were forced to engage with the personal accusations and defend themselves. Winfried Kretschmann, who at the time of the protests was the chairman of the Green party's parliamentary group in the Landtag of Baden-Württemberg and who is now governor of Baden-Württemberg, explained in a debate in the Landtag on 6 October 2010 that the main source of the protests was the government's refusal to take the protest seriously, and its assumption that the protesters did not have strong arguments.[8] In a similar vein, Dagmar Deckstein, in a commentary on 1 August 2010 in the German daily *Süddeutsche Zeitung*, wrote that the supporters of Stuttgart 21 were to a large extent responsible for the protests in that they categorised opponents of the project as "anti-progressive beraters".[9] Instead of being countered by factual arguments, the "ad hominem" arguments of the Stuttgart 21 supporters were recognised as such and answered by demands for respect.

Even the mediation process, introduced after the conflicts between protesters and the government had reached a rather violent climax, had as one of its major goals restoring the personal respect due to the protesters and the supporters of Stuttgart 21. To discuss the topic "on an equal footing" ("auf Augenhöhe") became a central concern of the mediation process, an expression that obviously refers to previous insults that had taken place, in particular with regard to the protesters and their motives.[10] The expression "on an equal footing" occurred at literally every session of the mediation process that consisted of eight generally day-long sessions. Heiner Geißler used it in the inaugural session, referring to governor Stefan Mappus who had initiated the mediation: "We have a governor who says of himself that it won't hurt him to sit down at this table with representatives of civil society. He is ready to proceed to this evaluation of facts and, moreover, not in a top-down manner, but on an equal footing."[11] As we will see,

---

8 | See Protocol of the 100th plenary session in legislation period 14 on 6 October 2010, p. 7092, URL: www.landtag-bw.de/wp14/plp/14_0100_06102010.pdf

9 | Dagmar Deckstein, "Prestige für sieben Milliarden Euro", in: *Süddeutsche Zeitung*, 1 August 2010, URL: http://www.sueddeutsche.de/politik/grossprojekt-stuttgart-prestige-fuer-sieben-milliarden-euro-1.981220

10 | Within the protest movement, very harsh insults towards the Stuttgart 21 supporters could be observed but they didn't enter into the "official" discourse of the protesters as this was voiced during the mediation or to the language of public representatives of the protests, above all politicians of the Green party and politically active people in Stuttgart. From these unofficial insults, we can distinguish the overtly voiced critiques and defences on both sides of the conflict.

11 | Verbatim transcript of the mediation session on 22 October 2010, p. 2; The following quotes from the mediation sessions will only indicate the session's date and the

Geißler repeated this expression throughout the sessions, a fact that underlines the importance of this motif in the mediation. In the second session, the expression was also taken up by Brigitte Dahlbender, the president of the environmental organisation BUND (Friends of the Earth, Germany) in Baden-Württemberg and part of the group opposing Stuttgart 21: "We had agreed that [all the information] needed to be on the table, we need to speak on an equal footing." (29 October 2010, p. 40). As we can see in Dahlbender's comment and as we can see throughout the entire mediation process, the "respectability" of the two parties involved in the discussions was also linked to questions of competence and access to information. Not only did the protesters want to be heard, they wanted to be treated as "experts" – a desire that signals the previous discrediting of the protesters' arguments or even of their capacity for argumentation. Boris Palmer, Green mayor of Tübingen, used the expression "on an equal footing" in a similar vein to Dahlbender when he complained about the secretive strategies of the DB (German National Railways) that in Palmer's view didn't give access to all relevant information: "But in general, if we talk about an equal footing, I also demand that you finally abandon your policy of concealment and actually put all the facts on the table." (27 October 2010, p. 131)

In addition to this demand for equal access to information, Palmer constantly hinted at his own expertise, showing that being on the protesters' side, this expertise was not easily accepted by the supporters: "What really upsets us and the reason why the people take to the streets is the following: If one brings this up during the planned assessment procedures, if one has been saying for ten years, using common sense, and in my case with a math major, that what you're doing there can't work, that it doesn't fit together, if one does the sums and finds that the trains don't fit, then you say: 'This is a centennial project, we're not talking about those kinds of things.'" (27 October 2010, p. 114)

Palmer repeated the fact that he was a mathematician several times, obviously counting on the perfect objectivity implied by this discipline. The reference to an objective discipline was intended to defuse charges of ressentiment and increase the level of acceptance of him as an adversary: "Now I may tell you as a mathematician – timetable construction is extremely difficult. It can't be done with computer programs. You need to do it with your head. There's no computer program for that. And if the best people can't accomplish a better preliminary result than this one, then it is something to be feared [...]" / "You realise that a mathematician is sitting in front of you. I'm sorry. This connection is purely and simply implausible." / "Now, I ask you as a mathematician: If we speak about optimisation [...]." (29 October 2010, p. 30 / p. 78 / p. 91) Palmer therefore used the fact that he is a mathematician in order to make his arguments count and to "prove" or rather to suggest that his critique was well-founded.

What is remarkable is that the reference to personal competence should have become an argument on the supporters' side as well. Kefer, the chief engineer,

---

page number referring to the verbatim transcripts as they are available online at URL: http://www.schlichtung-s21.de/dokumente.html. All translations are by the author.

"defended" his colleagues by stressing their competence and experience. "I am simply asking for a little respect for our people who do these studies. I want to clarify something: It is not the case that Mr. Weigand and everyone we have in charge there have only been doing this since the other day. We have in the main the know-how and experience of 15, 20, 25 years behind this." (22 October 2010, p. 86–87) It might be mentioned that the opponents did not question the intelligence of the planners and engineers, but merely the capacity of the infrastructure, as Palmer's utterances show: "Until yesterday, you didn't have a sound operational concept, not because you aren't smart – you even have the smartest people, we admit that – but because you had such big problems with your tracks and switches that you couldn't manage it until yesterday." (12 November 2010, p. 32)

The frequent underlining of intelligence and personal competence in the mediation process can certainly be seen as an answer to the implicit charge of ressentiment and presumed inferior motives. To this, one could add the claims of Palmer, Gangolf Stocker and other opponents of Stuttgart 21, to be friends of the railway or even politicians who actively support the railway:

> Gangolf Stocker: "[...] I'm telling you this explicitly – and I say this for the public as well – the opponents of Stuttgart 21 are friends of the railway. [...]" (12 November 2010, p. 8)

> Boris Palmer: "[...] If this infrastructure made possible considerably more railway traffic in Baden-Württemberg, I, as a politician supportive of the railway, could not be against it." (October 10, 2010, p. 78)

By presenting themselves as supporters of the railway, the protesters were reacting to the claim that they were simply "against" any kind of technological and infrastructural change, a claim they needed to repudiate in order to make their critique plausible.

With a similar goal in mind, the opponents had invited contributions from Alexander Kirfel, the owner of a freight train company who criticised the Stuttgart 21 project as being unhelpful for the improvement of freight transportation: "We as private train [companies] are only concerned with making money and working efficiently. We don't have any ideological concerns. Neither do we have regional interests on the site. We are not entwined with the region in such a way as to make us feel obliged to vigorously put forward a regional project, even if it doesn't help us at all. There are only economic interests at stake here." (4 November 2010, p. 148) Interestingly, perhaps, the reference to economic interests seemed to be a safe way of escaping the charge of ressentiment, which, as Kirfel makes clear, implies that one is acting out of ideological or other personal motives unrelated to the problem as such.

As we can observe, even in the microstructure of the mediation process, the ressentiment argument was palpable since the personal qualities of individuals became an important aspect of the exchange of arguments or even a prerequisite for the exchange of arguments. To guarantee this prerequisite proved to be a constant goal of the mediator, Heiner Geißler, which partly explains why he constantly came back to the Leitmotif of a discussion "on an equal footing", where all participants had an equal right to be heard. This aspect was often pointed out as the "democratic" facet of the mediation process, as alluded to here by Geißler: "I want to say that it's a project of unmediated citizen-democracy in a civil society. This means that in a case of conflict, both groups come to sit at one table, and discuss matters on an equal footing, with completely equal rights." (4 November 2010, p. 2) As becomes apparent in Geißler's explanation, the creation of situations where parties in conflict enter discussions on an equal footing is an experiment, a novelty, or to put it differently, an "exception". As such, it needs to be instantiated with a certain degree of effort and by taking particular measures which, by their very presence, highlight that it is more usual to discredit one's opponents' positions. Geißler's explanation also alludes to the fact that these measures need to precede a possible exchange of arguments, which is why – during the mediation process – talk about "participatory democracy" seemed just as pertinent as the talk about the pros and cons of Stuttgart 21.

In the same session, Florian Bitzer, a representative of the supporters of Stuttgart 21, used the expression "on an equal footing" in an attempt to clarify the weaknesses of the K21 project, the alternative infrastructural project developed by the opponents of Stuttgart 21. "Mr. Geißler, we agreed that in the context of this mediation we would meet 'on an equal footing' – on the train project as well as its variants. It is part and parcel of meeting on an equal footing that one does not simply explain the concepts with regard to the traffic, but that one also clearly states and makes apparent to the people what consequences these concepts have for the infrastructure." (4 November 2010, 19) Bitzer's use of the expression is interesting insofar as it implies an apparent difficulty in "criticising" the K21 project: instead of simply discussing the weaknesses of the project, Bitzer apparently finds it necessary to ask for permission to do so by using the expression "on an equal footing". This rhetorical effort again shows how complicated the simple exchange of arguments seemed to have become in the conflict surrounding Stuttgart 21.

The way mediator Geißler used the term in the sixth session sums up what was at stake in the mediation and testifies to the powerful influence of the charge of ressentiment: "You know, this here is actually an advantage: we meet on an equal footing, and the people who know something about the issue bring in their arguments and objections. One shouldn't make light of this all the time. After all, they also have an idea, a responsibility and don't do that for sheer fun. There are serious objections raised here. What you say is also serious." (22 October 2010, p. 204) What Geißler wished to clarify is the earnestness of the protesters' as well as of the supporters' arguments. An earnestness that apparently was called into question by both parties and that needed to be established in order for them to be able to listen and eventually even to learn from each other.

Unsurprisingly, as a main result and positive outcome of the mediation, Geißler noticed as early as in the fourth session:

We do things differently here. We sit together face-to-face on an equal footing and deal with each argument of each side and vice-versa. You on the screens can follow the arguments yourselves, see how good they are, and you can form an opinion of your own. This also contributes to the objectification and pacification of our discussion and of the overall situation. I want, in fact, to notice that the sessions and mediation talks until now have ensured that we all got down off our high horse. We just have to accept that there are good arguments for both projects. The people on the one side aren't criminal lobbyists and the others aren't backwoodsmen from the Stone age who haven't understood the modern age. This is already a success of our mediation talks, I believe. (12 November 2010, p. 2)

To bring people together eyeball to eyeball became the main result and success of the mediation. It was also a necessary step towards a pacification of the process, since the mutual discrediting and degree of oppositionalism of the differing parties had, up to this point, been particularly intense.

What needs to be noted is that the opponents as well as the supporters indeed adopted this interpretation of the mediation's "success" and thereby showed how important maintaining personal respectability had been in the discussion. The architect, politician and opponent of Stuttgart 21, Peter Conradi, commented on the mediation as follows: "The mediation has changed the perception of us in the public eye. [...] Geißler succeeded in creating something like an even-handed vis-à-vis."[12] The image of a discussion on an equal footing appears again in Conradi's words on the "vis-à-vis" and underlines the importance of the readjustments of positions in the discursive sphere. Werner Wölffle from the Green Party also stressed this aspect: "Our acceptability has grown, nobody can say anymore that we were only protesters [for the sake of being protesters]. We showed that with K21 we had an alternative project for the modernisation of the Stuttgart railway hub."[13] Only after the positions had been readjusted could the alternative project K21 find the attention it needed.

On the side of the supporters, Volker Kefer explained that he had learned something during the mediation process, namely how to discuss arguments in a way he hadn't previously done: "[...] humility, in order to engage in future discussions that I would have otherwise probably not engaged in in this way – that is what I learned during this mediation." (30 November, 2010, p. 8) As the term "humility" indicates, Kefer sees one of the mediation's positive effects in the modification of a personal attitude, an attitude ensuring precisely the openness to other positions regardless of the opponent's "status" or assumed competence. Johannes Bräuchle, a pastor who supported Stuttgart 21, summarised the success of the mediation process by pointing out values similar to humility, namely respect for other opinions and for the people expressing these opinions: "We see as a decisive success that supporters and critics have engaged in a dialogue. It is important that citizens even in times of conflict of opinions are nevertheless

---

12 | Quoted by Heiner Geißler in the verbatim transcripts of 30 November 2010, p. 38.

13 | Ibid.

able to live together peacefully side-by-side and accept the freedom of opinion of the dissenter." (30 November 2010, p. 14) In the light of these positive outcomes identified by the people involved in the mediation, it is not particularly surprising that the press as well as the political sphere commented on the mediation process as being a good example of "democratic participation" and even a model to adopt for further infrastructural projects and the conflicts they create.

Fundamentally, however, this focus on the "democratic" virtue of the mediation that we have analysed as being at least partly a response to underlying attributions of ressentiment and "inferior" motives, stands in stark contrast to the contents of the mediation which consisted in extremely detailed discussions about time-tables, railway station infrastructure, operating plans, journey times, pipe-routeing, calculations of costs, urban planning, species conservation (the track run-up at the station in Stuttgart is the habitat for endangered species), geology, and so forth. Since engineers and all kinds of specialists participated in the mediation, the discourse was, despite repeated requests by the mediator, Geißler, for comprehensible explanations, at times quite technical. The density of information was also rather high, and these two factors would normally be expected to drive away large numbers of the audience. Nevertheless, despite this at times dense technical discourse, there were over a million people following the mediation process on television, on the internet or on the radio. This indicates that the presentation of facts and contexts had become something highly attractive, notwithstanding the effort it demands of the audience. How else could one explain that a remarkable number of people watched all eight sessions of a very technical exchange of arguments about an infrastructural project that didn't even concern them locally?[14] For reasons that need further analysis, the press largely ignored this extremely "unlikely" public interest and instead kept commenting on the mediation process as a model for democratic participation which is at least worthy of explanation, since the mediation did not contain any kind of voting, did not have any legally binding outcome and did not have the authority to decide on any aspect of the issue, the project Stuttgart 21 having already passed the legal steps necessary. Of course, the journalists mentioned that this type of mediation process should happen prior to the decisions on big projects, but it still seems incongruous to comment on the remarkable public interest in the very content-loaded mediation by discussing issues of direct democracy and civil participation.

It is a very telling phenomenon that in the public discourse on the mediation and Stuttgart 21 in general, the discussion of facts concerning the project itself was a lot less intense than the one on democracy and participation. Only rarely could one find comments on the concrete issues discussed in the mediation. In general the information about the "content" of the discussion was limited to mentioning the difference between the "dead-end station" and the planned

---

14 | The audience was strong in Baden-Württemberg and the nearby Rheinland-Pfalz, but not limited to these states. On the channel PHOENIX which broadcasted the entirety of the sessions, the audience rate was the second highest ever attained on this channel.

"through-station", the trees that needed to be torn down in the park, the endangered species living in the track apron, the architecturally and symbolically important station building that would be mostly destroyed and to the real estate projects made possible by the space gained through putting the tracks underground. Very few articles focused on any one of these issues and discussed it in detail.[15] The majority of the articles just summarised matters and then proceeded with the "interpretation" of the protest movement[16] which shows how easily considerations of personal motives and eventual "ressentiment" overpower the discussion of facts. If one were to oversimplify a bit, one could say that frequently, the tenor of the articles was something like: "No matter what one might think of the actual railway project, the protests show that there's something wrong."

Instead of giving detailed facts, this type of "argumentation" instead suggested a sort of general "ressentiment" of the people against the decision-makers

---

15 | Concerning the architecture of the station and its historical role, one should mention Nicolai Ouroussoffs, "Last call for an elegant rail station", in: *New York Times*, 3 October 2009. Dieter Bartetzko from the German daily *Frankfurter Allgemeine Zeitung* followed the discussion of the architecture of the old and new stations. In the German weekly *ZEIT*, a few articles were concerned with the problem of endangered species in the station area.

16 | To quote but two typical examples of this structure consisting in a short resume followed by an interpretation in political terms: "In the planning for nearly 15 years, the Stuttgart 21 project calls for knocking down two wings of a century-old train station and replacing above-ground tracks with miles of tunnel that will allow Stuttgart to link into a high-speed rail system. The project, which will take about a decade to complete, requires cutting down nearly 300 trees in a popular park just behind the station. Opposition to the project has been steadily growing since demolition work started in the summer, with tens of thousands of residents of the conservative, wealthy area turning out for regular weekly demonstrations. But the local conflict became a national crisis last week for Chancellor Angela Merkel, who supports the project, when images of injured protesters were printed and broadcast around the nation." (Michael Slackman, "Germany Pulls Back on Demolition of Stuttgart Rail Station", in: *New York Times* 6 October 2010, A11) "The project, called Stuttgart 21, is complicated and ambitious. It is supposed to take fifteen years and cost 4.1bn. It would link Stuttgart to Germany's high-speed rail system with 55 new bridges and 63km of new tunnels, destroying two wings of the old station. By sinking the approaching tracks, the project will free up 10 hectares of land – a big fraction of Stuttgart's urban core – which can be used for building chic new neighbourhoods in the heart of the city. The plan was okayed by city authorities and approved by solid majorities in the Baden-Württemberg legislature. It provoked little opposition, until construction began. Then people decided they didn't want it. Everything hinges on whether they must now be listened to or told, 'too late, tough luck.' Maybe they are a majority, maybe not. But we are not talking about a handful of eccentric malcontents. Starting last summer, tens of thousands have been descending on the centre of the city every day." (Christopher Caldwell, "Tough luck on the train tracks", in: *Financial Times.com*, 8 October 2010, URL: http://www.ft.com/cms/s/0/50497584-d30d-11df-9ae9-00144fe-abdco.html#axzz10LzxTvOb.)

who decided things over their heads. An article published in the *Süddeutsche Zeitung* shows this drift in a quite typical way: "[...] [the protesters who] first of all want to keep the dead-end station and don't want an underground new building, who fear the overflowing costs of the project, who fear for the underground mineral springs in Stuttgart and who quite generally feel ignored and overrun by the politicians. Even though the history of the gigantic project has been paved with resistance and lawsuits that delayed the start of construction for ten years, now that the dredges are standing in front of the station, the mistrust in the powers-that-be manifests itself like never before."[17] *The Economist*, reporting on Stuttgart 21 in its "newsbook" blog, also referred explicitly to "the people-versus-power mood of the moment".[18]

Depending on the opinion of the journalist, this mood was then either supported or criticised, as one could observe in the comments on the referendum that had taken place on 27 November 2011 after the change of government in Baden-Württemberg in March 2011, bringing the Green party and the Social Democrats to power. The Green party had been opposed to Stuttgart 21 from the outset and the Social Democrats had supported it, but had also supported a referendum on the question, which is why the new government organised a referendum.

A lot could be said about this referendum – the opponents questioned its fairness, journalists reported on the strong influence of the parties supporting Stuttgart 21, particularly in small towns, the big marketing budgets on the side of the supporters was also an issue – but what matters in the context of our discussion is merely the fact that this referendum was seen as something like the natural "solution" to the Stuttgart 21 issue which had become a problem of participation, protest and ressentiment and in big parts of the press had never been anything else. As had been the case in the beginning of the coverage of the protests, the referendum was treated like a problem of protest and more or less legitimate ressentiment against the "people in charge".

Thus, it was either commented on as the proof that the "loud minority" does not necessarily reflect the majority opinion – Günther Nonnenmacher made this case in "Ein Sieg für die repräsentative Demokratie", published in the *Frankfurter Allgemeine Zeitung* on 29 November 2011 – or as a very good example of "civic participation", the result of which had to be accepted, now that it had been democratically achieved. Essentially, all political parties adopted this "interpretation" of the referendum. The possibility that this might not be the case and that the protests would go on was naturally also suggested, since Stuttgart 21 would now definitely be built and the reasons for protest and ressentiment had not disappeared.

---

17 | Dagmar Deckstein, Martin Kotynek, "Stadt der entgleisten Gefühle", in: *Süddeutsche Zeitung* 20 August 2010, (URL: http://www.sueddeutsche.de/politik/widerstand-gegen-stuttgart-stadt-der-entgleisten-gefuehle-1.990341)

18 | "Disoccupy Stuttgart", in: *The Economist*, 29 November 2010, URL: http://www.economist.com/blogs/newsbook/2011/11/german-railways.

Unsurprisingly, the opponents and supporters of the project remained quite clearly polarised in this press coverage. The pacifying effect of the mediation process had not lasted very long. It seems fair to comment that much of the press coverage didn't help to alleviate the situation since what was still largely missing was a discussion of the issues at hand, namely the railway project and its implications. This discussion might have been able to de-dramatise and nuance some of the oppositions.

Let's consider, for instance, the supposed opposition of "through-station" and "dead-end station": as the opponents of Stuttgart 21 stated during the mediation, they didn't criticise "through-stations" as such. They merely found that in the case of Stuttgart 21, the costs of "going under the earth" would be too high in relation to the benefit. They saw the benefit as threatened by overall costs, but also by risks of timetable interruptions which, in the special case of Stuttgart, were higher in the through-station than in the dead-end station. Besides this higher risk of unpunctuality, the opponents also raised some doubts about the operating plan of Stuttgart 21, questioning whether there were in fact going to be enough trains to benefit from the new infrastructure, the number of trains being limited for budgetary reasons. These considerations that the opponents backed-up by producing detailed simulations of timetables tied into their overall preference for a "Swiss railway model". The Swiss model is characterised by high punctuality, integrated timetables and an infrastructure that follows these priorities as opposed to the German system that first plans the infrastructure and then the timetables. Thus, the opposition to the through-station was mostly the result of holding a different priority. To this priority should be added Stuttgart 21's relatively low impact on freight transportation, something that for the Green party is of major importance in order to reduce traffic on the streets. This is why they claimed that the money spent on Stuttgart 21 should better be spent on other connections (for instance along the Rhine), crucial for freight transportation.

Interestingly, perhaps, the supporters of Stuttgart, namely the DB, didn't really oppose this view and admitted that Stuttgart 21 was mostly a project for passenger travel and not for freight transportation. It was therefore simply a different issue that the DB wished to push forward. The financing was regarded as a different problem. Whether the money spent on Stuttgart indeed stands in direct competition to money that could otherwise be spent on freight transportation infrastructure was difficult to ascertain during the mediation, but in any case, there was no real opposition between the parties concerning the focus of Stuttgart 21 on passenger travel or regarding the general importance of freight transportation.

In a similar way, the DB also stated that there was in principle nothing wrong with "dead-end stations" and of course nothing wrong with the "Swiss system" of integrated time-tables. But Stuttgart 21 was a project planned in Germany and thus, as Volker Kefer from the DB explained, it had to adopt the German procedures. The extent to which the Swiss system was in all aspects translatable to German conditions could not be answered in detail during the mediation, but in any case, the goal of integrated timetables seemed a shared one by both

parties. What distinguished the arguments was above all the different prioriti-
sation concerning travel-time, since the DB stated, based on research done on
the issue, that travel-time was the key factor in order to make people switch
from car or plane to the train, especially in travel between big cities where the
DB expects the biggest growth in passengers. Within this framework, the faster
way through Stuttgart with the help of the through-station made perfect sense,
although the probably bigger issue in this context is the construction of a fast
track line between Ulm and Wendlingen, a connection both parties hope for
(although lately the opponents have come to question its viability due to its high
costs and apparently pending financing).

Concerning the reduction of travel time, the opponents of Stuttgart 21 questioned the projected growth of travellers insofar as they compared it to possible
growth in freight transportation or improvements in non-urban areas, but they
did not oppose the goal of travel-time reduction as such. Again, the difference lay
more in prioritisations and related cost-benefit-considerations than in a general
opposition to the project as such.

This is not to say that these different prioritisations did not result in oppositional positions, but to explain the background of the positions and the arguments supporting them keeps one from buying into the simplistic oppositions of
progress-orientation versus hostility to progress. These oppositions were stated
particularly in the beginning of the conflict surrounding Stuttgart 21 and mentioned by the mediator, Heiner Geißler, who explained that the protesters could
not be seen as people who hadn't understood modernity. Besides being simplistic, the problem with the attributes "anti-progress" versus "progressive" was that
they were usually expressed without regard for contents and facts but more often
based on "psychological" attributions, on "ad hominem" strategies of discussion.
To be against a specific issue was seen as being against any kind of change. To
support a specific change was seen to be supportive of any kind of change. As
a reaction to these simplistic charges, opponents of Stuttgart 21 in particular
wished to appear in a different light. They managed to do so during the mediation and, as we mentioned before, saw this as an important achievement of the
mediation process.

Yet, large parts of the press, by neglecting the discussion of the concrete
arguments of opponents and supporters of Stuttgart 21, did not really back this
"result".[19] Instead, the mediation was praised as a model of civic participation,

---

19 | This is not to say that no articles tried a detailed overview of the pros and cons
of Stuttgart 21. The *Stuttgarter Zeitung* for instance issued a special supplement on
the project. But a few hints in the supplement are very telling concerning the overall
"absence" of facts: On page 4 of the supplement, the subtitle reads as follows: "While
the *New York Times* reports on Stuttgart 21 and the whole city is discussing the station, one question has been fading into the background: What exactly is the matter
anyway?" [translation mine] Furthermore, the journalists explain on page 1 that they
issued the supplement after many readers asked for a detailed summary of the concrete
facts – which precisely proves our theses that the public is craving factual information,
information that is not the predominant feature of the press coverage on Stuttgart 21, to

an experiment in direct democracy, or, on a smaller scale, as a clever coup of the-then governor Mappus to calm the situation down and to attenuate the critique of his government.[20]

While nobody questions the legitimacy of smart political strategies and the eventual benefits of civic participation, the question remains as to whether these were really the questions that interested so many people in the mediation process and that made it such a fascinating event even for people who weren't personally concerned by the railway transformation. It seems that the interest lay in a fascination with and a desire for facts, for argument, for rationality understood as a principle where decisions are based on goals and means that are organised in a comprehensible, traceable way in order to attain these goals, this traceability being crucial in order to find possible problems within the system, in order to improve it and in order to evaluate alternatives. And although these rational processes of decision-making can be very complex, as could be observed throughout the mediation, its audience seemed keen on finding out about the rationality of the projects.

It is very telling that in public discourse on the mediation and on its being a model for "citizen participation" in the future, not much was said of the goals of such citizen participation. What exactly would be better if citizens were to participate in decisions? It seems that this question was regarded as rather irrelevant, the very fact that citizens participated being sufficiently important in itself. It is not unlikely that this supposed evidence of the benefits of civic participation is a reaction to the underlying ressentiment reproach concerning all kinds of civic manifestation of dissent. From this standpoint, any kind of participation would be positive insofar as it responds to the people's "wish" to be heard and taken seriously.

Yet, it is problematic to "cut off" the issue at this point. Instead it would probably be helpful to ask the questions that researchers in the social sciences have started asking about "civic participation", namely its contribution to higher rationality in decision-making.[21] As the results of Bogner *et al.* (2011) suggest, the value of these contributions increases if the participating citizens are "experts" in the field and if they are personally concerned about the issue. These findings don't seem surprising since it does require knowledge of the facts in order to evaluate and improve propositions and since the acquisition of such knowledge requires an effort that one might only be ready to make if one is

---

say the least. One of the rather rare exceptions to this general tendency is Eckhard Buddruss from the regional daily *Rheinpfalz* who in his articles tried to support his arguments by focussing on factual issues concerning railway infrastructure, operational concepts and matters of this nature.

20 | This interpretation was put forward by Christoph Schwennicke in his commentary on the mediation "In Grund und Boden geschlichtet", in: *Der Spiegel*, 30 November 2010, URL: http://www.spiegel.de/politik/deutschland/0,1518,732042,00.html)

21 | See for instance: Alexander Bogner, Veronika Gaube, and Barbara Smetschka,"Partizipative Modellierung. Beteiligungsexperimente in der sozialökologischen Forschung.", in: *Österreichische Zeitschrift für Soziologie*, 36, (2011), p. 74–97.

directly concerned. Nonetheless, these findings should probably not hinder the attempt to raise civic participation. After all, while not everybody is an expert on everything, everybody is probably an expert on something. It seems crucial, however, to keep in mind something that should be a goal of participation, namely the improvement of decisions and projects. This is a goal that favours the participation of informed people and ways of participation where the exchange of arguments is central.

This focus on arguments and facts has another great advantage: while in decision-making, one can never be sure that the position one holds will be the one adopted, the exchange of facts at least always leaves the chance to learn. This chance, indeed, this opportunity is available to any participant in the process. At the end, arguments that did not make it into positions decided on may, at some point, become so relevant that they are ultimately adopted. Arguments can become discourses and discourses can become influential. As convincingly suggested by a recent dissertation, the negotiations on Stuttgart 21 show that ecological aspects are already part of the standard factors being considered in decision-making, on both the opponents' and the supporters' side.[22] One could say that the ecological arguments have now become an influential factor which goes to show that their success is not due to the "ressentiment" of the "ecologists" but to the fact that the ecologists at least in part had arguments on their side that could be implemented in the planning of projects.

Arguments, facts, complexity and the desire to learn, to uphold rationality even if it is in a minority position, are ideas not particularly en vogue at the present time, it seems. Personalisation – of which the ressentiment reproach is but one aspect – seems ubiquitous and philosophers such as Norbert Bolz see it as a necessary reduction of complexity.[23] While it is evident that complexity needs reduction and now maybe more so than ever, since the time-spans for decisions seem to constantly shrink, there is still probably no benefit in losing one's cool, in oversimplifying and in choosing easy oppositions. It is in view of these tendencies that a critique of protest movement makes sense.[24] As Luhmann so clearly put it: "Gegen Komplexität kann man nicht protestieren."[25]

---

22 | See Peter Owen Engelke, *Green city origins: democratic resistance to the auto-oriented city in West Germany, 1960–1990*. Ph.D. Dissertation, Georgetown University 2011, p. 337).

23 | Cf. Norbert Bolz, *Blindflug mit Zuschauer*, Munich: Fink 2004.

24 | As Mike Giglio mentions in an article on the protests in Stuttgart, the boundaries between protest and populism are easily blurred: "Even America's Tea Party had an open-source aspect at its outset, before it became closely allied with Republican donors: part of the movement's ostensible appeal was its aura of common people rising up in a 'we're mad as hell and we're not going to take it anymore' moment against bank bailouts and government stimulus spending." (Mike Giglio, "Hydra without a head", in: *Newsweek*, December 14 2010, URL: http://www.thedailybeast.com/newsweek/2010/12/14/hydra-without-a-head.html)

25 | "One can't protest against complexity." [translation mine], cf. Niklas Luhmann,

This kept in mind, one could say, to put it briefly: if public discourse wants to "support" protesters – and the calls for more civic participation indicate such a support – it might be more helpful to put forward their arguments, their premises and goals instead of underlining their personal integrity and the legitimacy of their protest. As long as arguments and factual discussions are missing, public discourse is stuck on the personal level, leading either to an *a priori* discrediting of protesters or to their *a priori* support. In both cases, what is at work is a powerful presumption of ressentiment that either disqualifies critique by reducing it to negative personal motives or idealises critique by inverting the negative attributions.

Instead of a concrete or at least identifiable problem with possible solutions or compromises, we then have groups fighting for prestige. Opponents protest, supporters start counter-protests,[26] both counting on the attention they will get from the media and public, attention they are sure to receive, since the media readily focuses on the very fact that there is apparently "lots of protest" going on. That the goal and even the raison d'être of protest is, and will be even more in the future, to attract the media's attention, has also been analysed by Luhmann.[27] And it might be utterly naïve to expect any changes in these relations between the media and protest movements, changes that would consist of a stronger focus on the facts and matters at issue. But naïve or not, the mediation process for Stuttgart 21 suggests that there is indeed an audience that wishes to discuss issues instead of people, and arguments instead of attitudes. The mediation in Stuttgart 21 was much less a model for direct democracy than the glimpse of a rationality that seems to have become less probable in the media age, but not less desirable.

Protest. Systemtheorie und soziale Bewegungen, ed. Kai-Uwe Hellmann, Frankfurt am Main: Suhrkamp 1996, 211.

26 | This co-appearance of "opponents' protests" and "supporters' protests" could be observed in Stuttgart where all kinds of "Pro Stuttgart 21" groups and activities came up and could then be observed in Frankfurt, where the airport operator *Fraport* is reacting to strong protests against night-flights by organising "Ja zu FRA" ("Yes to FRA")-protests. Whether employees were called on to attend these protests was discussed in the media as well as the reactions of the opponents who refused to be seen as opposing the Frankfurt airport in general – a general refusal suggested by the "Ja zu FRA"-dictum. But although the media reflected upon the oversimplified oppositions, the discussion of the issue on hand remained superficial. Key questions such as the following remained unanswered: How high is the loss for *Fraport* if it reduces or bans night-flights? How necessary are the night-flights? How much compensation could be handled? How can people learn to cope with aircraft noise? On which basis can people even ask for compensation? Indeed, such questions as these remained largely absent in the media coverage.

27 | *Protest. Systemtheorie und soziale Bewegungen,* p. 212.

Specular *Ressentiment*
San-Antonio, or the Art of Faking Resentment

Dominique Jeannerod

*Translated by Mary Gallagher**

Many of the labels applied to popular fiction, terms such as "industrial litera-ture" or "para-literature", emphasise its focus on the marketplace and its mar-ginality in relation to canonical literature. The reception of popular literature thus seems destined to reinforce a dichotomised, hierarchical understanding of the literary field, split between periphery and centre, ephemera and classics, exteriority and belonging, heteronomy and autonomy. Traditionally, those popu-lar authors who are lucky enough to be successful during their own lifetime are disdained by the critics. They are destined to remain forever the poor relations of literary history; their works are quickly forgotten, consigned as they are to the outer margins of literature, if not to complete oblivion.[1] However, the study of these "dominated" authors – and of their excluded, stigmatised or simply non-canonised works – enriches our understanding of the literary field. While much research is being carried out on the gigantic, though neglected, corpus of the popular novel, few studies focus on the frequently conflicted tenor of the relationship between popular[2] authors and "legitimate" literature.[3]

The concept of Ressentiment seems to offer a suitable critical tool with which to study this relationship, lending itself especially well to exploring the complicated underlying affects. The dialectical force of Ressentiment can help to identify the bad faith which is, as Pierre Bourdieu points out, such a pre-eminent characteristic of the relationship.[4] On the one hand, there is the financial resentment of "legit-

---

* | All translations from the French are by Mary Gallagher unless otherwise indicated.

1 | On canon formation and cultural selection, see the chapter entitled "The Slaughter-house of Literature" in Franco Moretti, *Distant Reading*, London: Verso 2013, pp. 63–89.

2 | See, in particular, Jacques Migozzi, *Boulevards du populaire*, Limoges: PULIM 2005; Jacques Migozzi and Philippe Le Guern, *Productions du populaire*, Limoges: PULIM 2004.

3 | Dominique Jeannerod, *San-Antonio et son double*, Paris: Presses universitaires de France 2010.

4 | Pierre Bourdieu, *The Rules of Art: Genesis and Structure of the Literary Field*, trans. Susan Emanuel, Stanford: Stanford University Press 1996.

imised" authors, whose rich literary capital renders it difficult for them to admit their envy of the less symbolic than all too real, material fortunes of the best-selling authors, whose books they might be expected to despise. On the other hand, there is the literary resentment of the authors who have sold millions of books but received no prizes, whose writing is not anthologised, and whose works receive little or no serious critical attention. This essay takes as its starting point the ways in which the envy and resentment felt by popular authors illustrates their internalisation of the structures and values of the literary field and of what Bourdieu terms its "inverted economics".[5] It focuses in particular, however, on showing that the greater and the more vehement the Ressentiment expressed by authors toward the literary institution, the greater their tacit affirmation of the latter's values. The case of one of the most illustrious representatives of French popular fiction, crime author San-Antonio, will serve to highlight this dialectic of Ressentiment, in which established literary hierarchies are paradoxically reinforced by the author's ostensible attack on literary critics and on the literary establishment in general.

San-Antonio (alias Frédéric Dard, 1921–2000) is the prolific author of a series of crime novels in which the detective protagonist is also called San-Antonio. Appearing at a steady rate from 1949 right up to 2000, the hundred and eighty-four novels of the series entitled *Les Aventures de San-Antonio* made their author the most read French writer of the twentieth century, but one whose writing was, in his own view at least, misunderstood and undervalued both by the literary establishment and by his peers.

Literary history offers a certain number of postures to successful writers. The posture of the rich and happy popular author was adopted with varying degrees of success by Peter Cheyney, Georges Simenon, Gérard de Villiers, *inter alia*. San-Antonio's choice, however, was ostensibly that of the unhappy popular author, rich and successful but frustrated by a lack of literary recognition and legitimacy. Frédéric Dard expressed very publicly many times and in many different ways, but most frequently through the voice of San-Antonio, his resentment regarding the reception and the status of his work.[6] If it is quite clear that his alter-ego's scathingly critical mockery of the literary establishment is inflected by a deep-seated Ressentiment, this is because Dard's literary values were not perhaps as far removed from those of canonical literature as some of his diatribes against it might suggest. As an adolescent, this one-time disciple of Georges Simenon was celebrated as the new Raymond Radiguet. He was an avowed admirer of both Louis-Ferdinand Céline and Jean-Paul Sartre, knew Pierre Benoit, worked with Francis Carco and wrote pastiches of Jacques Prévert. Moreover, his "genius" was recognised by Jean Cocteau and, in the final years of his long career, he was also praised

---

5 | Famously, according to Bourdieu (*The Rules*, p. 83), "The artist cannot triumph on the symbolic terrain except by losing on the economic terrain".

6 | Dominique Jeannerod, "Chateaubriand du coq-à-l'âne' ou dernier grand écrivain du siècle: La réception de San-Antonio dans la presse", in Françoise Rullier, Thierry Gautier, Dominique Jeannerod, Dominique Lagorgette (eds), *San-Antonio et la culture française*, Chambéry: Éditions de l'Université de Savoie 2011, pp. 25–53.

by the Académie française for the lexical inventiveness and verbal vigour of his novels. This acclaim, combined with sales of dozens of millions of copies of his books, sales that made him one of the wealthiest authors in French literary history, would not seem to warrant any sense of envy on his part, much less any Ressentiment. Yet Ressentiment can have a generic dimension and can be founded not on an individual author's personal frustration but rather on the lack of esteem accorded to the literary genre that he or she practices. It can also take the form of projections and fantasies on the part of the author, and a fortiori on the part of a "fictional" author/narrator/protagonist, and it can serve to reinforce a certain literary posture.[7] This would certainly appear to be the case for San-Antonio, whose expressions of Ressentiment can seem staged or faked. This is not merely because, as figments of Dard's imagination, they *are* fictions; it is also because their self-reflexive, meta-literary character imbues them with a spectral and strategic theatricality.

Devaluing the Detective Author and Staging the Ressentiment of the Popular Author

San-Antonio's detective novels have, from the outset, differed from others in this genre. This is largely because of the fact that the intra-diegetic narrator bears the same name as the pseudonymous author and also because of the meta-literary content of this author/narrator/protagonist's digressions.[8] These asides often consist of reflections on literature and on the place of San-Antonio within French literary history. Interrupting the central narrative line,[9] they create a space for reflection and commentary on the text, inviting the reader to leave behind the domain of the detective novel for literary criticism. In this way, the author can be seen as provisionally and intermittently abandoning the lucrative exercise of para-literature to focus on the less well-defined but more flattering or more highly valued one of meta-literature. Unlike, for example, Léo Malet, a direct precursor of San-Antonio, whose detective narrator Nestor Burma provides a running commentary on the arts and on literature, a commentary that underlines Malet's Surrealist inheritance, San-Antonio's practice is more narrowly self-reflexive; it explicitly invites the reader to observe the author's particular writing skills and to assess their value.

---

7 | This concept of literary posture is derived from the writings of Pierre Bourdieu, Alain Viala and J. Meizoz; the notion of the theatricality of authorship refers to the work of Dominique Maingueneau.

8 | In his first book, San-Antonio observes: "There are guys who have been relegated to the French Academy for less than that. I'm sure that if I wanted to take the trouble, I'd be able to make my writing amount to something in literature." ["Il y a des types qu'on a flanqués à l'Académie française pour moins que ça. Je suis sûr que si je voulais m'en donner la peine, j'arriverais à des résultats appréciables en littérature", San-Antonio, *Réglez-lui son compte* [Get even with him] (Lyon: Jacquier 1949, p. 131), Fleuve Noir 1981, p. 106.

9 | Jean Rousset, *Narcisse romancier*, Paris: Corti 1972, p. 69.

What is continually foregrounded in San-Antonio's meta-literary digressions is the fact that this detective writer is a frustrated author. Ostensibly, this is because he carries the stigma associated with a fictional genre born in the second half of the nineteenth century and yet still widely considered in the twentieth century as sub-literary. Despite the fact that writers of the stature of Jean-Paul Sartre, André Gide, Paul Morand, André Malraux and others took an interest in the work of popular authors such as Dashiell Hammett, Georges Simenon or James Cain, it is much more commonly the case that eminent literary writers and critics are disdainful, or even quite unaware, of this type of literary production. Paul Claudel expresses his contempt clearly, if not subtly, in an article published in the newspaper *Le Figaro* (April 1941) entitled "Detective novels are aimed at the lowest levels of human stupidity"["Le roman policier s'adresse aux couches les plus basses de la bêtise humaine"]. Claudel finds furthermore that, in reading crime novels, "the reader becomes conscious of his [sic] own stupidity through encountering that of the author" ["le lecteur devient conscient au contact de la stupidité de l'auteur de la sienne propre"]. While Claudel also admits to having read detective novels – albeit rarely – he roundly dismisses their literary value, declaring: "I never found a single one to be of any value, literary or otherwise"["Je n'en ai jamais trouvé un seul qui ait une valeur littéraire, ou autre, quelconque"]. In addition, the detective novel had at that time the relative symbolic disadvantage of being identified with new and often foreign, popular and media cultures far removed from academic literature, such as the culture of film, cabaret and comics, but also the popular theatrical traditions known as "Boulevard du Crime" or "Grand Guignol".

From the very start, Dard wrote his detective novels, unlike his other novels, under a pseudonym, thereby expressing a certain distance from his writing. It is clear that he had already as a very young man internalised the prevailing status of crime fiction, a genre that commanded scant literary respect. The production values of series such as the famous Fayard "65 cent" collection were both materially and visually very different from the classics; they looked and were cheaper than literary collections. While his generation witnessed a steadily growing critical appreciation of the genre, particularly in the 1960s, Dard himself remained, to a great extent, in the past, unduly influenced by the critical perception that had prevailed at the beginning of his career. Although their approach was actually quite far removed from the outright insults of Claudel or from the reticence of literary novelists concerned about the competition that might be forthcoming from the detective genre, the critics were still somewhat suspicious of the accelerated rhythms of publication of crime fiction.[10] Naturally, this criticism of mass production extended to the individual authors and to all involved in what was seen above all as a *trade* and despised as such for over a century. As early as 1839, Sainte-Beuve had attacked the industrialisation of literature, blaming "peo-

---

10 | Such reservations were not unique to literary criticism in French. For a review of criticism of the genre in Italy, see Jane Dunnett, "Crime and the Critics: on the Appraisal of Detective Novels in 1930s Italy", *Modern Language Review*, 106:3 (2011) pp. 745–65.

ple who knew nothing about literature invading the bookshops and dreaming of illusory profit" ["des hommes ignorants des lettres, envahissant la librairie et y rêvant de gains chimériques"].[11]

It remains, however, that Dard's experience of criticism was largely indirect and generic. Thus, when writing about what he perceived as critical hostility to his work, he was quite content for many decades – until the 1990s – to engage exclusively with the hostility that he had seen directed against crime fiction *per se* by conservative critics in the 1940s. Such critics had never mentioned his own writing, however. Indeed, serious criticism was only ever levelled against Dard in relation to his plays rather than his novels. If the critics about whom he complains are attacking the genre rather than his own work or himself personally, it is probably true that he was not spared as a result of some special indulgence on the part of the reviewers. In fact, though, Dard seems to have read this critical silence concerning his own work as mute hostility directed specifically against the latter. Indeed he took this apparent ignorance or disinterest very personally, interpreting it as a snub directed, not at the genre as a whole, but rather at his own writing. It remains, however, that the direct and explicit criticism described as having been levelled against San-Antonio himself and his work specifically are pure figments of the author's imagination.

The way in which San-Antonio refers to this putative critical hostility is by (ironically) undermining his own literary position, pretending to repeat the "received view" of the inferior status of his writing. Thus, in one novel, San-Antonio states: "If I'd been a writer, I would have entitled this book Blood and Darkness. But, luckily for you, I'm just Auntie Tantonio" ["Si j'étais un écrivain, j'aurais intitulé ce book « Sang et Nuit »]. Mais heureusement pour toi, je suis juste un San-Tantonio."][12] Another statement exaggerating the distance between his own position and the cultural legitimacy to which "real writers" can aspire, sees him pretend to count himself among those who are described as "weavers of sentences, upholsterers of an abject, sub-sub-sub-literature that is impure, depraved, crime-promoting, cynical, trashy, pornographic, obscene: in a word, commercial" ["tresseurs de phrases, vanniers de sous-sous-sous-littérature abjecte, polluante, dépravante, pousse au crime, cynique, ordurière, pornographique, obscène, bref commerciale"].[13] This exaggerated self-deprecation seems to signal more than a mere internalisation of genre divisions within the literary field; it also appears to express deep-seated nostalgia for a type of literature other than that which San-Antonio was writing. He admits as much indeed, declaring: "I'm just a cop with my right hand and a scribbler with my left and

---

11 | "De la littérature industrielle", *La Revue des Deux Mondes* (1er septembre 1939), repr. in Lise Dumasy (ed.), *La Querelle du roman feuilleton: Littérature, presse et politique, un débat précurseur (1836–1848)*, Grenoble: Editions ELLUG 1999, p. 36.

12 | San-Antonio, *Valsez, pouffiasses* [*Waltz on, you Sluts*],1989, Back cover. Unless otherwise indicated, all references to works by San-Antonio are to the Fleuve Noir (Paris) editions.

13 | San-Antonio, *La Vie privée de Walter Klozett*, [*The Secret Life of Walter Closet*], 1975, p.15.

I feel so weighed down with inadequacy" ["Moi qui ne suis qu'un policier de la main droite et un écrivaillon de la gauche. Je me sens si lourd d'inaccomplissement"];[14] "I'm ashamed of writing what I write, I'm ashamed of the money that it makes for me" ["J'ai honte d'écrire ce que j'écris, j'ai honte de l'argent que ça me rapporte"].[15] As Françoise Rullier has accurately observed,[16] the author appears to be caught between the temptation of the literary and his lack of faith in his chosen narrative vehicle: the parodic detective novel.

From Mere Envy to Ressentiment?

Having repeatedly agonised over the literary status of his writing, San-Antonio ends up by roundly rejecting literature and all its pomps. Thus, after thirty years of writing, he declares that "they are starting to drive me crazy, all of them, with their speculation about whether or not I belong with literary authors" ["ils commencent à me bassiner, tous, à chercher si j'appartiens ou non à la littérature"].[17] And he goes on: "A Sana (a San-Antonio) [...] has nothing to do with literature and, luckily, it never will!" ["Un Sana [...], c'est pas de la littérature, ça n'en sera jamais, heureusement!].[18] This abrupt transvaluation of literature provides the key to San-Antonian Ressentiment. In a rhetorical flourish of antiparastasis (condemnation of an object of praise), suppressed envy becomes Ressentiment. Reversing his prior interpretation of the elitist exclusion of books such as his from the world of letters, he claims – in obvious bad faith – to be proud of not belonging to that world. This move allows him to transform (putatively) negative judgements on his writing into a positive value, a certificate of (transgressive) authenticity. He positively cultivates, indeed, those qualities that he imagines or (supposedly) "quotes" as founding the criticism or exclusion of his work. Furthermore, this allows him to represent himself as an unjustly misunderstood, undervalued writer, neglected by the readers and critics of "serious" literature, and not taken seriously enough even by his own readers. He suggests, after all, that – deep down – his readership shares the prejudices of his non-readers for whom his books are mere entertainment.

San-Antonio's rhetorical pose is firmly based on a polemical interpretation of his own situation as a victim of, or even a martyr to, elitist persecution: "San-A... he should be banished... Should be denounced, decreed intolerable. His style should be castrated. [...] Make him submit ! Make him dry up!" [San-A ... Faut le bannir... Le dénoncer. Le décréter intolérable. Lui émasculer le style [...] Qu'il

---

14 | San-Antonio, *Si ma tante en avait*, [*If my Aunt had Some*],1978, p. 92.

15 | San-Antonio, *Je le jure* [*I Swear*], Paris: Stock 1975, J'ai Lu 1977, p. 125.

16 | Françoise Rullier, "Proust, Céline, Cohen et moi' ou San-Antonio et l'histoire littéraire", *Revue d'histoire littéraire de la France*, 2004, pp. 189–207.

17 | San-Antonio, *Morpions circus* [*Brats Circus*], 1983, p. 106.

18 | Ibid., p. 107.

s'incline! Qu'il décline!][19] As his critical and popular success, notably in the media, gathered pace, it became increasingly difficult, however, for him to maintain this posture.[20] Gradually, he had to invent an ever more intense or extreme parody of the criticism to which he was allegedly being subjected.[21]

In depicting himself as a victim of near-hysterical critical hostility, San-Antonio is implicitly blowing his own stylistic trumpet and triumphing over his supposed critics. First of all, the author's verbal and stylistic pyrotechnics mean that a San-Antonio book is, according to himself, "a missile made to be fired into people's faces" ["un projectile destiné à être flanqué à la gueule des gens"].[22] His transgressive – vulgar and neologistic – linguistic skill effectively allows him to make the popular vernacular audible over the conformist drone of the "little popes of syntax" ["petits papes de la syntaxe"].[23] Secondly, because of his non-conformist idiom and despite writing in a niche genre, San-Antonio's work could paradoxically be considered as more original from a literary perspective than that of many "literary" writers. And thirdly, compared to the prolific ease and brio of his production, the efforts of the latter seem precious and punctilious: "My God, how well I could write if I was one of those cocky posers poring over the slightest beauty spot! And what a prestigious career I'd drag around after me, like a dog trailing a saucepan tied to its tail by rascals" ["Mon Dieu, que je m'exprimerais bien, si j'étais un branleur d'écrivain à la recherche de ses grains de beauté les plus infimes ! Quelle carrière prestigieuse trainé-je à ma queue, comme le chien la casserole dont les polissons l'ont affublée"].[24]

This devaluation of literary success or recognition is, ostensibly, an expression of Ressentiment. It suggests that if San-Antonio himself wanted to garner such success, he could easily do so. And it also suggests that it is not for base

19 | San-Antonio, *Les Vacances de Bérurier* [*Bérurier's Holidays*], 1969, p. 33.

20 | See D. Jeannerod, "Chateaubriand du coq à l'âne", p. 23.

21 | See in particular the following example from *Mon culte sur la commode*, 1979, p. 12: "What bothers me? You want to know what bothers me? You really want to know? Once and for all? Right away? Straight up? Your devotees, San-Antonio. Your devotees. Simply and solely your devotees. You are surrounded by this unbearable veneration. At the sound of your name, people start smiling as though they were being promised the sun, the moon and the stars. There is too much talk of you. Too much written about you. You're being passed from hand to hand. You're borrowed and loaned. Worse still: you're being read!" ["Ce qui me gêne? Vous voulez savoir ce qui me gêne? Vous voulez le savoir vraiment? Pour de bon? Tout de go? Là, en plein? Votre culte, San-Antonio. Votre culte! Uniquement votre culte. Vous êtes entouré d'une sorte de vénération intolérable. À l'énoncé de votre nom, les gens se mettent à sourire comme si on leur promettait des choses plaisantes. On parle trop de vous. On écrit trop sur vous. On vous loue, on vous prête. Pire: on vous lit !".]

22 | San-Antonio, *Faut-il tuer les petits garçons qui ont les mains sur les hanches ?* [*Should we Kill the Small Boys with their Hands on their Hips?*], 1984, p. 20.

23 | San-Antonio, *Mes délirades* [*My Deliriabilia*], 1999, p. 149.

24 | San-Antonio, *Bacchanale chez la mère Tatzi* [*Orgy at Ma Tatzi's*], p. 179.

commercial reasons but rather out of contempt for conformity that he has chosen to abjure literary "success", choosing instead to write popular novels in an earthy, "plebeian" style. This message is particularly clear in his comments on the limitations even of members of the prestigious *Académie française*: "although I would be well able to produce a book in the style of Maurice Druon, Maurice Druon could never manage to write a San-Antonio, not in a million years".[25]

Why, then, is San-Antonio presented intra-diegetically as "the great French novelist, Mr San-Antonio" ["Monsieur San-Antonio, un grand romancier français"]?[26] It would appear that, self-flagellating and self-deprecating in places, self-aggrandising in others – especially in the commercial blurbs on the books' covers, the author is playing a double game. Thus, new editions of a series of books published very early on in his career (*Les Kaput*) were presented as revealing "the dark, hidden side of a hugely important writer" ["la face cachée et ténébreuse d'un immense écrivain"].[27] Similarly, the publication of a number of collections of aphorisms taken from his work, for example *Pensées de San-Antonio*, present him without apparent irony as a classic in the same league as Rabelais and Céline.[28] The press was also conscripted for this publicity campaign: thus,

---

25 | San-Antonio, *La Vie privée de Walter Klozett*, p. III.

26 | *San-Antonio chez les Mac*, 1961, p. 79 [San-Antonio in the Land of the MacPimps]. San-Antonio is, then, an imaginary novelist, who likes to reinforce his image as a popular author, downplaying the art and the status of writing and of literature: "I rhyme off, very fast and with the off-hand air of the master who doesn't want his modesty to be violated" ["je récite, très vite et très négligemment, en maître qui ne veut pas qu'on violente sa modestie : *La Dame aux hortensias* [The Lady with the Hydrangias], *Le Comte de Montebello* [The Count of Montebello], *A l'ombre des Vieilles Filles en pleurs* [In the Shade of the Old Maids in Tears], *Le Nœud de couleuvres* [Nest of Grass-snakes], *Un certain fou rire* [A Certain Hysterical Laughter], et *Aimez-vous Brabham ? Un bouquin sur les courses d'auto* [Do You Love Brabham? A Book about Motor racing]. The titles listed here are pastiches of the titles of classics and of two novels by Françoise Sagan: *La Dame aux camélias* [*The Lady with the Camelias*] ; *Le Comte de Monte-Cristo* [*The Count of Monte Cristo*]; *A l'ombre des jeunes filles en fleurs* [*In the Shadow of the Girls in Full Bloom*]; *Le Nœud de vipères* [*The Vipers' Nest*]; *Un certain sourire* [*A Certain Smile*] and *Aimez-vous Brahms ?* [*Do You Like Brahms?*].

27 | *Fleuve Noir*, 1971.

28 | "The verve of Frédéric Dard is inexhaustible. He is definitely cut out of the same cloth as Rabelais, Céline and Queneau. Beyond the earthiness of the colourful characters and situations, this writer knows how to blast prose into life, and his poetic drive and verbal wit have enriched the French language. He's better than anybody else at stirring and spicing up words to enchant us. San-Antonio is, quite simply, one of the classics of the twentieth century". ["La veine de Frédéric Dard est inépuisable. Il est bel et bien de la lignée des Rabelais, Céline et Queneau. Au-delà de la truculence des personnages et des situations, cet écrivain, dont les saillies verbales et les chevauchées poétiques ont enrichi la langue française, est un véritable dynamiteur de la prose. Mieux que quiconque il culbute, trousse et transfigure le vocabulaire, pour notre plus grand plaisir. San-Antonio ? Tout simplement un classique du XXème siècle", San-Antonio, *Les Pensées de San-Antonio*, Paris: Le Cherche Midi, 1996.

Marcelle Segal, the famous agony aunt for *Elle* magazine, provided the blurb for the novel *Béru Béru* (1970), endorsing it as follows: "[The] author is a real writer, a serious writer. A Rabelais for our times" ["Leur auteur est un écrivain véritable, sérieux. Le Rabelais de notre époque"]. Similarly, Jean Durieux, a journalist with the magazine *Paris-Match*, reminded readers that San-Antonio was "regarded by many as the greatest living French writer" ["considéré par beaucoup comme le plus grand écrivain français vivant"].[29] The responsibility for classifying or categorising San-Antonio and for discerning his literary pedigree and relations was thus assigned, not to academics and literary critics, but rather to the author himself and to the media.

One of the most striking of San-Antonio's Ressentiment postures, in which he expresses extreme hostility towards, and denigration of, literary criticism, is based on a self-vaunted ability to succeed without the critics. The author flaunts his independence through relentless self-promotion and by fully exploiting the channels provided by non-literary, mainstream media. Yet, while the irony of his self-aggrandisement is always obvious, as when he invites derision with pompous phrases like "as for us, the great novelists of the century" ["nous autres, les grands romanciers du siècle"], and with tongue-in-cheek references to his "chef d'œuvres",[30] the untiring repetition of this self-praise could be seen as nuancing the invited derision rather than simply reinforcing it. The hysterical quality of the self-endorsement signals perhaps a first-degree obsession with literary hierarchies and canons.

Meanwhile, however, the literary criticism that San-Antonio ridicules by quoting it ironically in his novels is unvarying in its focus. It is portrayed as entrenched and as clinging to dated and even obsolete positions. The author's supposed critics are thus depicted as holding on to literary values of the early 1940s, values that time has emptied of real currency. Appearing as generic, conventional and repetitive, this outdated criticism was then, of course, disqualified from being levelled at San-Antonio (even though it might have been in his case well deserved). As far as other, more traditional, writers were concerned, he confronted them with the anti-academic nature of his own style, presenting it as literary experimentation in order to make them seem dated, and mocking the literature admired and defended by the critics as "embalmed writing" ["littérature-tombeau"].

---

29 | Jean Durieux, *Frédéric Dard dit San-Antonio, un portrait*, Paris: Renaudot 1990, Monaco: Editions du Rocher 2011, from the back cover of the book.

30 | "We great writers of the current century have a definite preference for some of our children above others, because we think them more beautiful than the rest, or even more like ourselves. This is the case with this particular masterpiece. In writing it, I started to like it, even to like it quite a lot" ["Nous autres, les grands romanciers du siècle, avons une préférence marquée pour certains de nos enfants, parce que nous les jugeons plus beaux que les autres, voire même plus proches de nous. C'est le cas du présent chef-d'œuvre. En l'écrivant, je me suis mis à l'aimer, à bien l'aimer"], San-Antonio, *Tire-m'en deux, c'est pour offrir* [*Print Me Two of them, One is for Giving Away*], 1979, back cover.

The Detective Author in the Era of "Suspicion"

Is it possible to see the relationship between popular and "high" literature as being entirely determined by the Ressentiment inspired by a collective or generic sense of internalised inferiority?[31] Must the slight felt by the writer of detective novels develop into Ressentiment towards "high" literature and all its associates? In fact, San-Antonian Ressentiment is much less collective than it might appear. The author does not represent himself as belonging to any particular school; the San-Antonian "we" is, indeed, almost always ironic in tenor. Although this "we" might be read as San-Antonio extrapolating from his own Ressentiment to a host of popular writers, in fact he portrays himself as having little in common with, and little time for, those "popular" writers less successful and less wealthy than himself. Occasionally, indeed, he demonstrates a disdainful condescension towards, or even prejudice against, certain authors, works and readers of popular fiction.[32] Moreover, far from demonstrating automatic solidarity with other forms or genres of "dominated" or "subordinate" literature, San-Antonio's criticism of women's writing, of romance and indeed of women authors in general can be both harsh and obscene.

Although he shows scant solidarity, then, with his fellow authors of popular fiction, San-Antonio's contempt for those who write "literature" is particularly colourful and extreme: "They don't exactly break their backs, those so-called literary scribblers; they squat like cuckoos in the prose of their illustrious predecessors, pooping into their lumpy little sauces. Their Literature is a porridgy concoction spread over beautiful cold leftovers."[33] The main reproach levelled at "literary" authors, apart from a lack of originality, is a lack of vitality or intellectual fibre; he accuses them of producing "drawing-room prose for lobotomised

---

31 | Marc Ferro, *Le Ressentiment dans l'Histoire: comprendre notre temps*, Paris: Odile Jacob 2007.

32 | See for example in *Circulez ! Y a rien à voir* [*Move on there, Nothing to See*], p. III: "My poor pal has the same taste in books as in art. For him, the top writers are Pierre Loti, Claude Farrère and Anatole France" ["Ses goûts littéraires, à mon pauvre copain, rejoignent ses goûts artistiques. Pour lui, les grands auteurs sont Pierre Loti, Claude Farrère et Anatole France".] Cultural condescension can also be seen in the patronising tone of the following: "Mam has her own pet writers and reads and rereads them untiringly. Cronin – The Citadel falls apart, Pierre Benoit, Myonne, Gyp. Well, why not?" ["m'man a ses auteurs qu'elle lit et relit inlassablement. Cronin- la citadelle tombe en ruine, Pierre Benoit. Myonne. Gyp... Ça mange pas de pain", p.203; "The Comtesse de Ségur whose witterings will be one of the most shameful embarrassments of my childhood" ["La comtesse de Ségur dont l'œuvre à la con restera l'une des hontes de mon enfance"], San-Antonio, *Vol au-dessus d'un lit de cocu*, [*One Flew over the Cuckold's Nest*], p. 15

33 | San-Antonio, *Les Vacances de Bérurier*, p. 23. "Y se cassent pas les littératons; font leur nid dans la prose des grands devanciers en se contentant de cacater autour leur petite sauce à grumeaux. Leur Littré-rature, c'est une béchamel plâtreuse sur des beaux restes refroidis."

masturbators" ["prose de salon pour masturbé encéphalique"].[34] Their works are, he argues, dated as soon as they are published.[35] He attacks the so-called *nouveaux romanciers* with the greatest relish.[36] Likening the *nouveau roman* to "tepid piss",[37] he targets the work of Alain Robbe-Grillet in particular: this author is accused of knowing "how to not express himself while appearing to say nothing at all".[38] As for Claude Simon, he is a Nobel laureate by default or in absentia ["Prix Nobel par contumace"][39] and Marguerite Duras is "old Mother Boring" ["la mère Durasoir"][40] who only makes her slender novels ["minces romans"] "such a bloody yawn in order to make them appear longer than they are" ["très chiants, pour donner l'impression qu'ils sont longs"].[41]

Rather than exemplifying arcane literary theories or socio-cultural privilege and refinement, the literature that San-Antonio calls for is open, inclusive and craftsman-like; it depends only on the writer's inventive vigour and is killed by institutional conformity and prestige. He boasts about his own ability to bring a vital, rough and ready energy to writing : "Sana is the woodcutter of literature. He sculpts as he chops" ["Sana, c'est le bûcheron de la littérature. Il sculpte à la cognée"].[42] He declares himself open to all readers and all types of reading: "I'm just a small bistrot with a set menu... I'll never be a Michelin star" ["Je suis un petit bistrot à prix fixe. [...] Je ne serai jamais un Trois Étoiles"][43] or as he says in a footnote: "this pun might smack of pre-World War I cabaret but no style is beneath me" ["ce calembour fait un peu cabaret d'avant 14, mais je ne méprise aucun style"].[44]

The critical recognition received by San-Antonio from the mid-1960s, which gathered pace into the widespread acclaim of the 1980s, could be seen as cultural revenge. He persisted, however, in reiterating right throughout this period

---

34 | San-Antonio, *Le Loup habillé en grand-mère* [*The Wolf in Grandma's Clothing*], p. 124.

35 | These contemporary authors are treated in the same way as the great Romantic poet Lamartine, whose work is "sanatorium poetry", San-Antonio, *Mange, et tais-toi !* [*Eat Up and Shut Up*], 1966, p. 156.

36 | See F. Rullier's article, quoted above, and also R. Milési, "Les Pattes de mouches sodomisées: image de la littérature chez San-Antonio", in: *San-Antonio et la culture française*, pp. 225–36.

37 | San-Antonio, *Un os dans la noce* [*A Bedding in the Wedding*], 1974, p. 147.

38 | "[...] it would put me to sleep to have to write like that" ["[...] ça m'endormirait de narrer dans de telles conditions"], *Mon culte sur la commode*, 1979, p. 175.

39 | San-Antonio, *Le Trouillomètre à zéro* [*Off the Charts Terror*], p. 220.

40 | Ibid, p. 12.

41 | San-Antonio, *Princesse Patte-en-l'air* [*Cock-a-leg Princess*], 1990, p. 169.

42 | San-Antonio, *Du bois dont on fait les pipes* [*What you Smoke in Your Pipe*], 1982, p. 31.

43 | San-Antonio, *Je le jure*, p. 106.

44 | San-Antonio, *N'en jetez plus* [*Don't Ditch any More of them*], p. 91.

his ironic disdain for literary glory and in maintaining the pose of the *auteur plébéien.*[45] The limited and belated recognition that he received does nothing to diminish the force of his decades of sarcastic attacks on the blindness of the critics and on the injustice and misunderstanding meted out to him by the literary world:

> On all sides, people come up to me in the street, thinking I'm somebody. They congratulate me, take their hats off, and are all over me. "Howdy, Mr San-Antonio, how very fine you look, how easy on the eye!" Some of them would kiss my ass if I let them. As for me, I want to raise them up, magnanimously, in the style of Charles the Seventh doing a Joan of Arc. I want to say "Don't overdo it, my darlings, pipe down. Pop your idolatry back into your tub of Vaseline. I'm just a waster, a chancer, a mousetrap, a poxy flycatcher."[46]

Specular Ressentiment: San-Antonio Mirroring Céline

1949, the year in which Dard decided to write the first San-Antonio potboiler, is also the year that saw the publication of a new edition of the masterpiece of self-styled literary pariah, Louis-Ferdinand Céline,[47] *Voyage au bout de la nuit* (1932).

---

45 | Early on in the series, the narrator signals this aspect of his choice of genre: "People lean towards where they're going to fall. I myself fell into the arms of the law because I had the makings of a good cop. There's no point in pushing yourself against the grain. When you're playing cards, it's no use envying your opponent's luck; you have to make the best of your own hand and use it to block him.", [" 'un homme penche du côté où il doit tomber. Moi, je suis tombé dans la rousse parce que j'avais des dispositions certaines. Inutile de se frapper. Quand on joue à la belote, faut pas envier les brèmes de son adversaire, on doit se contenter des siennes et s'en servir pour le mettre capot". San-Antonio, *Passez-moi la Joconde [Pass me the Mona Lisa]*, 1954, p. 52.

46 | "On me croit quelqu'un, de-ci, de-là. On me gratule. Les coups de bitos pleuvent. Les salamalecs à n'en plus finir 'Eh bonjour, Môssieur San-Antonio, que vous êtes joli, que vous me semblez beau.' Y me baiseraient les burnes, certains, si je leur en faisais part. Et moi j'ai envie de les relever, magnanime, façon Charles VII retapissé par Jeanne of Arc. Envie de leur dire « Vous fatiguez pas mes drôles, calmez vous la frénésie. Rangez vos dévotions dans votre pot à vaseline, j'suis qu'un fumiste, un charlatan, un piège à cons, un gobe mouche à merdes", *N'en jetez plus*, 1971, p. 14. This self-deprecation needs to be compared to the comments on serious authors: "There are some really twisted writer-types, I know them well; their prose is sacred. Especially the theatrical ones. You change a comma on them and they send you a solicitor's letter, or affidavits, or even better, some punches. Merci to God, I'm not cut out of that particular cloth. As far as my books are concerned, guys, you can assemble them as you will" ["Y a des tordus plumassiers, je les connais ; leur prose, c'est sacré. Les théâtreux surtout. Une virgule qu'on leur change, les voilà qu'envoient du papelard timbré, ou bien leurs témoins; ou mieux encore, des gifles. Dieu thank you, je ne suis pas de ce tonneau. Mes bouquins, les gars, vous pouvez les bricoler à votre idée"] San-Antonio, *Béru et ces dames [Béru and the Ladies]*, 1967, p. 381.

47 | See J. Meizoz's studies on Céline's posturing, in particular his *La fabrique des singularités : Postures littéraires II*, Lausanne: Slatkine 2011.

In his preface to this new edition, Céline claimed that his only reason for writing was to earn a living. San-Antonio, who had admired Céline from his teenage years, re-cycles these and other lines from Céline, making his own of that celebrated, transgressive stylist's ostentatious self-distancing from the literary world.[48] As was the case for Céline, San-Antonio's rejection of the status of a "man of letters" is expressed in the pose of the "anti-man of letters", in other words in an oppositional, negating, critical stance.[49] When he refers to himself as a "workman", San-Antonio is recalling Céline's use of the same term. He identifies with Céline as an author who prefers the idea of workmanship to that of artistic creation and who legitimates writing as a mercenary activity, not in a purely cynical manner but with some sincerity. Like both Céline and Simenon, San-Antonio represents his writing as a craft, and refers to himself as being a writer "in spite of himself". The metaphors that he uses to describe his work are borrowed from Céline, as when he borrows the latter's comparison of his writing to the secretions of a snail.

The implicit and explicit references to Céline and the superimposition of a Célinian twist upon his expression of Ressentiment reinforce San-Antonio's recriminations regarding the lack of serious critical recognition of detective fiction. The heterodiegetic "I" who intervenes in the novels to talk about literature adds a deeper resonance to that of the detective narrator. His is a powerful authorial voice, reminiscent of that of Céline, and is entirely taken over by a jubilant Ressentiment towards the literary institution. In imitating Céline's invectives and counter-attacks, San-Antonio associates his own misunderstood prose with the literary legitimacy of the author of the *Voyage*. In adopting as his model a literary author who triumphed over his detractors, San-Antonio seems to suggest that he too deserves, and will attain, literary eminence, despite his own avowed lack of interest in such anointment. If he cannot claim to be the greatest writer of the century, that place being reserved, at least in his own personal Pantheon, for Céline, he will, like Céline, be a literary monster ["monstre"].[50] If he can't be a giant, towering over other writers in height, he will be the biggest in girth: "I may not be a literary giant, but I am a sumo colossus" ["Je ne suis pas un géant mais un obèse de la littérature"].[51] He may not reach the same heights as the

---

48 | See François Gibault, *Céline II : Délires et persécutions*, Paris: Mercure de France 1985.

49 | See Philippe Roussin, *Misère de la littérature, terreur de l'histoire: Céline et la littérature contemporaine*, Paris: Gallimard 2005.

50 | See on this point Nicholas Hewitt, "Céline: The Success of the *Monstre Sacré* in Postwar France", *SubStance*, 102, 32:3, (2003) pp. 29–42.

51 | San-Antonio, *Concerto pour porte-jarretelles* [Concerto for a Suspender-Belt], 1976, p. 152. Behind this derision it is possible to recognise Jules Renard's oft-quoted comment that "[...] in literature there are only oxen. The genius is the biggest of these beasts of burden, the one who labours for eighteen hours each day, indefatigably" ["[...] en littérature il n'y a que des bœufs. Les génies sont les plus gros, ceux qui peinent dix-huit heures par jour d'une manière infatigable"]. Jules Renard, *Journal 1887–1910*, (ed.) Henri Bouillier, Paris: Robert Laffont 1990, p. 4.

giant, but he will be just as hard to ignore and will surpass all other authors in output.

It is chiefly, then, as a falsely proletarian and ambiguously populist author that Céline offers San-Antonio a way of positioning himself as a popular novelist while also satisfying his literary ambitions. Yet, however much he imitates the timbre of Céline's "me and them" or "me against them" invective, he was not in conflict with the literary institutions, nor even with his publisher. Also unlike Céline, he had to wait a long time to be consulted on his views on contemporary literature. For many decades, although clearly constrained by the demands of productivity, San-Antonio would continue to pen his entirely unsolicited literary criticism in novel after novel. This undoubtedly added to the richness of his writing, injecting it with a multi-layered, reflective (inter-) textual and semantic depth.

There is a celebrated passage in Céline's *Voyage au bout de la nuit* in which the young and unknown author expresses his disdain for Marcel Proust.[52] For Céline, who remained "faithful during his entire life to this execration of Proust" ["toute sa vie fidèle à cette exécration de Proust"],[53] the author of *In Search of Lost Time* is the archetypal literary enemy. The fictional world created by Proust is targeted by Céline almost as much as the writer's personal situation. What Céline resents is both Proust's choice of subject matter, namely the lives of the privileged, and also his own privileged status as a writer of independent means, who did not have to produce literature to earn his living. All the targets of Céline's criticism – the putatively empty aestheticism of Proust's style, his depictions of privileged, leisured individuals and his excessively long sentences, for example – contrast diametrically with the spontaneous, non-intellectualised descriptions of the lower classes in Céline's own work.

It is, of course, the same type of criticism that San-Antonio levels not so much at Proust (whom he admired and with whom he has occasionally been

---

52 | The following celebrated passage, commented on by Marie Christine Bellosta, may be cited for comparison (see Bellosta, *Céline ou l'art de la contradiction. Lecture de voyage au bout de la nuit*, Paris: Presses universitaires de France 1990, pp. 96–110) : "Proust, who was half-ghost, immersed himself with extraordinary tenacity in the infinitely watery futility of the rites and procedures that entwine members of high society, those denizens of the void, those phantoms of desire, those irresolute daisy-chainers still waiting for their Watteau, those listless seekers after implausible Cythereas. Whereas Madame Herote, with her sturdy popular origins, was firmly fastened to the earth by her crude, stupid and very specific appetites", Céline, *Voyage to the End of the Night*, trans. Ralph Manheim (1983), New York: New Directions 2006; ["Proust mi-revenant lui-même, s'est perdu avec une extraordinaire ténacité dans l'infinie, la diluante futilité des rites et démarches qui s'entortillent autour des gens du monde, gens du vide, fantômes de désirs, partouzards indécis attendant leur Watteau toujours, chercheurs sans entrains d'improbables Cythères. Mais Madame Hérote, populaire et substantielle d'origine, tenait solidement à la terre par de rudes appétits, bêtes et précis"], Céline, *Voyage au bout de la nuit*, Paris: Gallimard 1932, p. 74.

53 | Bellosta, *Céline, ou l'art de la contradiction*, p. 98.

compared) but rather at all the writers included in what he derides as *"la lit-térature-tombeau".*[54] As we have seen, San-Antonio's Proust was Alain Robbe-Grillet, the pope of the Nouveau Roman. He also attacked Raymond Queneau and Marguerite Duras. For all of this criticism, however, San-Antonio's model was Céline's insulting hostility towards "Farty Proust" ["Prout Proust"], including the hostile criticism of Proust's literary decadence which Céline linked, of course, to the writer's bourgeois identity and (obsession with) homosexuality.[55]

What is particularly striking about San-Antonio's literary criticism is its "generic" quality. The entire Célinean matrix is transferred and applied without any significant modification from Proust to Robbe-Grillet, two very different authors whose only apparently shared characteristic is their prominent and prestigious position in the literary field. And it is this hostile self-positioning in relation to the two "masters" that seems, above all else, to define and explain the Ressentiment of the two (self-styled) "popular" author/critics. Unlike Céline, however, San-Antonio is recycling a discourse that is not his own. In other words, even his literary or literary critical asides are, fundamentally, imitative and derivative. On a formal level, these meta-literary passages, which might be supposed to represent the most personal and direct authorial self-expression and which puncture the more conventional and impersonal detective narrative inspired by the American hard-boiled tradition, are themselves deeply mimetic. Even – if not especially – in their transgressive, vulgar, neologistic verve, they are themselves a form of pastiche (of Céline).

In terms of content, San-Antonio's embedded (literary) criticism is above all a type of staged posturing. The author seems, in other words, to be acting out, in order to keep his readers on side, poorly-concealed indignation. He deploys to this end a rhetoric which dates back to the end of the 20s and which sets proletarian writers against elitist or "snobbish" literature. However, this same pose and this same rhetoric had already been deployed by Céline; and San-Antonio adds little of substance. He does, however, extend the reach and the power of the posturing, bringing it to bear on millions of readers and using it thereby to defend a certain type of popular literature, the burlesque detective novel. And yet, in incorporating a critique of "high" literature and in mimicking the poetics of Céline, San-Antonio's writing contradicts in practice the ideals of proletarian literature. Ressentiment, faked or otherwise, has led him to perpetuate in his nov-

---

54 | San-Antonio, *Ça ne s'invente pas*, 1973, p. 77 and see also F. Rullier, "Proust, Céline, Cohen et moi".

55 | This theme is particularly evident in Céline's aggressive dismissal of Proust's subject matter as being limited to "little tales of pederasty" ["des petits drames de la pédérastie"], which are furthermore chronicled in too much detail : ("300 pages just to make us see that Tutu is sodomising Toto: it's over the top." ["Trois cents pages pour nous faire comprendre que Tutur encule Tatave c'est trop"]) "Louis-Ferdinand Céline vous parle" in Céline, *Œuvres II*, and Lettre à Milton Hindus, 11 juin 1947, p. 147). These criticisms can be usefully compared with the treatment of a plethora of San-Antonio's homosexual characters, notably in *Napoléon Pommier* (2000).

els, increasingly removed from the depiction of society, a type of criticism which was no longer able to focus on, or even to see, the literature it was talking about.[56] He has thus come full circle back to the point from which both proletarian authors and Céline wanted to break free. And he does so without moving beyond secondary or subordinated practice, whether critical or mimetic. In that sense, since it lacks the primary stylistic originality that characterises literary writing, the "would-be critical" dimension of San-Antonio's work remains locked into the reactive Ressentiment of the sub-literary, generic writer. It is not when writing about literature that San-Antonio shows himself at his most literary. Moreover, despite its bad faith, his real/fake Ressentiment ultimately reinforces the status and values of the literary institution, reaffirming its implicit hierarchies.

---

56 | To paraphrase Emmanuel Berl's famous 1929 pamphlet, *Mort de la pensée bour-geoise*, Paris: Laffont 1970, p. 85: *"la critique ne voit plus la littérature dont elle parle et la littérature ne voit plus la société qu'elle devrait peindre"* [literary criticism is no longer capable of distinguishing the literature on which it is supposed to be commenting just as literature can no longer distinguish the society that it is supposed to be depicting].

Criticism or *Ressentiment*?
Literary Studies and the Politics of Interdisciplinarity

Christine A. Knoop

Empirical Humanities and Literary Studies

In 2011, the *New York Times* published an exchange between Alex Rosenberg, professor of philosophy at Duke University, and William Egginton, chair of the Department of German and Romance Languages and Literatures at Johns Hopkins University. In their contributions, Rosenberg and Egginton debated the extent to which the sciences and the humanities respectively contribute to the production of knowledge. Egginton, focussing mostly on examples from literature, argued that epistemological models created by the humanities constitute the very core of any concept of knowledge (and in fact make such concepts conceivable in the first place).[1] Rosenberg opted for a rather different perspective by construing an opposition between the 'traditional' humanities, which he defines as "indispensable parts of human experience but not to be mistaken for contributions to knowledge", and scientific approaches, which, he asserts, provide "a basic picture of reality".[2] He suggests that the humanities should turn to the sciences, notably neuroscience, for help, and that only such collaborations can "save"[3] their right to exist. Rosenberg maintains:

> Neuroscience's explanations and the traditional ones compete; they cannot both be right. Eventually we will have to choose between human narrative self-understanding and science's explanations of human affairs. Neuroeco-

---

1 | William Egginton, "The Cosmic Imagination", in: *The New York Times*, 6 November 2011, URL: opinionator.blogs.nytimes.com/2011/11/06/bodies-in-motion-an-exchange. See also: "'Quixote,' Colbert and the Reality of Fiction", in: *The New York Times*, 25 September 2011, URL: opinionator.blogs.nytimes.com/2011/09/25/quixote-colbert-and-the-reality-of-fiction.

2 | Alex Rosenberg, "Galileo's Gambit", in: *The New York Times*, 6 November 2011, URL: opinionator.blogs.nytimes.com/2011/11/06/bodies-in-motion-an-exchange.

3 | Ibid.

nomics, neuroethics, neuro-art history and neuro-lit-crit are just tips of an iceberg on a collision course with the ocean liner of human self-knowledge.[4]

In this passage, Rosenberg evokes the debate on neuroscientific approaches to the humanities, a debate that touches upon his own discipline (philosophy) as much as it touches upon Egginton's (literary studies). Both fields have seen an increasing interest in scientific findings, especially a fascination with the workings of the brain. Neuroscience is treated like a promise that we will finally be able to access what people "really" think or feel – or, more realistically, that we might get a glimpse at a "real" reader response, not only the response we ourselves or a construed ideal reader, model reader, historical reader, or implied reader might have. If handled with care, collaborations with neuroscience have vast intellectual potential. However, the risks and pitfalls of such endeavours in both philosophy and literary studies have also been pointed out, maybe most prominently and extensively in Bennett and Hacker's *Philosophical Foundations of Neuroscience*.[5] In the field of literary studies, defenders[6] and critics[7] of empirical cognitive literary studies have yet to discuss systematically the methodological, theoretical, and practical implications for the future of the discipline – a particularly difficult task, since the methods and findings of cognitive neuroscience are in a state of continuous development.[8]

Rosenberg's image of the collision course positions the sciences against the humanities without accepting the possibility that the two might complement each other in a more comprehensive view of knowledge, as more moderate

---

4 | Ibid.

5 | M.R. Bennett/P.M.S. Hacker, *Philosophical Foundations of Neuroscience*, Oxford: Blackwell 2003.

6 | See, for instance: Gerhard Lauer, "Going Empirical. Why We Need Cognitive Literary Studies", in: *Journal of Literary Theory*, 3.1, (2009), pp. 145–54; Jonathan Gottschall, "Quantitative Literary Study: A Modest Manifesto and Testing the Hypotheses of Feminist Fairy Tale Studies", in: Jonathan Gottschall/David Sloan Wilson (eds), *The Literary Animal: Evolution and the Nature of Narrative*, Evanston: Northwestern University Press 2005, pp. 199–224. While these two mainly praise the new approach, many empiricists have the urge to defend it against accusations instead of developing it in relation to existing literary studies and thereby showing its worth (see Mark J. B Bruhn, "Introduction: Exchange Values: Poetics and Cognitive Science", in: *Poetics Today* 32.3, 2011, pp. 403–60, 424).

7 | See, for instance: Frank Kelleter, "A Tale of Two Natures. Worried Reflections on the Study of Literature and Culture in an Age of Neuroscience and Neo-Darwinism", in: *Journal of Literary Theory*, 1.1, (2007), pp. 158–89; a rhetorically more moderate, yet equally critical assessment is provided in Kilian Koepsell/Carlos Spoerhase, "Neuroscience and the Study of Literature. Some Thoughts on the Possibility of Transferring Knowledge", in: *Journal of Literary Theory*, 2.2, (2008), pp. 363–74.

8 | Consequently, accounts about empirical literary studies that date back longer than ten to fifteen years are no longer entirely representative of the current trends.

approaches[9] have long advocated. Like him, many scholars from either end of the spectrum tend to think that "they cannot both be right", and that therefore the respective other is approaching the subject area from a wrong angle, an angle that simply does not fit the subject matter or meet the scholarly objectives. Heightened by the reality that empirical interdisciplinary approaches are frequently in competition for funding with non-empirical, 'traditional' ones, tensions have emerged. However, while it might be easy to detect an occasionally hostile tone in face-to-face exchanges, it is much more demanding to determine where the boundary between valid criticism, polemics, and *ressentiment* is crossed in scholarly *writing*, as the conventions for academic publications obviously set narrow limits to any display of affect.

In this article, I propose to examine the boundary between criticism and *ressentiment* in relation to the politics of interdisciplinarity, and more specifically in relation to empirical and experimental literary studies involving the sciences.[10] This approach will focus mostly on the new paradigm's fierce critics and defenders, leaving out the many researchers who believe in the possibility of overcoming the rifts between the disciplines, but who do not themselves engage with the new paradigm. I will begin by discussing the role of the sciences in the history of literary studies, and the current political and economic situation dividing the two, in order to identify a number of reasons for potential *ressentiment*. Then, I will analyse ways in which traces of *ressentiment* appear in scholarly texts by looking first at argumentative positions, then at argumentative strategies, and lastly at individual rhetorical aspects; finally, I will examine how the notion of *ressentiment* is used as a charge against others.

The sciences in literary studies

In the midst of current discussions about a paradigm shift due to the influence of neuroscience,[11] it is often forgotten that interdisciplinarity, even involv-

---

9 | For a historical example, see, for instance: Wilhelm Windelband, *Geschichte und Naturwissenschaft. Rede zum Antritt des Rektorats der Kaiser-Wilhelms-Universität Straßburg am 01.05.1894*, URL: www.hs-augsburg.de/~harsch/germanica/Chronologie/19Jh/Windelband/win_rede.html. See also: Patrick C. Hogan, *Cognitive Science, Literature, and the Arts: A Guide for Humanists*, New York: Routledge 2003. Hogan points out that knowledge can be acquired and explained on different levels, including the physical or neurobiological, the mental, the social and the cultural (pp. 202ff.); no one of these levels can replace another.

10 | The term "empirical literary studies" is thus here used to address quantitative, experimental, cognitive literary studies. It does not refer, for instance, to works based on corpus analysis, sociological, economic or historical empiricism, such as William St. Clair's undoubtedly equally interdisciplinary, empirical, and quantitative *The Reading Nation in the Romantic Period*, Cambridge: CUP 2004.

11 | This debate is primarily important in Germany, where the notion of the paradigm shift ("Paradigmenwechsel") is not only used for scientific disciplines as intended by Thomas

ing the sciences, is not new to literary studies. On the contrary, the discussion of literature is informed by findings from sociological and historical research, philosophy, logic, psychology, linguistics and other disciplines. Indeed, these influences are frequently so well incorporated into our discipline that they are not even considered interdisciplinary, but simply necessary prerequisites for being able to think about literature at all – although technically they represent knowledge from other fields. Scientific influences are admittedly less frequent than, for instance, historical or philosophical ones, but they are by no means completely alien to the study of literature. Concepts as deeply rooted in the discipline as catharsis, logos, ethos, pathos and the sublime, all draw on the physiological dimension of experience.[12] Links between scientific discovery and its aesthetic value and representation are, for example, explored in the works of Alexander von Humboldt.[13] Experimental approaches to understanding aesthetic emotions and reactions as well as their physiological correlates date back to Gustav Theodor Fechner's experimental aesthetics. Fechner attempted to find common denominators in individual reactions to art by construing carefully crafted aesthetic stimuli[14] – attempts mirrored and developed nowadays in studies trying to measure cognitive and emotional reactions to aesthetic experiences. The most famous example linking narrative and psychological conditions is certainly Sigmund Freud, whose findings have been appropriated so eagerly and rooted so deeply in literary studies that their success in that discipline has by now outlasted their success in psychology itself. And in recent years, the field of linguistics, traditionally a close ally to literary studies, has become more and more influenced by cognitive science and neuroscience.

In this context, interdisciplinary endeavours could be seen as merely continuing the joint history of the myriad disciplines involved in the production and

---

Kuhn, who coined the term (see, e.g., Thomas Kuhn, *The Structure of Scientific Revolutions*, Chicago: University of Chicago Press 1970, pp. 149–50), but also for the humanities.

12 | Indeed, some of these notions have attracted the attention of the empirical disciplines for a while now, especially the idea of catharsis. See, for instance: Brad J. Bushman *et al.*, "Catharsis, Aggression, and Persuasive Influence: Self-Fulfilling or Self-Defeating Prophecies?", in: *Journal of Personality and Social Psychology*, 76.3, (1999), pp. 367–76; Sidney A./Manning, Dalmas A Taylor, "Effects of Viewed Violence and Aggression: Stimulation and Catharsis", in: *Journal of Personality and Social Psychology*, 31.1, (1975), pp. 180–88; Lauren M. Bylsma et al, "When Is Crying Cathartic? An International Study", in: *Journal of Social and Clinical Psychology*, 27.10, (2008), pp. 1165–87.

13 | Cf. Oliver Lubrich, "Alexander von Humboldt: Revolutionizing Travel Literature", in: *Monatshefte*, 96.3, 2004, pp. 360–87. Humboldt's work at the interface of science and aesthetics is also cited in the context of interdisciplinary literary studies: James Williford, "Humanities on the Brain", in: Humanities 33.1 (2012), URL: www.neh.gov/news/humanities/2012–01/HumanitiesBrain.html.

14 | Cf. Gustav Theodor Fechner, *Zur experimentalen Ästhetik*, Leipzig: S. Hirzel, 1871. See also: Theodor Lipps, "Aesthetische Einfühlung", in: *Zeitschrift für Psychologie und Physiologie der Sinnesorgane*, 22, 1900, pp. 415–50.

reception of literature. Hans-Ulrich Gumbrecht's observations regarding the nature of Comparative Literature as a multi-faceted bouquet of approaches, for instance, might be read as encouraging such a conclusion.[15]

While the historical propensity of literary studies for incorporating knowledge from other disciplines might make the current tensions regarding experimental, cognitive approaches seem superfluous, one short-term, practical fact needs to be borne in mind. In recent years, funding bodies in the US, the UK and continental Europe have developed a partiality to funding interdisciplinary research; external sources of funding are often made available for such research to supplement shrinking university budgets. At the same time, interdisciplinarity is, gradually, also making its way into teaching. According to data from the US National Center of Educational Statistics, the number of interdisciplinary Bachelor's degrees in the United States has risen significantly since the 70s, not only in absolute numbers, but also relative to the general increase of Bachelor's degrees.[16] In addition, interdisciplinary approaches in a variety of disciplines are explicitly invited by funding bodies, such as the NIH or the German Research Foundation (DFG), and strongly supported by educational institutions such as the Boyer Commission or the American Association for the Advancement of Science.

Hence, the tension not only arises from concerns that empirical, experimental studies in the humanities might be poorly conceptualised, but also from the fact that even being at their beginnings and having not yet proven their full intellectual worth, they are already very successful politically – simply for being interdisciplinary. In the light of recent UK and US budget cuts which led to the closure or merging of whole literature and other humanities departments, and in the light of the notoriously small university budgets in continental Europe, which tend to result in short-term contracts and cuts in university staff, it may seem to many that the humanities are at a crossroads. They need to prove their productivity and social worth in order to receive sufficient funding; and this search for a new profile becomes manifest in conferences such as the annual MLA meeting. Stanley Fish points out that this conference, while no longer dominated by great theoretical discussions, is much concerned with the (uncertain) future of the field:

A session on "The Future of Higher Education" plays off against other sessions suggesting there may not be one. In the latter we find papers with titles like "The University of Disaster", "The Ripeness of Decay", "Are the

15 | Hans-Ulrich Gumbrecht, "The Origins of Literary Studies – And Their End?", in: *Stanford Humanities Review,* 6.1, 1998 (*Disciplining Literature,* ed. Jeffrey Schnapp), pp. 1–10.

16 | See National Center for Education Statistics, "Bachelor's degrees conferred by degree-granting institutions, by field of study: Selected years, 1970–71 through 2008–09", in: *Digest of Education Statistics: 2010,* URL: nces.ed.gov/programs/digest/d10/tables/dt10_282.asp?referrer=list and "Master's degrees conferred by degree-granting institutions, by field of study: Selected years, 1970–71 through 2008–09", in: *Digest of Education Statistics: 2010,* URL: nces.ed.gov/programs/digest/d10/tables/dt10_283.asp?referrer=list.

Humanities Worth Saving?", "What Do Students Need From the Humanities?", "Why Literature Teachers Should Stop Being Cheap Dates" and "When Literature Mattered and Why."[17]

Not all attempts to find new ways into the future are interdisciplinary; others engage with the concept of World Literature or try to remember old virtues of the discipline, for instance by paying renewed attention to traditional philology. All of these attempts to broach new paths, in one way or the other, lead to criticism. And in all of these cases, it is vital neither to dismiss just and potentially productive criticism as mere *ressentiment* nor to mistake *ressentiment* for a valid objection.

Although an interest in scientific influences on literary study is palpable in today's academic landscape, these have not yet been examined in a systematic theoretical fashion that might comment on their merits and shortcomings. The existing scholarship on general problems of interdisciplinarity, such as the work of Gould,[18] Klein[19] and Snow[20] mostly adopts a multidisciplinary perspective, as do the approaches of C.S. Peirce[21] and Merleau-Ponty.[22] Research considering the effects of interdisciplinarity on the area of literary studies in particular tends to leave aside the theoretical and methodological implications for the discipline and its self-conception, as well as its interdisciplinary past, instead analysing individual interdisciplinary angles.[23] Many approaches tend to argue either against liter-

---

17 | Stanley Fish, "What's Next for Literary Studies?", in: *The New York Times*, 26 December 2011, URL: opinionator.blogs.nytimes.com/2011/12/26/the-old-order-changeth /?pagemode=print. Interestingly, of course, instead of the debate being open to those who are seen as challenging the discipline, it is frequently limited to participants from within literary studies who agree that the humanities are indeed worth saving, that students do need the humanities and that literature does matter for good reason. The futility of discussing such matters only within groups of like-minded peers was pointed out by David Castillo at a conference entitled "Humanities at the Limit" (SUNY Buffalo, November 2011).

18 | Stephen Jay Gould, *The Hedgehog, the Fox, and the Magister's Pox: Mending the Gap Between Science and the Humanities*, New York: Harmony 2003.

19 | Julie Thompson Klein, *Interdisciplinarity: History, Theory, and Practice*, Detroit: Wayne State University 1990.

20 | Charles Percy Snow, *The Two Cultures and the Scientific Revolution*, Cambridge: Cambridge University Press 1959.

21 | Charles Sanders Peirce, *The Logic of Interdisciplinarity. The Monist Series*, ed. Elize Bisanz. *Deutsche Zeitschrift für Philosophie*, special issue, 2009.

22 | Maurice Merleau-Ponty, *Phenomenology of Perception*, New York: Humanities Press 1962.

23 | See, for instance, Mary Thomas Crane/Alan Richardson, "Literary Studies and Cognitive Science: Toward a New Interdisciplinarity", in: *Mosaic*, 32, 1999, pp. 123–40; Mary Thomas Crane, *Shakespeare's Brain: Reading with Cognitive Theory*, Princeton: Princeton University Press 2001. An exception to this rule is the work of Joe Moran,

ary empiricism[24] or in favour of it and at the expense of traditional approaches,[25] but neither side offers a unifying perspective which dialectically discusses the potential benefits and risks. Virginia Richter's paper on empiricism in literary studies comes much closer to this, but due to the necessarily confined scope of her article, she, too, adopts a discursive, general stance rather than offering a systematic analysis of different methods, approaches and ideas.[26] Similarly, the collective volume *Directions in Empirical Literary Studies* covers an impressive range of individual aspects, thus presenting "the state of the art in empirical studies of literature", but does not offer a systematic discussion of their place in, and impact on, the discipline at large.[27] The same is true of Richardson's and Spolsky's *The Work of Fiction: Cognition, Culture and Complexity*. The absence of a systematic exploration of the implications of literary empiricism, which often leads to incomplete conclusions and generalisations, can in some cases add an air of *ressentiment* to mere attempts at valid scholarly assessment.

Distinguishing *Ressentiment* from Criticism

The *Oxford English Dictionary* defines *ressentiment* as "an attitude which arises, often unconsciously, from aggressive feelings frustrated by a sensed inferiority of one's situation or personality, frequently resulting in some form of self-abasement". Criticism, on the other hand, is defined as "the action of criticizing, or passing judgement upon the qualities or merits of anything; esp. the passing of unfavourable judgement; fault-finding, censure". In a slightly different manner, the *Oxford Dictionary of English* defines *ressentiment* as "a psychological state resulting from suppressed feelings of envy and hatred which cannot be satisfied". The *New Oxford American Dictionary* combines these two definitions, labelling *ressentiment* as "a psychological state arising from suppressed feelings of envy and hatred that cannot be acted upon, frequently resulting in some form of self-abasement". Consistent with the *Oxford Dictionary of English*, it further

---

who, however, presents a concise overview of many different interdisciplinary takes on literary studies rather than focussing on scientific ones (Joe Moran, *Interdisciplinarity*, New York: Routledge 2002).

24 | See, for instance, F. Kelleter: "A Tale of Two Natures".

25 | See, for instance, J. Gottschall: "Quantitative Literary Study: A Modest Manifesto and Testing the Hypotheses of Feminist Fairy Tale Studies", p. 219; G. Lauer: "Going Empirical".

26 | Virginia Richter, "'I cannot endure to read a line of poetry.' The Text and the Empirical in Literary Studies", in: *Journal of Literary Theory*, 3.2 (2009), pp. 375–88, 385.

27 | Sonia Zyngier, M. Bortolussi, A. Chesnokova, J. Auracher (eds),: *Directions in Empirical Literary Studies. In Honor of Willie van Peer*, Amsterdam/Philadelphia: John Benjamins 2008, p. xii.

defines the term "criticism" as "the expression of disapproval of someone or something on the basis of perceived faults or mistakes".

These definitions show a fundamental difference between criticism and *ressentiment*: While criticism is an *expression* of disapproval, *ressentiment* is a psychological state, that is, an *affective condition*. In other words, it would be possible to express criticism on a purely logical and cognitive level without the emotional involvement characteristic of *ressentiment*, whereas it would be possible to feel *ressentiment*, but not express criticism. Secondly, *ressentiment* is related to hatred and envy, two base emotions implying intense *personal* dislike. We hate or envy someone – or someone for something – whereas we can criticise not only a person, but also an individual action, view, or position without necessarily harbouring hostile feelings towards the person performing the action or holding the view or position. Unlike the closely related term 'resentment', a "sense of grievance; an indignant sense of injury or insult received or perceived; (a feeling of) ill will, bitterness, or anger against a person or thing", as the *Oxford English Dictionary* defines it, *ressentiment* often remains suppressed. It indicates a futile, unwholesome affective state that is essentially more negative for the person feeling it than for the person against whom it is directed, as Nietzsche has pointed out.[28] Michael André Bernstein adds another quality to *ressentiment*, namely that of "[the sufferer's] hope of someday forcing others to suffer in his place."[29] *Ressentiment* is thus personal, emotional, and not necessarily logical; it entails ill-wishes and potentially *Schadenfreude*.

While this differentiation may easily be understood in terms of definitions, it is rather more difficult to differentiate between *ressentiment* and criticism where they appear in the context of individual utterances; firstly, because they frequently co-occur; and secondly, because utterances, by nature, are expressions, not affective states, while *ressentiment* is an affective state, not an expression. This difference lies at the heart of Deleuze's definition of *ressentiment*: "La réaction cesse d'être agie pour devenir quelque chose de senti." [The reaction stops being something that is performed and becomes something that is felt.][30] It follows that if we assume that *ressentiment* can be detected in scholarly interactions, the utterances themselves must betray it: their affective baggage must somehow be traceable within the message itself, and formally capable of being distinguished from merely critical content. This begs the more extensive question of how we detect affectivity in general, and *ressentiment* in particular, in a written text. For the context of this article, this larger question must be narrowed down to ask how we can detect *ressentiment* in a *scholarly* text, which, due to the

---

28 | See Friedrich Nietzsche, "Menschliches, Allzumenschliches", II.60, in: *Werke* 1, ed. Rolf Topman, Dortmund: Könemann 1994. See also: Friedrich Nietzsche: "Ecce Homo" I.6, in: *Werke* 3, ed. Rolf Topman. Dortmund: Könemann 1994.

29 | Michael André Bernstein, *Bitter Carnival: Ressentiment and the Abject Hero*, Princeton: Princeton University Press 1992, p. 27.

30 | Gilles Deleuze, *Nietzsche et la philosophie*, Paris: Presses Universitaires de France 1970, p. 127. (Translation mine).

conventions of academic writing, by necessity encounters certain formal limits which may not apply to other forms of writing.

Since *writing*, for any scholar, involves being *active*, no scholarly text, polemical, critical, self-pitying, hostile and/or illogical as it may be, reflects the "intensely focused, but *impotent*, hatred"[31] characteristic of *ressentiment*: through writing, the researcher becomes active and shows that she is not yet defeated. Nonetheless, there are certain argumentative positions which bear traces of *ressentiment*. While it cannot be said with absolute certainty that their authors felt *ressentiment*, it is likely that those traces may be read as such. On the other hand, there are texts which do not, themselves, show any traces of *ressentiment*, but which attribute this affective state to other writers.

Traces of *Ressentiment* in Scholarly Texts

Ressentiment can often be detected in two main argumentative positions. The first is the position of the defeated party, whose *ressentiment* is caused by the triumphant party, as Michel de Montaigne puts it with reference to situations of war. The defeated party who survives a battle only due to the victor's mercy is forced to admit to himself that he has been overpowered. For him, the consequence is *ressentiment*: not only has he been defeated, but the victor evidently considers him weak enough to risk his rebound and potential revenge.[32] In scholarly texts, a variation of this type of *ressentiment* becomes evident when scholars write against what they construe to be the dismissive gesture of "mainstream" discourse. In the case of interdisciplinary literary studies, this occurs very frequently. Ironically though, both sides, the "traditional" literary scholars as much as the empiricists, tend to attempt to define themselves as the marginalised party fighting for intellectual survival, and the respective other as representative of the condescending majority position. In a way, they are both right: while "traditional" literary studies undoubtedly are having a hard time securing funding in an increasingly science-dominated environment, empirical literary studies are finding it difficult to take root within a long-established field marked by mostly interpretive and/or historical approaches.

The second position, as put forward by Friedrich Nietzsche, consists of the urge to turn an argument into a moral question by imposing one's own values on all others, thereby creating a frame of mind in which it makes sense, for moral reasons, to object personally to those who do not share these values; thus moral indignation replaces the urge to fight back. In this instance, morality becomes a reason for despising others and not coming to terms with oneself.[33] In the con-

---

31 | M. Bernstein, *Bitter Carnival*, p. 27, my emphasis.

32 | Michel de Montaigne, "Couardise mère de la cruauté", in: Michel de Montaigne, *Essais*, Vol. II, ed. Albert Thibaudet, Paris: Gallimard 1950, pp. 776–87, 777, 779.

33 | Friedrich Nietzsche, *Zur Genealogie der Moral*, ed. Volker Gerhart, Stuttgart: Reclam 1993, I.10.

text of scholarly writing, this type of *ressentiment*, again, exists only as a variant (not least because morality, here, is usually also based on argument): a person's own assumptions and research questions are declared to be the only right way of approaching the subject, a presupposition logically leading to the conclusion that everyone who does not work the same way must be off the mark. This happens mostly in publications which make it their goal to point out what empirical literary studies fails to offer, instead of discussing what it does offer. Indeed, the unwillingness to accept a pluralism of methods and/or opinions often proves to be a thin veil for *ressentiment* in the debate on empirical literary studies, and the simple fact of *not* belonging to a group accused of methodological or theoretical naïveté is erroneously taken for proof of the academic superiority of one's own approach. This is another point which Deleuze raises as characteristic of *ressentiment*: "Tu es méchant, donc je suis bon" [You are bad, therefore I am good].[34] This is supported by a tendency to focus only on particularly weak texts or arguments represented by the 'other side', emphasising problematic research that vindicates criticism instead of acknowledging the wider field and more representative examples.[35]

On a more direct level, what might be read as traces of *ressentiment* can be expressed by resorting to *ad hominem* arguments. The latter are directed against the *ethos* of the attacked person; that is, against his or her authority and credibility.[36] This is not to say that all *ad hominem* arguments are displays of *ressentiment* (or vice versa).[37] Nonetheless, *ad hominem* arguments very often entail the key ingredients of *ressentiment*: personalised feelings of ill will, a shaken sense of self-esteem, and frustration and/or fear induced by someone else's achievements, as Douglas N. Walton explains:

---

34 | Deleuze, *Nietzsche et la philosophie*, p. 136. See also Nietzsche, *Zur Genealogie der Moral*, I.10; M. Bernstein, *Bitter Carnival*, p. 68.

35 | In the context of the debate on New Historicism, Brian Vickers charges Stephen Greenblatt with such *ressentiment*, claiming that he "regularly misrepresents the text he cites" in order to justify a "New Historicist *ressentiment*" against hermeneutical approaches (Brian Vickers, "Masters and Demons", in: Daphne Patai/Will Corral: *Theory's Empire. An Anthology of Dissent*, New York: Columbia University Press 2005, pp. 247–70, 254).

36 | This definition of *ethos* is taken from: Aristotle, *On Rhetoric. A Theory of Civic Discourse*, trans. George A. Kennedy, Oxford: Oxford University Press 1991, book I, 2.5–11; book II, 1.6–16.

37 | There are also polemical and ironic uses of the *ad hominem* argument; one example is Carol Tarvis's review of David Brooks's *The Social Animal*, in which she depicts David Brooks as "an intoxicated lover" who has "fallen in love with psychology" and is now, blinded by love, unable to differentiate between good experiments on the one hand and "pop-psychological, inflated and often unsubstantiated claims" on the other (Carol Tarvis, "Porch Companions", in: *Times Literary Supplement*, 2 September 2011, p. 13). This passage, however, is clearly marked as irony, and involves the concession that some of psychology's findings as reported by Brooks are useful for the study of literature.

The *ad hominem* or personal attack argument is frequently the immediate defensive response to any new and powerfully upsetting argument on a controversial and polarized issue, especially when interests are threatened, and emotions are running high on the issue.[38]

If *ad hominem* arguments express *ressentiment*, they usually remain argumentatively weak and fundamentally unsuited to changing the situation.

Walton distinguishes five main types of *ad hominem* arguments: the abusive argument, which is directed against the character of the person whose opinion is being challenged; the circumstantial argument, which requires a "practical inconsistency between the [attacked individual's] argument and something about the [her] person or circumstances";[39] the bias argument, where the impartiality of the attacked person is challenged; the "poisoning the well" type of argument, which claims that the person has no impartial credibility whatsoever; and the "tu quoque" type of argument, where a person is accused of arguing hypocritically or in bad faith. In addition, Walton identifies three types of "fallacies" which can, but need not, take the form of personal attacks: the genetic fallacy, an attempt to prove a conclusion wrong by condemning its source; the "two wrongs" fallacy, "an argument that attempts to justify what is considered wrong by appealing to other instances of the same or similar action";[40] and the "guilt by association" fallacy, which attacks someone's argument by way of "reference to the alleged character of some of his friends or relatives."[41]

In the case of attacking scholarly positions in academic writing, these arguments appear in slightly altered forms. For obvious reasons, the abusive argument hardly ever occurs. The circumstantial argument and the bias argument seem to fall in one with the "two wrongs" fallacy – a person's research background inevitably entails a bias towards certain theories and methodologies, as well as a number of blind spots in areas less well-explored; therefore, the circumstances of the person can often be matched with their academic background and environment. This can be used to claim that a scholar lacks the necessary expertise and training to do what she proposes and that therefore her results are not to be trusted. Indeed, scholars in interdisciplinary projects sometimes stand accused of lacking the necessary training to understand all facets of their own research properly, from which it is then concluded that said research must be faulty.[42]

---

38 | Douglas N. Walton, *Ad Hominem Arguments*, Tuscaloosa: University of Alabama Press 1998, p. xi.

39 | Ibid., p. 6.

40 | Vincent Soccio/Douglas Barry, *Practical Logic. An Antidote for Uncritical Thinking*, New York: Harcourt/ Brace 1992, p. 129; also quoted in D. N. Walton, *Ad Hominem Arguments*, p. 19.

41 | Philip Wheelwright, *Valid Thinking. An Introduction to Logic*, New York: Odyssey Press 1962, p. 327; also quoted in D. N. Walton: *Ad Hominem Arguments*, p. 20.

42 | See, for instance: Raymond Tallis, "The Neuroscience Delusion", in: *Times Literary Supplement*, 9 April 2008, URL: http://tomraworth.com/talls.pdf. This type of

While doubts regarding anyone's ability to fully comprehend a foreign discipline without formal training do not constitute *ressentiment* or qualify as *ad hominem* arguments,[43] they become problematic as soon as they produce a hard-and-fast rule of discounting other approaches, that is, as soon as the very possibility of success is categorically ruled out without regard for the individual case. Ironically, the argument is also reversed – those engaging in interdisciplinary research occasionally point out that their mono-disciplinary colleagues do not grasp the scientific foundation of their work.[44]

The "poisoning the well" type of argument works as an extension of this, while the "tu quoque" type tends to appear where flaws in someone else's research are employed to justify the arguer's own (different) approach. The "guilt by association" fallacy dismisses whole scholarly movements without necessarily looking at their entire range of academic contributions. The aim, in all of these cases, is not to attack the researcher's personality, but her academic credibility and authority.

It is important, however, to distinguish between *ad hominem* attacks that are expressions of *ressentiment*, and those that are mere displays of polemics, or side-effects of valid critical arguments. In the following, I will discuss a number of examples from the debate on interdisciplinarity that may help to make this distinction. The examples will also show if and how personalised attacks can be read as *ressentiment*. These examples are linked to particular rhetorical strategies which frequently concur with *ad hominem* arguments and which in some cases can be interpreted as signs of *ressentiment* themselves, namely in the use of verbal imagery (here metaphor), and the use of emotional vocabulary.

---

charge is denied by Ellen Spolsky (Ellen Spolsky, "Preface", in: Alan Richardson/Ellen Spolsky, *The Work of Fiction. Cognition, Culture, Complexity,* Aldershot/Burlington, VT: Ashgate 2004, pp. vii–xiii, xii). Similar criticism has been directed against Comparative Literature (see: Stathis Gourgouris, "The Poiein of Secular Criticism", in: Ali Behdad/Dominic Thomas: *A Companion to Comparative Literature,* Oxford: Blackwell 2011, pp. 75–87, 77–78).

43 | This scepticism applies not only to interdisciplinary endeavours involving the sciences. In an article on interdisciplinary work between law and literary studies, Jane Baron asks: "What does a scholar from one discipline need to know in order to 'employ' another discipline? Can we really learn another discipline (late in life? without formal training?)? And if we cannot, what is it we borrow from the other discipline? Facts? Theories? What kinds of interdisciplinary work represent 'rigorous' scholarship, as opposed to what one sceptic has called 'intellectual voyeurism'? Most importantly, what are the underlying ways in which we categorize knowledge?" Jane B. Baron, "Interdisciplinary Legal Scholarship As Guilty Pleasure: The Case of Law and Literature", in: Michael Freeman/ Andrew D. E. Lewis (eds): *Law and Literature,* Oxford: Oxford University Press 1999, pp. 21–45, 22.

44 | See, for instance, Herbert Simon, "Literary Criticism: A Cognitive Approach", in: *Stanford Humanities Review,* 4.1, 1995. (Bridging the Gap. Where Cognitive Science Meets Literary Criticism, eds, Stefano Franchi/Güven Güzeldere), URL: www.stanford.edu/group/SHR/4-1/text/simon1.html.

Ad hominem Arguments and Metaphor

Under the graphic title "Oberflächliche Augenwischerei" ("Superficial Window-Dressing"), Peter André Alt, professor of German and president of the Freie Universität Berlin, criticises recent interdisciplinary developments between the sciences and humanities as often poorly-conceived and detrimental to the in-depth education and training of early career researchers.[45] It is the title that qualifies his text as an example; the criticism voiced in the article itself is sophisticated and entirely avoids generalisations and *ad hominem* arguments. In the title, however, the credibility of the interdisciplinary researchers is under attack. They are guilty of "superficial window dressing" instead of conducting reliable, in-depth research: they are pretenders. This *ad hominem* argument bears traits both of the abusive and the circumstantial argument, and of the "guilt by association" fallacy. But is it a case of *ressentiment?*

The second example is taken from the opposite end of the spectrum. With his article "Bekämpfen Sie das häßliche Laster der Interpretation! Bekämpfen Sie das noch häßlichere Laster der richtigen Interpretation!" [Fight the ugly vice of interpretation! Fight the even uglier vice of the right interpretation!][46] from 1979, Siegfried J. Schmidt dismisses traditional criticism. Interpreting literature, to Schmidt, is subjective and irrational, a pleasurable divertissement that should in no way be allowed to lay claims to the production of knowledge. In this, Schmidt's argument matches Rosenberg's in the passage quoted earlier. (See footnote 2). But Schmidt goes even further by saying that literary studies, if based on interpretation, has no place in the ranks of a university; to deserve even to be counted among the academic disciplines, he claims, it would need to adopt the methods of empirical social research, psychology and psycholinguistics. What turns his merely polemical point into an *ad hominem* argument is, as in Alt's case, the title: a vice is a moral failing; it is always personal. Hence, Schmidt not only attacks the method, but also those employing it; they are vice-ridden individuals entertaining their personal hobby during paid work-time and pretending that this creates academic knowledge. Again, this is clearly an *ad hominem* attack, but does it constitute *ressentiment?*

Comparing these examples, the following becomes evident: Schmidt and Alt formulate attacks, as does Rosenberg, on a particular type of scholar, but do not link this argument with proper names. Hence, it might seem that their *ad hominem* argument is not really personal. However, Alt, Schmidt and Rosenberg clearly direct their criticism at people, not only positions, and it is to be expected that these people will understand that the criticism is directed at them. All of the examples share a tendency to use metaphors to turn their argument from

---

45 | Peter-André Alt, "Oberflächliche Augenwischerei", in: *Süddeutsche Zeitung*, 21 December 2010.

46 | Siegfried J. Schmidt, "Bekämpfen Sie das häßliche Laster der Interpretation! Bekämpfen Sie das noch häßlichere Laster der richtigen Interpretation!", in: *Amsterdamer Beiträge zur neueren Germanistik*, 8, (1979), pp. 279–309.

object-bound into personal criticism; whether it is the image of someone's ugly vice, the person fooling the eye by means of window-dressing, or, in Rosenberg's case, the sinking ship which is steered into disaster by a clueless crew – these metaphors imply that the actions or objects criticised can be blamed on individuals. The use of metaphor also adds an affective value to the points made.[47] The context of Alt's and Schmidt's contributions indicates a potential feeling of powerlessness and of writing against the dismissive gesture of mainstreaming. Alt criticises a politically powerful trend in Germany in general and in his very own university in particular (Freie Universität Berlin is the home of a large interdisciplinary research centre and part of the German Research Foundation's so-called *Exzellenzinitiative* [excellence-initiative], a large grant scheme explicitly encouraging interdisciplinary collaboration); and Schmidt, back in the 1970s, attempted to shake up the discipline from within. However, Alt's, Schmidt's, and Rosenberg's texts lack two key ingredients of *ressentiment*: their authors seem to believe that they can instigate the changes they deem necessary; and while the polemical tone of their articles clearly implies emotion, it does not betray a ruffled sense of self-worth (although Alt and Schmidt seem to lament their causes' lack of academic worth). Furthermore, the opponents they describe are not real-life colleagues, but, so to speak, implied or ideal opponents that serve to make a particular point. Lastly, in Alt's case (but not so much in Schmidt's and Rosenberg's), the text itself puts the title in an argumentative perspective that, while critical, is not akin to *ressentiment*.

If *ressentiment* cannot be unambiguously found in these texts, however, can it be found in arguments employing emotional vocabulary?

Ad hominem Arguments and Emotional Vocabulary

Collaborations between literary studies, experimental psychology and neuroscience represent a new paradigm in an old discipline. As such, they are obviously only in their incipience, combining tentative steps forward with ambitious aims and dreams. This makes them vulnerable to criticism; and many critics do not offer a constructive analysis, but instead question the intellectual justification of the whole paradigm's very existence on the basis of some unfortunate examples. This tendency to a general dismissal can be found in Frank Kelleter's "A Tale

---

47 | Rhetorical theory attributes threefold potential to verbal imagery: it renders the argument more plausible (*docere*), aesthetically pleases the addressee (*delectare*), and influences her affectively (*movere*) – while winning her over (*conciliare*). Classical rhetoric in the tradition of Aristotle, Cicero, and Quintilian considers verbal imagery as a particularly effective means of persuasion on a cognitive as well as an emotional level (see, e.g., Aristotle, *Poetics*, trans. Malcolm Heath, Penguin Classics: 1996, §21; Id.: *Rhetoric*, book III, 2.6–12, 3.4–4.4, 10.2–7, 11.1–15). Regarding the affective potential of metaphorical speech, see also: Pradeep Sopory: "Metaphor and Affect", in: *Poetics Today*, 26.3 (2005), pp. 433–58.

of Two Natures", which focuses on a number of problematic examples of inter-disciplinary research, but disregards others that have become milestones in the new paradigm.[48] This impression is further enhanced by the use of emotional vocabulary. For example, Kelleter considers the tone of the so-called "neo-naturalists" to be "patronising"; their view of literature is described as "strikingly impoverished" and as sometimes expressed in "a crassly dilettantish manner and without the least interest in the methods, goals, and questions of the fields they dismiss". He conjures up a future in which they will be but "quaint fantasies", and suspects that their methods in dealing with texts are occasionally "due to wilful misunderstanding and polemics."[49] Kelleter may not be entirely wrong in his evaluation, but the manner of its presentation and the generality of his claims nonetheless have a slight air of *ressentiment*. The charge of "wilful misunderstanding and polemics" betrays a sense of having been treated unfairly. Kelleter's mentioning of the empiricists' alleged "lack of interest" und dismissal of traditional approaches shows that Kelleter believes himself to be fighting a losing battle, trying to win over someone who will not listen.

On the opposite side is Schmidt's aforementioned manifesto against the "ugly vice of interpretation". Here, as in Kelleter's case, we hear from a scholar whose view did not conform to what was successful in his field at the time. The attempt to establish the so-called Empirical Constructivist Literary Studies which wanted to do away with interpretation was neither particularly popular nor successful. The ideas voiced here did not resonate much on an international level, and even within Germany were only short-lived.[50] This is not to imply that Schmidt lost hope in his endeavour – to this day, he (both nationally and internationally) publishes on the role of constructivism for the humanities. However, like Kelleter's, Schmidt's text uses emotional vocabulary which betrays anger and disdain in the face of a development he cannot change. As in the above case of metaphor, it is difficult to determine conclusively whether Kelleter and/or Schmidt felt *ressentiment* against their objects of criticism. Nevertheless, their respective stances might be perceived as stemming from *ressentiment*.

---

48 | In this respect, he is guilty of a strategy which he, in turn, accuses the empiricists of using and which Gabriel Stolzenberg defines as follows: "people hunt for nonsense in statements of authors suspected of being partial to it and, when they find what looks like it, they consider themselves done. Yet had they hunted instead, or in addition, for more generous interpretations, they almost surely would have found them." (Gabriel Stolzenberg, "Reading and Relativism: An Introduction to the Science Wars", in: Keith M Ashman/ Philip S. Bahringer, (eds), *After the Science Wars*, London 2001, pp. 33–65, 34. Quoted in F. Kelleter: "A Tale of Two Natures", p. 159, n.3.)

49 | F. Kelleter: "A Tale of Two Natures", pp. 161, 162, 183, 186, 166.

50 | See Steven Tötösy de Zepetnek,: "Empirical Science of Literature/Constructivist Theory of Literature", in: *Encyclopedia of Contemporary Literary Theory. Approaches, Scholars, Terms*, ed. Irena R. Makaryk, Toronto: Toronto University Press 1993, pp. 36–9.

The *Ressentiment* of Others

The above examples illustrate how difficult it is to identify *ressentiment* unambiguously in scholarly texts. Yet while there are good reasons for suppressing one's own potential *ressentiment* in writing, it is relatively common to accuse others of it implicitly. Only very few scholars openly do so in the manner of Christine Mielke[51] from the University of Karlsruhe, who laments her "Unglück" [misfortune] in having had a secondary supervisor during her studies who fostered *ressentiment* against interdisciplinarity.[52] Susanne Baer confirms that criticism and *ressentiment* against interdisciplinarity are often voiced "hinter vorgehaltener Hand" [in hushed whispers],[53] especially where they rely on individual experience only. Nevertheless, texts defending approaches to experimental literary studies reveal a tendency to charge more traditionally-minded colleagues with *ressentiment*, attributing this mostly to fear or to a lack of knowledge (which, in itself, constitutes an *ad hominem* argument).

Marissa Bortolussi's and Peter Dixon's *Psychonarratology*, which outlines the advantages of employing psychological methods and theories in literary studies, for instance, suggests that some traditionally-minded critics from literary studies react to empirical work with a mixture of fear for their own academic raison d'être and also show a simple lack of knowledge in doing so – a mixture that, indeed, shows many traits of *ressentiment*. While Bortolussi and Dixon concede that fear of empirical approaches in the humanities is "no trivial or unfounded concern",[54] their first chapter is nonetheless preceded by the quote, "fear is a failure of the imagination".[55] This overarching epigraph implicitly belittles those who are later identified as fearful of empiricism. They are effectively dismissed as unimaginative, unknowledgeable critics who reject something that exceeds their understanding, the inference being that this failure amounts to academic self-aggrandisement and is similar, perhaps, to *ressentiment*. This stance is particularly problematic, since, contrary to Bortolussi's and Dixon's assertions,[56] psychological research has not yet been entirely able to counter the methodological and theoretical concerns voiced by critics included in the volume regarding an empirical, experimental analysis of literature.

---

51 | Mielke works in a different interdisciplinary environment than the one discussed in this article, namely at the interface of literary studies and film studies.

52 | Christine Mielke,: "Zyklisch-serielle Narration. Von 1001 Nacht bis zur TV-Serie", in: Homepage der Andrea-von-Braun-Stiftung. URL: www.avbstiftung.de/fileadmin/projekte/AVB_LP_Christine_Mielke.pdf.

53 | Susanne Baer, "Interdisziplinierung oder Interdisziplinarität – eine freundliche Provokation", in: *ZiF-Bulletin*, 19, 1999, (Institutionalisierung und Interdisziplinarität. Frauen- und Geschlechterforschung an der Humboldt-Universität zu Berlin), pp. 77–82, 77.

54 | Marissa Bortolussi/Peter Dixon, *Psychonarratology. Foundations for the Empirical Study of Literary Response*, Cambridge: Cambridge University Press 2003, p. 22.

55 | Ibid., p. 1.

56 | Ibid., p. 23.

The charge of fear is occasionally linked to that of low self-esteem; it is also frequently linked to the term "threat". In these instances, it is sometimes implied that the more traditionally-minded side of literary criticism sees neuroscience as a danger because of its supposedly superior techniques in assessing and accessing the human mind. However, while it is certainly true that many literary scholars view the interdisciplinary surge involving neuroscience as a threat, it would be premature to assume that they feel threatened by the force of the new approach, as Brian Baxter suggests when he claims that the "arrival of biology at the door of the [...] humanities poses a serious threat to much that human beings have come to hold dear".[57] Rather, many seem genuinely convinced that their traditional access to literature is simply better than an empirical one, but might be at risk in a changed political climate. In other words, if scientific approaches – mistakenly or otherwise – are associated with a greater objectivity, political decisions could favour these and harm the humanities. In that sense, the empiricists professing their wish to bridge the gap between the sciences and the humanities are perceived as "re-enact[ing] the very division" they have "set out to bridge".[58]

But even this fear of being disadvantaged politically and economically, which need not involve any academic self-doubt, can be read as bearing traces of *ressentiment*, as Ann Mroz demonstrates:

> Although the humanities may feel that they have been betrayed by philistines and politicians, they themselves must shoulder some blame: through academic navel-gazing they have failed to live up to their true mission and potential, often making themselves irrelevant.[59]

In Mroz's view, the humanities simply chase the blame and present their own misfortune as a lack of fairness instead of (re-)acting in a constructive manner – the classic gesture of *ressentiment*. Mroz overlooks the fact that, in spite of certain faults of the humanities, scholars in these disciplines might not be wrong in feeling betrayed by others; their possible *ressentiment* does not render their criticism entirely invalid.

These examples show that the charge of *ressentiment* or of feelings akin to *ressentiment* is used to unmask a discursive strategy which presents itself as criticism, but entails self-pity, self-abasement, the feeling of having been treated unfairly, ill-concealed yet impotent hostility, and/or potentially a lack of knowledge. At the same time, however, the examples attest to a serious problem, in that by dismissing criticism as *ressentiment*, the validity of this criticism is

---

57 | Brian Baxter, *A Darwinian Worldview: Sociobiology, Environmental Ethics and the Work of Edward O. Wilson*, Aldershot/Burlington, VT: Ashgate 2007, p. 91.

58 | Sylvia Wynter, "But What Does 'Wonder' Do? Meanings, Canons Too?" In: *Stanford Humanities Review*, 4.1, (1995), (Bridging the Gap. Where Cognitive Science Meets Literary Criticism, eds S. Franchi/G. Güzeldere), URL: www.stanford.edu/group/SHR/4–1/text/wynter.commentary.html.

59 | Ann Mroz, "Leader: Factor In the Human Equation", in: *Times Higher Education*, 7 January 2010, p. 5.

implicitly questioned. Yet even where criticism voiced against interdisciplinary endeavours does bear traces of self-pity and/or fear, it might not be unfounded. Ignoring it because of (real or imaginary) *ressentiment* means risking the perpetuation of error. It is only to be expected that a new branch of interdisciplinarity as controversial as experimental literary studies should provoke affective reactions along with theoretical and methodological concerns. This need not mean that the criticism is in itself incorrect or faulty, although it must of course be handled with care.

In fact, no one should understand the affective impact of such large methodological and theoretical shifts better than people already working in interdisciplinary contexts. It might be for this reason that between 2011 and 2013 most job postings for early-career researchers at the interdisciplinary Swiss Center for Affective Science included the remark that suitable candidates must show not only interest in, but also "the necessary personality" for interdisciplinary research.[60]

Political Solidarity, Intellectual Divergence

Interdisciplinary approaches have been an integral and unavoidable part of literary studies throughout their history, but the latest developments involving the sciences and the subsequent criticism from within the discipline require a thorough discussion of the reasons for this criticism, as well as its foundations.

It appears that a lot of the *ressentiment* voiced in relation to interdisciplinary literary studies from both sides of the spectrum is motivated politically rather than intellectually. While many do not agree with the methods, theories, goals, and assumptions of the opposite side, and believe that "they cannot both be right", as Rosenberg puts it, their unwillingness to co-exist is heightened affectively by the fact that they still constitute one discipline and thus have to compete for funding and social influence. It seems important, in this context, not to perpetuate old stereotypes of the opposition between the humanities and the sciences. While the question of whether or not the two are compatible should be debated rationally, hostility towards the respective other means directing one's frustration in the wrong direction. The sciences are not to blame for the funding crisis and for society's fascination with the workings of the brain; neither are the more traditional humanities to blame for pointing out flaws and methodological problems with newly emerging approaches. Instead, working together politically (while perhaps disagreeing intellectually) is surely a more constructive path towards what is likely to be, after all, a joint future. The justified doubts that much empirical work evokes could then be used to spark discussions that would strengthen its methodological basis. Certainly, the dismissal of criticism as *ressentiment* is a reductive reflex that poses a real risk to the quality and the development of interdisciplinary work in the context of literary studies.

---

60 | Swiss Center for Affective Research, job listing. URL: www.affective-sciences.org/jobs.

Ressentiment and Dissensus: The Place of Critique in the Contemporary Academy

Mary Gallagher

Reflection on the present, and on the present state of the academy in particular, is constrained by the limits of insight fundamental to all self-reflexive effort. Within those restrictions, this essay considers the place of critique in, or in relation to, the contemporary academy. More specifically, it reflects on the distinctions and connections between an affect (Ressentiment), a diffuse cognitive disposition (dissensus) and a focused and responsive intellectual positioning (critique).

An important meta-discursive or meta-epistemological point about legitimacy and authority needs to be made at the outset of this discussion. Its author is neither an historian nor a philosopher, nor indeed a human scientist. Moreover, beyond linguistic analysis and beyond the nebulous notion of critique, it would be difficult to identify the academic field to which the study belongs, or in which its author might properly or willingly claim, certainly not "expertise", but some discursive legitimacy or authority. Although the distinction between the academic and the "expert"[1] is a problematic one, it might seem plausible to suggest that either expert or academic discourse (historical, sociological, philosophical etc.) on the ontology of the academy is relatively more authoritative and more legitimate than non-expert, non-academic discourse. This commonsense assumption is, however, as we shall see, highly contestable and has indeed been

---

1 | "Il faut en finir avec la tyrannie des experts style Banque Mondiale ou FMI, qui imposent sans discussion les verdicts du nouveau Léviathan, et qui n'entendent pas négocier, mais 'expliquer'; il faut rompre avec la nouvelle foi en l'inévitabilité historique que professent les théoriciens du libéralisme." ["An end must be put to the tyranny of these World Bank or IMF style 'experts', who impose without any debate the verdicts of the New Leviathan and who are interested not in the discussion, but in the exposition, of ideas. We have to sever our ties with the new credo of historical inevitability professed by the theoreticians of liberalism."], Pierre Bourdieu, *Contre Feux: propos pour servir à la résistance contre l'invasion néo-libérale* [Counter-Fire: Suggestions for Resistance to the Neo-Liberal Invasion], Paris: Liber/Raisons d'agir 1998, p. 31. (Note: in this instance and in all others in the present essay, translations from the French are mine, unless otherwise indicated.)

contested both within and around the aforementioned disciplinary discourses themselves; moreover, the grounds of the challenge relate both to the notion of critique and to the idea of the academy or the academic.

The tense relation between critique and disciplinarity – more specifically the connection between self-reflexive critical reason and the epistemological legitimacy of distinct academic disciplines – is addressed by Immanuel Kant in the context of the organisation of the academy (in *The Conflict of the Faculties*).[2] Michel Foucault, as we shall see, returns to this same question in his essay "What is Critique", when he observes that critique is for him a "project that keeps taking shape, being extended and reborn *on the outer limits of philosophy, very close to it, up against it, at its expense*, in the direction of a future philosophy and in lieu, perhaps of all possible philosophy".[3] For her part, Judith Butler also acknowledges the necessarily liminal positioning of critique and its para- or extra-disciplinary reach, when she notes that "[a]lthough critique clearly attains its modern formulation in philosophy, it also makes claims that *exceed* the particular disciplinary domain of the philosophical".[4] Bill Readings, author of *The University in Ruins*,[5] sees in the humanities disciplines in general the contemporary equivalent of what was for Kant the "lower" faculty of philosophy: namely, the foundational discipline that must model for all the others the very essence of critique, thus enabling but not, of course, conducting – their separate and constitutional self-critiques.

One of the principal questions raised in the present essay concerns the possibility or impossibility for critique and for dissensus to (continue to) take place around and about academe today and more specifically where it might do so: in which "excess-ive", liminal or interstitial space? Within or outside the academy itself? And if the former, will that space be supra-disciplinary, infra-disciplinary, intra-disciplinary and/or inter-disciplinary?

Critical Lexicon

(1) Ressentiment

Remaining, to begin with at least, upon the – for this author – relatively stable ground of philological or linguistic analysis, it will be immediately obvious that the title of this study contains three non-English words. At first sight, these borrowings might appear as a gratuitous or even pretentious stylistic affecta-

---

2 | Immanuel Kant, *The Conflict of the Faculties*, trans. Mary J. Gregor, University of Nebraska Press 1992 [*Der Streit der Fakultäten*, 1798].

3 | Michel Foucault, "What is Critique" in: Foucault *The Politics of Truth*, ed. Sylvère Lotringer, trans. Lysa Hocroth and Catherine Porter, Los Angeles CA: Semiotext(e) 2007, pp. 41–81, p.42. Emphasis mine.

4 | Judith Butler, "Critique, Dissent, Disciplinarity", *Critical Inquiry*, 35 (Summer 2009), pp. 773–95, p. 775. Emphasis mine.

5 | Bill Readings, *The University in Ruins*, Harvard Mass.: Harvard University Press 1996.

tion. The fact is, however, that the notion of "Ressentiment" was first theorised in German, a language in which the French word sounds immeasurably more foreign than it does in English. The extreme phonetic unfamiliarity of the term "ressentiment" to the language in which Friedrich Nietzsche and Max Scheler – in the late 1880s and early 1910s respectively – constructed their theories of morality and (in)equality around it, is part of its meaning; and the implications of its lesser – but still recognisable – foreignness to the language of the present study are also significant. More specifically, it is important to note that it is neither pretentiousness nor affectation that prompts the non-translation here of the word out of the French; it is rather the fact that the best, if not the only, English translation of "ressentiment" (the cognate term, "resentment") is what French linguists call a "faux ami" or a "false friend". Although seeming to the non-initiated to spell out the same meaning as its English near-homonym, the French word, particularly when used in a language other than French, has been intellectually (re-)defined by Nietzsche and then by Scheler to mean far more than either "ressentiment" in French or "resentment" in English. Scheler, indeed, already regarded the French word, deployed after Nietzsche, as a "termus technicus".[6]

(2) Critique

"Critique" is also a non-English term. What is the point of this second gesture to a concept referenced by a foreign term for which a perfectly functional English synonym apparently exists? Why invoke here "critique" rather than "criticism", the word that features, after all, in the title of this volume of essays as a whole? Use of the term "critique" in English is significant in three different ways. Firstly, like all loan words, it is surrounded in the host language with connotations of foreignness. Moreover, as a function of its foreign – more specifically Gallic – phonetic and graphic form, use of the loan-word in English suggests the somewhat rarefied cachet of intellectually specialised discourse. Independently of whether "critique" *as commonly used in French* has or does not have different connotations to those of the English term "criticism", a choice has been made *not* to use the cognate English term, but rather to deploy a translingual word. This selection, in itself, suggests a certain, intellectually discriminating, stylistic distinction. Secondly, the status of the word "critique" as an import from a different language allows its functional meaning to be distinguished or redefined

---

6 | "We do not use the word 'ressentiment' because of a special predilection for the French language, but because we did not succeed in translating it into German. Moreover, Nietzsche has made it a *terminus technicus*". Max Scheler, *Ressentiment*, edited with an Introduction by Lewis A. Coser, trans. Lewis A. Coser & William Holdheim, New York: Schocken Books, 1972, p. 39 [*Das Ressentiment im Aufbau der Norden*, 1915]. The translator writes that "[i]n the translation as well, the French term 'ressentiment' has been maintained for the reasons which Scheler indicates: Nietzsche has made it a technical term, and it would be difficult to find an English word which adequately expresses the same nuances. The English word 'resentment' is too specific. Its use has been avoided throughout the translation", Max Scheler, *Ressentiment*, p.175, n. 3.

in relation to that of the closest synonyms in the host or "borrower" language. Thirdly, for a combination of reasons, including specific morphological factors, the combined semantic effect of the French term's translingual connotations in English is to attenuate, neutralise or even completely efface the more directly censorious or condemnatory force associated with the English term "criticism". In other words, the term "critique" as used in English could be seen as bearing considerably less negativity than the term "criticism", and as evoking a less reactive, less normative and perhaps more speculative intellectual operation.

The title of the present volume of essays makes the implicit transitivity, reactivity and even negativity of the term "criticism" and *a fortiori* of the English verb associated with it ("to criticise"), eminently clear; it refers, after all, to the "critics" of "criticism", meaning those who criticise – ie. find fault with or otherwise reject or dismiss – criticism, rather than those who "critique critique". The English verb derived from the noun "criticism" is, of course, "to criticise". But although the French verb corresponding to the noun "critique" is "critiquer", the loan-word "critique" is commonly used in contemporary English both as a verb and as a noun (as in "to critique this or that"). In French, the same word "critique" can be an abstract noun ("criticism") and can also translate both the verb "to criticise" as in "je/tu/il/elle/on critique" and the noun "critic" (le critique). Unlike English, the French thus conflates the abstract activity, the concrete action and the agent or subject of the act. This, one could argue, is why the French term suggests a more diffuse and speculative valency quite absent from the full frontal force of "criticism". It is, indeed, precisely because of its more concrete, focussed and agonistic connotations that "criticism" is more likely than "critique" to be undermined or criticised as being animated or fuelled by "Ressentiment". The US critic, Barbara Johnson, in her comments on deconstruction in the introduction to her translation of Jacques Derrida's *La Dissémination* (1974), makes the importance of this semantic divergence between the two notions quite clear.

> A critique of any theoretical system is not an examination of its flaws and imperfections. It is not a set of criticisms designed to make the system better. It is an analysis that focuses on the grounds of the system's possibility. The critique reads backwards from what seems natural, obvious, self-evident or universal in order to show that these things have their history, their reasons for being the way they are, their effects on what follows from them and that the starting point is not a (natural) given but a (cultural) construct, usually blind to itself.[7]

(3) Dissensus

Use of the third foreign word, the unreconstructed Latin term "dissensus", is no more gratuitous than the use of "ressentiment" is emptily pretentious. It might be argued, certainly, that "dissensus" is perfectly well translated by the

---

7 | Jacques Derrida, *Dissemination*, trans. Barbara Johnson, Chicago: University of Chicago Press 1981, p. xv.

English word "dissent". Yet the connotational meaning of "dissensus" is significantly different from that of "dissent". To begin with, there is the ablation in "dissent" of the Latinate ending of "dissensus", ie. of the suffix that ensures that the word "dissensus" immediately brings to mind its antonym, "consensus". "Dissent" rhymes, of course, not with "consensus" but rather with "consent". This consonance, in a way, highlights the fact that "dissent" can refer to a limited, localised instance of disagreement or divergence, just as the connotations of "consent", unlike the much more diffuse connotations of "consensus", are almost exclusively associated with discrete acts of acceptance or agreement (of a very particular proposition or state of affairs). In other words, "dissent" can designate a singular act of disagreement (as when one or more persons dissent from a given decision). Use of the word "dissensus", on the other hand, like use of the word "critique" instead of "criticism", suggests that the word "dissent" has been rejected in favour of a "foreign" word, this time a Latin term, with all the connotations of classical learning borne by that language. However, it is the phonetic pairing with "consensus" that is significant here. Like "consensus", "dissensus" suggests less a single concrete action than an abstraction, a state of affairs; it seems, in other words, to point to the existence of a diffuse multiplicity of differing viewpoints. Moreover, the latter do not necessarily differ in relation *to the same* proposition, decision, value, action, etc. Thus, the word "dissensus", as deployed in French and in English by contemporary thinkers, can evoke not just the existence of different perspectives on the same question, but a multiplicity of questions and perspectives which, in its diffuse, unfocussed divergence from a state of consensus, enacts dissensus.

It could perhaps be said, then, that the title of this essay points to a spectrum of divergence which moves from the reductive, obsessive compulsiveness of Ressentiment, through the normative (a)stringency of criticism and the more speculative tenor of critique, to the altogether more diffuse freedom of dissensus. However, given the focus of this essay on education, more especially "Higher Education", it must be pointed out that, around or beyond this spectrum of divergence, the ideal of Socratic dialogue hovers, suggesting a paradigm beyond dissensus, a paradigm of thinking together that involves not just thinking and talking divergently – whether separately and apart, beside one another or together –, but also listening, responsively and responsibly, to and with each other.

The Academy's Historical Relation to Critique

The present study turns on essentially political and ethical questions of value. To begin with, the notion of Ressentiment was first developed by Friedrich Nietzsche in a genealogical study of morality; hence matters of value, of revaluation and transvaluation are at its heart. As for dissensus, it is, as we shall see, increasingly conceptualised today as having a certain non-dialectical value – epistemological, social, political, even ethical or moral – said to be protective of equality, justice, democracy and politics. Finally, critique too has been described in moral or ethical terms, most notably perhaps by the French philosopher Michel Foucault, for whom it is a *synonym of virtue* ("There is something in critique which is akin to virtue").[8]

Clearly, academic concerns are not historically, and therefore not axiomatically, associated with Ressentiment, dissensus or even critique. The word "academy" found its way into English from the Greek *akadēmeia*, the name of the grove or garden where Plato taught, and that was in turn named after the legendary hero *Akadēmos*. Plato's academy was a space not just of philosophy, but of philosophical dialogue. Significantly, the philosopher Diogenes of Sinope, also known as Diogenes the Cynic, was an early figure of marginality, who liked to mock the pretentions of the original academy. Perhaps paradoxically, it is to this figure that the German thinker Peter Sloterdijk turns when seeking a way out of the generalised Ressentiment informing cynical reason today. The irreverent "Frechheit" or cheekiness and the deliberate marginality of Diogenes's "gai savoir", as invoked by Sloterdijk, could thus be seen as a manifestation of critical or academic freedom *avant la lettre*.[9] However, as its referent evolved, the multilingual or indeed translingual term "academy" came to denote a space far more closely connected with power, dominance and investiture than with marginality or critique. This is made particularly clear by the role of specialised consecration vested in academies dedicated to scholarship in the arts and the sciences: for example, visual, musical, military, medical academies but also more generalist academies of learning such as the French Academy or the Royal Academies. During the long, post-classical nineteenth century, the relegation of some outstanding artworks to various "salons des refusés" did somewhat tarnish the reputations of mono-academies (devoted to the visual arts, for example), casting them as bastions of the doggedly reactionary conservatism consecrated by the term "conservatory" (designating academies of music – in France for example). The aura of anointment is indeed what still distinguishes most "academies" from other "academic" institutions: schools, colleges and, most notably, universities. The latter, which came into being in medieval Europe, are – along, of course, with schools – the oldest and most globally preeminent of academic institutions in operation today and they continue to be distinguished by the number of *diverse* faculties or disciplines that they usually accommodate. Despite their "universal(ist)" tenor, they are often associated, however, with quite particular, nationally inflected, histories.

Certainly, a ratio of critique or self-interrogation has not been invariably central to the academy. However, as Bill Readings recalls, it was Immanuel Kant

---

8 | Michel Foucault, "What is Critique", p. 43.

9 | Sloterdijk invokes the sensuality and sarcasm with which Diogenes of Sinope challenged the moral arrogance and complacency of idealism. He devotes a chapter of his book *Kritik der zynischen Vernunft* (2 vols), Frankfurt am Main: Suhrkampverlag 1983 to Diogenes: "Diogenes von Sinop – Hundmensch, Philosoph, Taugenichts", Vol 1, pp. 296–319. The chapter title is explained by the fact that the Greek word *Kynikos* means "dog" or "Hund".

who founded the mission of the (early) modern university on critical reason, which thus became the basis of the institution's legitimacy. In contrast, the medieval university had been founded on the famous disciplinary units of the trivium and quadrivium, a curriculum that had no immanent unifying principle but was guaranteed rather by the external authority of superstition, theodicy, etc. For Kant, the foundational academic role of critical reason is played essentially by the discipline of philosophy, which belongs to the "lower" faculties of the university, as opposed to the so-called "higher" faculties. The content of the latter – law, theology and medicine – was founded, historically at least, on the sort of transcendent authority upon which critique, especially self-critique, had little purchase. In contrast, the lower faculties (the humanities and philosophy) might be seen as having little or no content apart from the freely critical exercise of rational inquiry. In other words, whereas the so-called higher faculties were heteronomously authorised (by "received wisdom", "established authority", "superstition" or "magic"), the "lower" faculties were – more autonomously – based on critical reasoning.

> Each particular inquiry, each discipline, develops itself by interrogating its own foundations with the aid of the faculty of philosophy. Thus, inquiry passes from mere empirical practice to theoretical self-knowledge by means of self-criticism. Each discipline seeks [...] what is essential to it. And what is essential to philosophy is nothing other than this search for the essential itself: the faculty of critique.[10]

The fundamental principle informing the Kantian university and indeed the later Humboldtian, or research university, is that of enlightenment. Kant's university model was based on a tension between rational inquiry or enlightenment, on the one hand, and, on the other hand, not so much revelation, as established tradition. However, the main basis of the (Kantian) university's divergence from the model of the "specialised academy" or conservatory lies in the dynamic, friction or "dissensus" arising between or amongst the varied knowledge claims of different faculties or disciplines. In other words, the link between the project of critical reason underlying the university and the opening of dissensus is based *both* on the foundational (and fundamentally philosophical) self-critique of all academic work in the "uni-versity" and also on the co-location within the same institution of a plurality of inherently divergent disciplines or faculties.

The research university, a notion usually traced back to the linguist-philologist Wilhelm von Humboldt and thereby to early nineteenth-century Prussia, was, above all, the university of knowledge or *Wissenschaft*. Humboldt was at one time the Prussian minister of education; he was also the founder (in 1810) of the University of Berlin. His idea of the research university was much influenced by the thinking of other Idealist German thinkers such as Johann Gottlieb Fichte and Friedrich Schleiermacher, and it centered on the development of a strong nation state and national culture. In the shift of emphasis between the

---

10 | Kant, quoted by Bill Readings, *The University in Ruins*, p. 57.

Kantian university founded on critical reason and the Humboldtian idea of the university emphasising rather the culture of the nation state, the "progressive" notions of science or knowledge (Wissenschaft) and of education as self-development (Bildung) had a very clear role to play, arguably indeed a more important role than that of critical reason.[11] "Bildung" lay at the heart of the Humboldtian university, and while this term does refer to "formation" in the sense of "education", it could also be translated as "acculturation". Bill Readings suggests that Humboldt's university is emblematic of a shift "[...] from philosophy to literary studies as the major discipline entrusted by the nation-state with the task of reflecting on cultural identity".[12] Clearly, "Bildung" describes a process of self-accomplishment that is more unambiguously constructivist in tenor than Kant's notion of critical reason. The ideal of 'Bildung' could also be seen as suggesting a more unifying or consensual tenor for the university, a knitting together or uniting of faculties that had been represented by Kant as being, if not in critical "conflict", then at least in a relationship of tension with each other. Whereas critical reason supposes a prior object upon which it is brought to bear (reactively), "Bildung" looks more positively, or at least less reactively, to the shaping of an enlightened, but also a cultured, national subject. It would seem, then, that the ideal Humboldtian university is less a space of tension or even conflict, and therefore of critique, than is the Kantian one. Moreover, it stresses the development of an integrated body of knowledge in tandem with a national culture based on the national language, German (rather than French or Latin), an imperative entirely consonant with Humboldt's training and outlook as a philologist. This emphasis explains the new importance of national literature.

Three central principles informed Humboldt's notion of the university: first, the dual mission of totally unified, mutually sustaining education and scholarship or research based on a shared activity of "learning together"; second, the principle of academic freedom; and third, the reference to the nation state and the formation of a national culture. As we have seen, the emphasis on individual self-accomplishment and collective cultural moulding contrasts with the Kantian emphasis on the institutionalisation of critique, which appears closer to the Platonic idealisation of the philosopher-ruler; closer, in other words, to Plato's conviction that there will be "no end to the troubles of states or indeed [...] of humanity itself until political power and philosophy come into the same hands".[13] In other words, the Humboldtian university plays a particularly clear role of national consolidation through its vocation of acculturation, whereas the role played by critical reason in the Kantian university is more in tune with the representation of the academy in Plato's *Republic* as a school of governance.

---

11 | Of Wilhelm von Humboldt's work on education, only vestiges survive: for example, a fragment of a treatise on the *Theory of Education*. Bill Readings's book provides, however, a cogent discussion of Humboldt's views on the "research university".

12 | Readings, *The University in Ruins*, p.22.

13 | Plato, *The Republic*, trans. D. Lee, 2nd edition Hammondsworth: Penguin 1978, p. 263.

Although his academy was itself, discursively, a "space apart", Plato saw it as closely connected to the "real world", arguing that the creation of a civilised and just society required that "political power should be in the hands of one or more true philosophers".[14] Little appears to have changed in the rhetoric of the New World academy of 1905, the year in which the inaugural President of the University of Chicago declared that "it is the university that fights the battles of democracy, its war-cry being: "Come, let us reason together".[15]

Three important questions arise from that grandiloquent statement. They concern, first of all, the meaning of democracy, then and now; secondly, the identity of the "we" being called upon to "reason together"; and finally the relation between the idea of democracy, the idea of the university and the project of Western imperialism that had dominated nineteenth-century world history. As twentieth-century history was driven forward by the mass murder machines not just of the two world wars, the Shoah and the wars and genocides of imperial engagement, disengagement and their fallout, but also of Stalinism and Maoism, and then by the diversionary sink of the Cold War, the idealist notion of the university seemed to survive more or less intact. Alongside all this upheaval, the academy apparently developed and expanded its quixotic self-image and recognised standing as a space underpinned by a commitment to enlightenment and democracy, a commitment itself guaranteed by the institutionalisation of academic freedom and of parliamentary reason. Clearly, however, universities in the West were also tuning in throughout this time to *Realpolitik*, as witnessed by the accelerating academic integration and development of engineering and technological faculties, mainly as a response to the aforementioned demands of war and empire. Universities continued to adjust in the second half of the century to the changing demands of states caught up simultaneously in the Cold War, in the unravelling and eventual dismantling of Western colonialism and in the latter's triggering of the counter-cultures of the 1960s. They similarly adapted to the economic globalisation that took hold in the long postcolonial ebbtide and that sharply accelerated after the collapse of communism and indeed of the Left per se. It was over this last period that the value of critique came to be most radically altered in relation to the construction of the academy's civic, social or political role.

In *The University in Ruins*, published posthumously in 1996, Bill Readings writes that the imperatives of the nation-state and of national cultures had been definitively superseded by the end of the twentieth century as founding and determining factors of the university's constitution and role. In fact, as globalisation gathered force across the millennium divide, it became clear that universities were being conscripted into an apparent consensus regarding the supremacy of trans-national, if not post-national and post-political economic realities over all others. In a post-industrial age, necessarily focused on global problems such as

---

14 | Ibid., p. 354.

15 | William Rainey Harper was the founder of the University of Chicago. The quotation is from his 1899 Charter Day address. (in W.R. Harper, *The Trend in Higher Education* (1905), London: Forgotten Books 2013, p. 17).

climate change, urbanisation, migration and terror, the emphasis of the academy has shifted away from the tension around epistemological (self-)critique within, between or amongst the different faculties, towards global Higher Education rankings based on imperatives of throughput, output and excellence which are not easy to reconcile with those of critique or self-critique.

Towards the end of the twentieth century, two important "post-modern" critiques of the political narratives on which the university was based were articulated in France by the sociologist, Pierre Bourdieu, and by the philosopher, Jean-François Lyotard. Bourdieu for his part emphasised how the narrative of emancipation (through knowledge, critique, education) was undermined by the logic of social reproduction (the reproduction of privilege, elites, distinction, etc) that dominated academic institutions even, or most of all, in social democracies.[16] The student revolution of May 1968 in France followed roughly two decades of emancipation for the former French colonies in Asia and Africa, a process which, thanks to the spectacularly bloody disengagement from Indochina and Algeria, brought to a head the unsustainable contradiction between the French Republic and "its" Empire. A decade after the May Revolution, Jean-François Lyotard was commissioned by the Quebec authorities (more specifically the Universities Council of the Quebec government) to write a steering report on the future of Higher Education in the province, or at least on the status and nature of knowledge in the contemporary world. Published in 1979, Lyotard's analysis, entitled *La Condition Postmoderne,* and subtitled *Rapport sur le Savoir* [*Report on Knowledge*] fully foresaw the future in which academia is currently positioned.[17] Lyotard traces the history of philosophy as the "legitimising discourse" ["discours de légitimation"] entrusted for a time with defining the status of knowledge or science. Recalling the founding principle of the Kantian university, he thus credits philosophy with having been charged with laying down the ground rules – that is, the ethos, values and goals – of academia. For Lyotard, postmodernity is identified above all with a certain incredulity or scepticism regarding what he terms the "grands récits" (transcendant narratives) of Western history: for example the "récit des Lumières" (the "Enlightenment narrative"), driven by values of universal progress and emancipation. He underlines the stakes of this scepticism, acknowledging that it was these debunked narratives that had determined not just the workings of Higher Education but also the value

---

16 | Pierre Bourdieu is the author of *Homo Academicus,* Paris: Minuit 1984. The English translation by Peter Collier was published by Stanford University Press in 1988. In that work and also in his co-authored book, Pierre Bourdieu & Jean-Claude Passeron, *La Reproduction: Éléments pour une théorie du système d'enseignement,* Paris: Minuit 1970, Bourdieu situates the academy as a site of reproduction of cultural capital and of higher-class *habitus.* He notes that it is, above all, a "site of permanent rivalry for the truth of the social world" (Preface to *Homo academicus* [English translation], 1988, p. xiii).

17 | Jean-François Lyotard, *La Condition post-moderne: rapport sur le savoir,* Paris: Minuit 1979. *The Postmodern Condition: A Report on Knowledge,* trans. Geoffrey Bennington and Brian Massumi, Minneapolis: University of Minnesota Press 1984.

and legitimacy of all of the institutions governing social relations ("la validité des institutions qui régissent le lien social").[18] He also credits them with defining and articulating what constitutes justice and truth.

The contemporary university (or the "university of excellence",[19] as Readings terms it) functions from the late 60s onwards with less and less reference to (national) culture. This is in strong contrast to the culturalist mission of Humboldt's university, based partly, as we have seen, on a principle of national identity and difference. The academy today is certainly seen as having been severed from the notion of serving the national culture and indeed from the notion that cultural difference, divergence or diversity might have a value other than marketable vestigiality. It is, in other words, widely viewed as servicing above all a globalised economy. As Readings puts it, the contemporary university follows the "capitalist logic of general substitutability"[20] and so aspires to being global or internationalised, both in terms of its student and staff demographic and in terms of the cash transfer that fuels it. The same formatting is apparently applied in every university in the world. A particularly extreme example is the global linguistic levelling that led to French education legislation being changed in order to authorise the instruction of French students in French universities, alongside international students, *in English*.[21] Some French academics (in, for example, in the famous HEC (École des hautes études de commerce)) are conscientious objectors, while others – in areas that include humanities subjects such as history and philosophy – seem to be quite willing to "teach" in a language foreign to themselves and to the majority of their students and to the country in which the latter are studying. They are happy, in other words, to jettison French for the more global language, English. Similar developments in universities in Italy (Milan) and Germany (Munich) attracted international media attention in 2013–14. It would be impossible to overestimate the implications for dissensus of this linguistic and cultural reduction. The re-formatting of European universities in particular along the lines of Globish-speak bureaucracy has seen a most remarkable de-Babelisation of the academy across the polylingual continent and this erasure of linguistic diversity cannot but have an impact on the ecology of dissensus.

However, it is principally in its deficit of radical or foundational self-critique and self-reflection that the contemporary academy diverges from the Kantian idea of the university. For Jean-François Lyotard, the narratives of critical enlightenment and emancipation have been jettisoned in the postmodern age, and have

---

18 | Ibid., p. 7.

19 | Readings, *The University in Ruins*, p. 22.

20 | Ibid., p.188.

21 | This bill was voted into law by the French parliament at the end of May 2013. In lifting the linguistic trade restrictions on Higher Education in France, the Loi Fioraso reversed much of the impact of the 1994 Loi Toubon, which had sought to protect the French language against competition from Globish.

been replaced by strategies of efficiency and performance. Similarly, both the critical autonomy of the teacher/scholar and the Humboldtian ideal of the eternal scholar-(re-)searcher have been replaced by the positivist figure of the expert and/or, more frequently, the expert-led team. Lyotard notes that information and knowledge have been made available by technology on such a massive scale that the academy no longer has the same level of responsiblity for, or the same authority in relation to, the transmission role of education. The other main role of the academy, writ large, is knowledge creation, which the contemporary university has re-named "innovation". Lyotard has substantial reservations about the primitive input/output model on which the postmodern academy's innovation role is based. His reservations concern most crucially the need for disjunctive or interruptive thinking in knowledge creation and, more specifically, the need to go beyond communicational transparency or contracted rationality, in order to puncture or disrupt consensus. In other words, Lyotard insists that we cannot regard the values of consensus, efficiency or performance as being congruent with the creative or critical "transcendence" of existing knowledge.

The Contemporary University and the Role of Critique

Before considering the fortunes of critique and of dissensus in the contemporary university, it might be useful to consider how Michel Foucault answered the question "What is Critique?":

> [B]etween the high Kantian enterprise and the *little polemical professional activities* that are called critique, it seems to me that there has been in the modern Western world (dating, more or less, empirically from the 15th to the 16th centuries), a *certain way of thinking, speaking and acting, a certain relationship to what exists, to what one knows, to what one does, a relationship to society, to culture and also a relationship to others that we could call, let's say, the critical attitude.*[22]

Foucault goes on to observe that critique, or the "critical attitude" is based on "some kind of [...] general imperative – more general still than that of *eradicating errors*".[23] Even more significantly, he suggests that this general imperative consists in a "certain way of refusing, challenging, limiting" the rule of those who would govern us. He suggests that critique is a "kind of general cultural form, both a political and moral attitude, a way of thinking, etc.". It is "the art of not being governed or better, the art of not being governed like that and at that cost"[24] and it is "the movement by which the subject gives himself [*sic*] the right to *question truth on its effects of power* and to question *power on its discourses of*

---

22 | Michel Foucault, "What is Critique", p.42. Emphasis mine.

23 | Ibid., pp. 42–3. Emphasis mine.

24 | Ibid., p. 45.

truth".[25] For Foucault, then, the critical attitude is the "art of voluntary insubordination", of "reflected intractability", ensuring the *"desubjugation of the subject in the context of what we could call, in a word, the politics of truth"*.[26]

One of the most noteworthy aspects of the contemporary university as François Lyotard observed its workings in the late 1970s and as Bill Readings and many others describe them from the 1990s, is the extent to which the self-critique founding the "high Kantian enterprise" of academia seems to have become surplus to requirements and, instead of lying at the instititional and constitutional heart of the academy and of academic practice itself, is corralled, where it still subsists at all, in what Foucault scathingly minimises as the "little polemical professional activities that are called critique".[27] According to Jean-François Lyotard, this shift was achieved not just by the exclusive promotion of the values of excellence and efficiency, but also by a combined process of technologisation and bureaucratisation.

It would be difficult to deny that the ethos of today's "faculties" is dominated by a positivist rather than a critical tenor. Both in its ("Higher") educational role and in its role in knowledge creation, the contemporary university promotes what it measures as "excellence", "efficiency" or "impact", largely through the (supposed) calculation, evaluation, management and optimisation of the quality and performance (or at least of the spectacle of quality and performance) of academic work: teaching, research and administration. Can we say, then, that these positivist paradigms have displaced or replaced "critique" and "dissensus" in the contemporary academy? Can their hegemony be seen to have supplanted some previous and comparable hegemony of the paradigm of (self-)critique? Surely it could be argued that "true" or "significant" self-critique can still lie at the heart of a given academic's work or at the heart of a given academic discipline or inter-disciplinary node? However one answers those questions, what seems clear beyond doubt is that there exists immense cognitive dissonance between Foucault's "critical attitude" on the one hand, and the governance and structuring of the university as it functions today, on the other.

The democratisation and indeed the "massification" of the academy and its expansion, partly through the integration of areas of endeavour that would heretofore have been considered to be non-academic such as "marketing", "patent development" or "event management", have significantly altered the way that universities relate to critique. Arguably, however, the proliferation of disciplines and faculties since Kant's time should give to foundational academic "self-critique" more rather than less of a role, and should lend more rather than less scope to the general dissensus or "conflict" between the various disciplines and faculties. In fact, however, two crucial factors of the contemporary Higher Education ethos play an even more important part in determining the place of

---

25 | Ibid., p. 47. Emphasis mine.

26 | Ibidem. Emphasis mine.

27 | Ibid., p. 42.

critique in the university of today. These are, first of all, the standardisation, modularisation, commodification and branding of a "student experience" that is often only marginally or inauthentically academic in nature (having more to do with consuming bite-sized packages of knowledge than with actually working, studying or thinking across and beyond limits). And secondly, the UK-led, comprehensive, managerialist and industrialist reconfiguration of academic labour.

The main question that arises in relation to the contemporary university paradigm is whether, in between two academic moments – that of what Foucault affectionately, if sceptically, terms the "high Kantian enterprise" and that of contemporary academic capitalism or entrepreneurialism – academic institutions really offered, for a time, a space propitious to critique and dissensus, rather than a locus of dressage and competition. Universities certainly were, and continue to be, spaces of individual intellectual competition and of the Ressentiment that such competition inevitably arouses. And although they were, and again continue to be, configured in the apparently durable double helix of transmission/conservation and invention/transcendence of knowledge (teaching and research), they were – up to the twentieth century at least – the preserve of small social elites. However, a major and steadily progressing expansion of Higher Education took place in the West over the century following World War I. Prior to that crescendo of massification, the university might have claimed a privileged relation to critical thinking, but those claims must now be regarded as somewhat delusional, given the entrenched, socially and culturally exclusive elitism of the institutions themselves, and just as importantly, given their implication in the subordination and exploitation of most of the planet by a handful of disunited European nation states and their united American and Soviet offshoots. Although the problems of social reproduction restricting access to Higher Education may not have been fully resolved, they are now acknowledged. Consequently, the academy's claim to critical thinking is now discredited for reasons other than social exclusiveness: namely, because of the incompatibility of that claim with the evaluation and self-evaluation of contemporary academic work principally, if not exclusively, in economic terms. In other words, the fact that the meaning and value of academic work is determined largely in relation to cash (student fee revenue, income from technology transfer, research funding, graduate employment etc), means that the *intrinsic academic value* of what is being performed, of what is being classified in extrinsic (economic) terms as excellent or efficient, is in many cases unexamined or even comprehensively emptied both of intrinsic, and of critical, meaning and value.[28]

Functioning as a space of (Higher) education or learning, the contemporary academy is embodied above all in the corporate university, which is distinguished by at least five fundamental characteristics. First of all, it is formatted as an industry or a business, in which a commodity, an output or a service, is traded by ever-proliferating institutions promoting competing brands of so-called Higher

---

28 | For a lucid critique of the notion of "excellence" as applied in relation to the work of universities, see Bill Readings, *The University in Ruins*, pp. 21–43.

Education. Higher Education may or may not have adopted the global franchise or the national consortium model, but in all cases it has donned the corporate structures associated with the promotion of branded outputs. In that sense, students are constructed as clients entitled – either as directly paying customers or as citizens whose tuition fees are either loaned to them or paid or subsidised for them by the state – to the purchased certification. Secondly, the commodity for which students pay tuition fees, often by contracting debts, is not just a branded qualification, however, but also a branded "experience" (hence, no doubt, its exorbitant cost). It is, indeed, as consumers of an "experience" that students are required to provide the university with feedback on their degree of client satisfaction. Their (sometimes only putatively or partially) academic experience, "captured" in the tautological tangles of reciprocal evaluation of instructors by students and of students by instructors, then feeds into the international competitive rankings of whole institutions in a continuous feedback loop. The third characteristic is the appearance of greater democratisation of Higher Education in certain respects (minimally selective mass admissions to third-level institutions, for example); this appearance is belied, however, by the very high costs of attending "top" institutions in an international context where, increasingly, a culture of student debt has resulted from the displacement of the costs and risks of "higher education" from the state to the individual. The fourth is the dominance of the circular and purely economic values of de-referentialised and competitive excellence, efficiency and performance as the core "values" driving the system. And the fifth and final trend is the increasing divergence of instruction and research, with 70% of instructors in US Higher Education institutions being employed outside the tenure-track positions guaranteeing research platforms.[29]

Universities might point to the dispensing of "modules in ethics" to undergraduates studying, for example, in university "faculties" or "schools" of pharmacology (in some cases re-named as Schools of "Drug development") as evidence of an ongoing investment in academic self-critique. However, the supposedly critical value of this provision can scarcely be seen as congruent with the message sent by the deeply embedded commercial interests often present within such schools: for example, endowed chairs of Translational Medicine financed by major drug companies. The chief commercial traction of contemporary universities is provided essentially by the so-called internationalisation of the student body, notably in the lucrative technology sector, most especially bio-tech-pharma and information technology. Irish Higher Education in the English language and in medical and information technology trades quite competitively, for example, across the globe, but principally in the cash-rich nexus formed largely by more or less opaque crypto-dictatorships located in South-East Asia and in the Persian Gulf states. It is difficult to imagine a role for self-critique in such unfree and patently commercial contexts and any such self-scrutiny on or around the home campus, within philosophy or human science or humanities or social sci-

---

29 | See G. M. Reevy & G. Deason, "Predictors of Depression, Stress and Anxiety among Non-Tenure Track Faculty" in: *Frontiers in Psychology*, 5:701, July 2014.

ence faculties, must surely, at the very least, be compromised or undermined by the arguably inglorious role played in the cash nexus by the corporate university as a whole.

Clearly, right across the contemporary academy, regardless of the specific disciplines under consideration, power, success and even legitimacy adhere to cash. There seems, indeed, to be no higher value than that of money for the corporate university. Excellence or productivity in research translates precisely, with no remainder, into cash funding or sponsorship just as educational excellence translates into cash tuition fees. Indeed, for philosopher Alisdair MacIntyre, author of an influential re-thinking of ethics, entitled *After Virtue*,[30] today's research universities are "wonderfully successful business corporations subsidised by tax exemptions and exhibiting all the acquisitive ambitions of such corporations".[31] MacIntyre notes that the contemporary university lacks the sense of an overarching, coherent *telos* like that prescribed by John Henry Newman for the National University of Ireland.[32] Archbishop Newman's explicitly theological "idea" of the university is based on the "teaching of universal knowledge". The word "teaching" is key here, for Newman, unlike Humboldt, regarded the university's mission as inhering not in what we call "research" today, but in the "diffusion and extension of knowledge rather than [its] advancement". Regardless of the (significant) distinctions that one can make between Kant's, Humboldt's and Newman's unifying "ideas of the university", it is clear that each of these ideas posits a single, shared enterprise. Today's university may not lack a common purpose, but it does lack – in MacIntyre's view – "any large sense of and concern for enquiry into the relationships between the disciplines".[33] In the new millennium, universities and most other academic institutions prioritise the entrepreneurial spirit of applied research and the lucrative competitive mining of intellectual property; they have, in this respect, definitively distanced themselves not just from the historical association with ivory towers and sylvan groves but also from Kant's priorities. Thus, behind the reconfiguration of dual-mandate (education/research) academic institutions towards ever-increasing and ever more (self-) vaunted and minutely benchmarked relevance, excellence and efficiency, and *in fine* towards ever greater directly economic instrumentalisation, a much more significant shift than a mere rejection of academic pastoral or indeed a move to greater, more equal access to, and tighter social integration of, the university, has taken place. Its anti-Kantian thrust can be seen in the contraction within the academy of self-reflexive critique and of dissensus. An eloquent illustration

30 | Alisdair MacIntyre, *After Virtue*, London/New York: Bloomsbury Academic 2013 (1st edition, Bristol Classical Press 1981).

31 | Alisdair MacIntyre, *God, Philosophy, Universities: A Selective History of the Catholic Philosophical Tradition*, New York: Rowman and Littlefield 2009, p. 174.

32 | John Henry Newman was the Rector of the Catholic University in Dublin and his magnum opus, *The Idea of the University*, was published in 1873.

33 | MacIntyre, *God, Philosophy, Universities*, p. 174.

of the anti-Humboldtian tenor of this epistemic shift is the major academic cur-
tailment of the dissensus associated with the speaking and study of non-global
or "less global" languages. A much more pervasive example of the overall devia-
tion is the transformation of universities into institutions run as a collection of
"Schools", the latter word underlining their regression towards the "scholastic"
or the primary/secondary levels of education in which "critique" plays a lesser
role. This regression is reinforced, not to say copper-fastened, by the replacement
of collegial self-governance by an infantilising managerialism, as a standardised
and streamlined, top-down structure operated by transmission belt replaces parliamentary debate and discussion. In this context, where the university is formatted as a uniform, even totalitarian discursive space, critique and dissensus will
be, at best, counter-cultural, at worst unimaginable.

Certainly, the potentially make-believe value of critique was already acknowledged in the so-called Frankfurt "School" of Critical Theory. As Theodor
Adorno's essay "Cultural Criticism and Society" shows, neither an "anti-exclu-
sionary assault" on elitist or High Culture, nor an apparently elitist assault on
mass culture (as the opiate that diverts the masses from their own alienation
and expropriation) can hold any real critical validity or efficacy. The critical exposure of culture as an inherently oppressive, manipulative and mendacious ideology can only function if culture has an "outside". Adorno had already foreseen,
in other words, a world in which there are no separate "vested interests" lying
behind culture:

> There are no more ideologies in the authentic sense of false consciousness,
> only advertisements for the world through its duplication and the provoca-
> tive lie which does not seek belief but commands silence.[34]

As Bill Readings puts it, cultural critique depends on the assumption that culture
is organised in terms of truth and falsehood rather than in terms of successful or
unsuccessful performance. Hence, when performance is apparently "all that there
is", "[r]ather than posing a threat, the analyses performed by Cultural Studies
risk providing new marketing opportunities for the system".[35] However reductive
that view may appear to be in relation to contemporary Cultural Studies, it seems
plausible to suggest that even the most theoretically sophisticated contemporary
academic critique can be recuperated for the contemporary academy's "provoca-
tive lies" of excellence and impact, which do indeed appear to command silence.
It is this sense of there being no real inside or outside (the Academy) because of
the latter's total absorption along with all other social and political institutions
within the global cash nexus, that makes it difficult to articulate a critique that
will register as critique, rather than being instantly translated into the dominant

---

34 | Adorno's article entitled "Cultural Criticism and Society" dates from the early
1940s and was later, in 1967, reprinted in his book, *Prisms*. For this quotation, see
Prisms, trans. Samuel M. Weber, Boston: MIT Press 1981, p. 34.

35 | Readings, *The University in Ruins*, p. 121.

currency of cash or credit. It is important, however, to understand exactly how the machinery of contemporary university operation disarms critique.

Consideration of the limiting effect on the academic role of "critique" of the structural packaging of education deliverables through the semesterisation and modularisation first devised in the US lies beyond the scope of this essay. However, the effect on critique of the managerialist tenor of UK-led "reform" is too significant to be omitted. Just before the global university rankings race, supposedly based on the competitive delivery of excellence, took hold across international academia, UK and UK-influenced universities moved under Thatcher and then Blair to impose on universities a programme of managerialist re-structuring, supposedly designed to maximise and optimise academic output. It is worth considering in detail exactly how these reforms have turned the academy, in line with other public institutions and organisations, into a space of standardisation and subjugation and how this *modus operandi* makes real critique and dissensus unlikely, if not impossible. It is obvious that Western academic institutions as well as individual academics have widely and irreversibly internalised Taylorist and Fordist managerial norms that spread globally on the winds of Anglo-American cultural dominance. And what is equally evident is the incompatibility of the latter "governmentality" with what Foucault defines as the "critical attitude".[36]

In some contexts, the Orwellian neo-liberal reform of the academy involved the renaming of "faculties" or "disciplines" as "colleges". These units were, and in many cases still are, headed by officers known as "Principals" and are in turn divided into various "schools" or "cost centres" and sub-schools or "sections". The "colleges" in question contradict their etymology, however: instead of consisting in a horizontal community of peers engaged in parliamentary-style self-governance, reformed Colleges of Arts, Human Sciences, Engineering etc, are bureaucracies run according to business plans rubber-stamped by executive committees, which are often led by appointed heads rather than by elected chairs. As is the case in all bureaucracies, the language of standardisation dominates, as education is delivered and coordinated in modules, partly controlled (by the clients to whom they are dispensed) via centralised and again, largely standardised, client satisfaction feedback overwhelmingly centred on module delivery technique. There is little place in such contexts for the ethos of the collegium, in the sense of bodies or communities of peers (students and scholars) thinking and talking together, listening and responding to, and learning with and from, debating and discussing. In some contexts, particularly in the US, direct contact with "students" has become so divergent from industrialised "research" outputting, that it is essentially entrusted to adjunct academics on precarious short-term or temporary contracts, a practice which further reduces the room for free inquiry or critique.

As Jean-François Lyotard recognised, wherever a culture of efficiency depends on a "say or do this, or else you'll never speak again, we are in the realm of terror

---

36 | Thomas Lemke, "The Birth of Biopolitics: Michel Foucault's Lectures at the Collège de France on Neo-Liberal Governmentality", in: *Economy and Society*, 30:2 (2001) pp. 190–207.

and the social bond has been destroyed".[37] In an article on the rule of administration in contemporary academe,[38] Richard Roberts argues that the modern-day Leviathan of Human Resource Management is indeed totalitarian and terrorising in tenor, requiring the total submission of all employees. The difficulty of engaging critically with the phenomenon is explained by Roberts in terms of its pervasiveness: it operates as a "totalising reality seemingly without boundaries or graspable externalities".[39] In other words, Human Resource Management (HRM) installs an "entire Lebenswelt", leaving no room for dissensus. One of the ways in which it preempts divergence is by extinguishing the idea of "any fundamental antagonism between capital and labour", assuming instead a "single common interest".[40] For Roberts, managerialism implies "a banal societal *Aufhebung*, a passing beyond social contradiction into a putatively higher form of existence".[41] It is this assumption of an absolute consensus that makes the power of HRM "seemingly unchallengeable".[42] Instead, submission is guaranteed and critique rendered impossible, as employees, including or even especially "knowledge workers", are transformed "from fully human status to commodified 'resource' [...] subject to sourcing, refining and to value-adding".[43] In universities, the two most effective "command and control" mechanisms, beyond promotion and tenure reviews, full economic costing exercises, performance management programmes, quality assessment and improvement reporting etc, are audits of so-called "research excellence" and of client enrollment and satisfaction. In the case of UK universities, these audits are organised by the state through the REF (Research Excellence Framework) and the NSS (National Student Survey). Again, as Roberts explicitly states, the "development of viable and realistic critiques of this form of social power is not simple or easy"[44] because one would have to decide first of all "[u]pon what basis might a fundamental critique be developed".[45]

---

37 | Lyotard, *The Postmodern Condition*, p. 46.

38 | "Contemplation and the Performative Absolute: Submission and Identity in Managerial Modernity", Richard H. Roberts *Journal of Management, Spirituality and Religion*, Vol. 9, no. 1, March 2012, pp. 9–29. While this essay quotes extensively from this article, two other studies have also examined the question with particular cogency: Bronwyn Davies & Peter Bansel, "Governmentality and Academic Work: Shaping the Hearts and Minds of Academic Workers", in: *Journal of Curriculum Theorizing*, 23: 2 (2010) and Rosemary Deem, Sam Hillyard and Michael Reed (eds), *Knowledge, Higher Education and the New Managerialism*, Oxford: Oxford University Press 2007.

39 | Roberts, p, 12.

40 | Ibid, p. 13.

41 | Ibidem.

42 | Ibid., p. 11.

43 | Ibid., p. 14.

44 | Ibid., p. 15.

45 | Ibid., p. 16.

Indeed, for Roberts, academia has regressed to a "quasi-theocracy", namely a "programme of submission, regulation and surveillance in which 'Supreme Leaders' – the executive class – command, and all others mediate and regulate intricate structures of supervision and conformity".[46] Roberts diagnoses not just the "diminution of responsible agency of academic staff in British higher education through a long and inexorable process of neo-soviet managerialisation" and an "attack upon and a reconfiguration of the [academic profession]", but also the fundamental "[a]brogation of the Kantian principle that each human being should be treated as an end in her or himself, and not simply as means to end".[47]

As described by Richard Roberts, the academy is no less a space of submission for the student than for the academic. In the contemporary university "repeated acts of submission become an essential part of the training of the self in both the work-place and the education that may precede it."[48] Crucially, the tropes of "quality" and of "excellence" "subvert [the] critical resistance"[49] not just of the professor or the tutor, but of the student as well: "[e]ducation has largely become knowledge transfer, training in competences, and facilitation of the capacity for receptivity and submission".[50] A very acute problem arises, however, when the tutor, lecturer or professor cannot "embody" or "model" critical freedom for the student, but is rather just as constrained as the latter. While there is a spectrum of possible responses to the academy's counterproductive empowerment of HRM, ranging from full compliance to full rejection (ie. exit), none are really compatible with the values of critique or dissensus, least of all those occupying the middle ground of self-deception or passive resistance. Czesław Miłosz has written of the self-deception known as "ketman",[51] while Richard Roberts evokes Jaroslav Hašek's *Good Soldier Schweik* and the eponymous Schweikism by which the "non-compliant subject" engages in "flawed obedience", " truculent dissociation" and "passive subversion".[52] However, Roberts has no real answer to the question as to how one might articulate a frontal "critique of this fundamentally unaccountable power", acknowledging instead that "[...] at this juncture we are confronted by some extremely difficult questions about the *status of the critic*, and of the *standpoint of any critique*."[53]

---

46 | Ibid. p.23.

47 | Ibid. p.16.

48 | Ibid., p.18.

49 | Ibid., p. 21.

50 | Ibidem.

51 | Czevlaw Milosz, *The Captive Mind*, London: Secker & Warburg 1953, p. 578.

52 | Roberts, p. 20.

53 | Ibid., p.23. Emphasis mine.

Critique and Dissensus: the Wider Political Stakes

In *The Postmodern Condition*, Lyotard explains that the role of the philosopher (critique) is quite distinct from that of the scholar (erudition) and from that of the expert (expertise).[54] For him, both erudition and expertise are antithetical to critique: instead, they "combine to prevent social critique, whether by defusing critical energies or by recuperating them so as to refine the functioning of the existing social order".[55] In Lyotard's view, the role of the philosopher, in contradistinction to that of the expert or the scholar, is precisely to play the part of somebody "who is not sure what it is that he [sic] does and does not know".[56] Like Socratic uncertainty, this fundamental, searching unsureness resounds as dissensus in what otherwise, according to Bill Readings, functions as a closed economy of knowledge. As Readings observes, the "capitalist logic of general substitutability (the cash-nexus) presumes that *all obligations are finite and expressible in financial terms*, capable of being turned into monetary values. This is the logic of the restricted or closed economy."[57]

The implications of a "closed economy" of knowledge are not just epistemological; they are also ethical, moral and political. Readings draws them out in an argument that leans towards the ethics of Emmanuel Levinas. While recognising the apparently mystical charge of the language of "incalculable obligation", "unknowable debt" or "non-finite responsibility toward the Other",[58] Readings insists that "[t]o believe that we know in advance what it means to be human, that humanity can be an object of cognition, is the first step to terror, since it renders it possible to know what is non-human, to know what it is to which we have no responsibility, what we can freely exploit"[59] (or annihilate). The link between cognition and terror is related to the connection between consensus and terror, and this connection is made perfectly clear by the way in which the French political thinker Jacques Rancière tries to distinguish the critical "we" of "political" dissensus (unstable and diffuse) from the (identitarian) terrorist "we" of "policing" and of "consensus". Readings for his part emphasises the diffuse, uncertain and unbounded character of the "we" of dissensus when he states that "the political as an instance of community is a sharing that does not establish an autonomous collective subject who is authorized to say 'we' and to terrorize those who do not, or cannot, speak in that 'we'".[60] And he goes on to posit that unstable "we" as the

---

54 | Lyotard as quoted in: Readings, *The University in Ruins*, p. 221.

55 | Ibid., p. 221, n. 1.

56 | Lyotard, quoted in Readings, *The University in Ruins*, p. 220.

57 | Readings, p. 188. Emphasis mine.

58 | Ibid., p. 188.

59 | Ibid., p. 189.

60 | Ibid., p. 188.

basis of a community that he describes in terms of the "uncertain experience of being together that no authoritative instance can determine".[61]

Considered in this light, the distinction between critique and dissensus comes into clearer focus. Whereas critique may have, as Foucault recognises, an interest in discovering and correcting *error*, the opening of dissensus (or the absence of such an opening) is perhaps a better indicator of the relative tolerance of a given community, society or academy for *terror*. The characteristic closure of cognition, a closure in which critique is surely complicit to a degree, albeit dialectically, is quite foreign to dissensus. Dissensus is marked, indeed, by a lack of the transitivity, reactivity and negativity that we might associate with criticism, and even with critique or self-critique. But there is more to the distinction than that. As Readings puts it: "thinking together is a dissensual process; it belongs to dialogism rather than dialogue".[62] This means that, unlike critique, dissensus is not necessarily dialectical nor is it even, necessarily, responsive: not only does dissensus not (necessarily) emerge, like criticism, as a reaction to something else (some action, value, discourse, proposition, position, etc.), but it can arise spontaneously, non-dialectically. And it can do so within, beside or at an angle to a given situation or discursive context. Moreover, whereas criticism or critique can be enunciated from outside or from inside a given institutional or discursive situation, dissensus has no location as such; rather it draws the outside in and the inside out. Most crucially, critique is an intentional move, whereas dissensus can emerge in a much more aleatory or random manner, as a result of actions as well as reactions, and indeed, where its production is not necessarily volitional.

Critique and Dissensus

As we have already seen, there is a strong tradition of thinking from Plato right through Kant, Humboldt, Newman, Harold Bloom, Lyotard, and up to the present day, that situates the role of the academy, particularly of the university, and especially the role of the academic philosopher or of the humanities thinker within the University, in relation to politics. For Michel Foucault, as we have seen, critique is first and foremost a way of resisting blind or blanket submission to (self-)government or governance. He stresses that it developed historically from a relation with ecclesiastical rule, imposed via the "direction of conscience" and the "relationship of obedience".[63] So, while recognising in critique "[a] kind of general cultural form, *both a political and moral attitude*, a way of thinking"[64] and even, as we saw at the start of this essay, as "virtue", Foucault does link it quite specifically with a questioning or challenging relationship to the legitimacy

---

61 | Ibidem.

62 | Ibid., p. 192.

63 | Foucault, "What is Critique?", p. 45.

64 | Ibidem. Emphasis mine.

or authority of government, and thereby with power and politics. The switching off of radical, foundational, constitutive (self-)critique inside the contemporary university could be seen as mirroring certain social and political trends outside the academy. However, rather than simply mirroring or mimicking wider social bonds, the university might have been, or might still be, regarded as a different order of institution: as a prime institutional locus of critique, intellectual dissent and even conflict (as in the "Conflict of the Faculties"). If it is perceived as functioning as a space of critical freedom, in which the exercise of critical reason has been, at least since Kant, not just legitimate, but constitutionally enshrined, then any closing of this space, or any consequential shrinkage or annulment of the (self-) critical function of thinking within this space will have deep and wide implications for the entire *res publica*.

Outside the institution of the university, in the wider world, certain contemporary thinkers have noted a general contraction of dissensus, a development that has been linked to globalisation and to the traction gained thereby for a totalising economic model that has supplanted most other political or social paradigms, formats and languages. The preeminence of this replicant idiom across all manner of institutions, organisations, professions, cultures and languages (hospitals, schools, universities, churches, private companies, parliaments) confirms the idea that the academy is no longer (conceived as) a space apart. Rather it is can be seen as serving the same values, applying the same standards, following the same formats, conforming to the same benchmarks (or "key performance indicators") as the wider social world.

Bill Readings has argued that "the disappearance of 'the political', which Lyotard calls 'depoliticisation', does not mean an end of politics, but rather an end to 'big politics': that is, an end to the positioning of the political sphere as the site where the question of *being together* is to be solely raised and exhaustively answered".[65] In his *The University in Ruins*, Readings argues that the university is the principal space where the meaning of *"thinking together"* can be, should be, and is being, thought about. And Readings believes that "thinking together" necessarily involves dissensus. In this, he echoes the thought of Jacques Rancière. Rancière has written several studies on the politics of literature and of education, as well as on politics in general, but his major contribution has been an analysis of the state of democracy in the contemporary world. For him, democracy has been, since Plato, the object of (intellectual) hostility. However, he suggests that today, politics itself is increasingly being dispensed with, and is being replaced instead by the triple logic of policing, administration and economics.

Rancière proclaims that the very essence of politics is dissent or "dissensus", which he defines as the encounter between different, co-existing worlds.[66]

---

65 | Bill Readings, *The University in Ruins*, p. 219, n. 16.

66 | Jacques Rancière, *Aux bords du politique*, Paris: La Fabrique 1998, p. 241: "L'essence de la politique est la manifestation du dissensus, comme présence de deux mondes en un seul." This book is translated as *On the Shores of Politics*, trans. Liz Heron, London: Verso 1995.

His writings on politics are entirely based, in fact, on the value of dissensus. Indeed, Steven Corcoran's collection of Rancière's shorter texts, which he has edited, introduced and himself translated, is entitled *Dissensus: On Politics and Aesthetics*.[67] What is particularly important about Rancière's notion of dissensus is that it is not merely a matter of disagreement, but a matter of the disruption of the power relations and arrangements of a certain social order. For him, consensus is not peaceful discussion and rational agreement as opposed to violence and conflict. And he defines dissensus very broadly as the disruption of the *self-evident reasonableness, or naturalness of any given order*; it is the interruption and thereby the exposure of what he terms "le partage du sensible", which is the perceptual and conceptual framework or grid that purports to make sense of the world, classifying it, dividing it up and ordering it in a certain way.

In *Chroniques des temps consensuels*,[68] Rancière notes that we are living in a time of consensus in which there is general agreement that there is *no reasonable alternative* to the way in which things are currently perceived, understood or made sense of. He argues that "[t]he consensus holding sway over us today is a machine of power insofar as it is a machine of vision" and he goes on to identify the two principal messages of that machine: "one maintains that we have at last come to live in times of peace, and the other states *the condition of that peace – the recognition that there is no more than there is*".[69] Rancière's word for this reductive, ironic totalitarianism is consensus, which he defines as follows: "Consensus as a mode of government says, it is perfectly fine for people to have different interests, values and aspirations, nevertheless there is one unique reality to which everything must be related, a reality that is experience-able as a sense datum and which has only one possible signification".[70] As well as acting as a prevailing blanket of doubt-suffocating certainty and inevitablity, consensus reduces the "people" to the sum of the various parts of the social body, just as it also reduces political community to the various interests and aspirations characterising the different social segments or modules.

How does Rancière explain the manner in which consensus cancels politics and in which dissensus defines it? What does he mean by arguing that the "essence of politics" is dissensus and that "consensus is the reduction of politics to policing/policy" (the word "police" in French means both policing and also policy)?[71] For Rancière, society is heterogeneous. If it is in myriad ways dif-

---

67 | Jacques Rancière, *Dissensus: On Politics and Aesthetics*, ed. Steven Corcoran, London: Continuum 2010.

68 | Jacques Rancière, *Chroniques des temps consensuels*, Paris: Seuil 2005; *Chronicles of Consensual Times*, trans. Steven Corcoran, London/New York: Continuum 2010.

69 | Rancière, *Chronicles*, p. viii.

70 | Rancière, *Dissensus*, p.44.

71 | Rancière, *Aux bords du politique*, p.252: "Le consensus est la réduction de la politique à la police". The police state, he argues (*Dissensus*, p. 107), is based on a "community of fear".

ferent, and even unequal, to and within itself, it is so by virtue of its ability to create and to recognise distinctions; and dissensus is the manifestation of these differences and divergences. He explains dissensus as the opening up of a space, a gap or a crack, separating what can be perceived or felt or understood or made sense of, from itself. It shows that things are *not* (just) what they are; that there *is* more than there is, or than there appears to be. This excess is made manifest, for example, in linguistic translation. The "messsage" of apparent equivalence associated with translation is akin to that of consensus in that both of these 'optics' cancel or deny the "excess of subjectivity" or the "remainder of meaning" that dissensus produces by creating or recognising distinctions, for example, the distinction between "critique" and "criticism", an excess that translation produces by revealing its own impossibility.

Rancière does not accept that our so-called globalised and decentred world of migrancy and of nomadic knowledge workers carries within itself the possibility of equality. Instead, he argues, the de-centred power of capital, of wealth or property and government are just as mutually reinforcing as they ever were, just as united in a "single and identical expert management of cash and population flows" ["seule et même gestion savante des flux d'argent et de populations"].[72] Expertise and management are self-evidently pejorative terms in his vision of the obstacles to real equality: (supra-)state power and the power of capital both continue to deploy expertise and managerialism in order to reduce, if not annihilate, the space of the political. If, however, Rancière defines politics as dissensus, he sees democracy as inhering in action: it is, more specifically, the double action that ceaselessly tears away from oligarchic governments their monopoly on public life, and from the rich, their total power over human lives ["Elle est l'action qui sans cesse arrache aux gouvernements oligarchiques le monopole de la vie publique et à la richesse la toute-puissance sur les vies"].[73] Democracy, he reminds us, "is neither that form of government that allows oligarchies to rule in the name of the people, nor is it that form of society ruled by the power of the market."[74] He thus distinguishes democracy, not merely from contingencies of birth, or inheritance, but also from contingencies of the market.[75]

Bill Readings, in locating the phoenix-like future of the university in dissensus, underlines the relevance of this concept for the contemporary academy. Readings states that "a distinction must be drawn between the political horizon of consensus that aims at a self-legitimating, autonomous society and the heteronomous horizon of dissensus".[76] To explain the difference between the two, he

---

72 | Jacques Rancière, *La Haine de la démocratie*, Paris: La Fabrique 2005, p. 104.

73 | Ibid., p. 105.

74 | Ibidem. "La démocratie n'est ni cette forme de gouvernement qui permet à l'oligarchie de régner au nom du peuple, ni cette forme de société que règle le pouvoir de la marchandise."

75 | Rancière, *Aux bords du politique*, p. 31.

76 | Bill Readings, *The University in Ruins*, p. 187.

argues that "[i]n the horizon of dissensus, no consensual answer can take away the question mark of the social bond" which inheres in the simple fact of other people and in the necessity of language [...] no universal community can embody the answer; no rational consensus can decide simply to agree on an answer [...] Thought can only do justice to heterogeneity if it does not aim at consensus".[77] The value of dissensus and that of consensus relate to the academy not as a bounded space of knowledge transmission or transcendence (whether we think of sylvan groves, secret gardens, ivory towers or silos), but as a meta-society or community. And in this connection the thinking of Jean-Luc Nancy is particularly instructive. For Nancy, author of an influential work entitled *La Communauté désoeuvrée*,[78] any attempt to design a specific kind of society according to a prescriptive or pre-planned programme will inevitably result in violence or even terror. Nancy's central thesis in this book is that community cannot be dictated into existence; it is not a product and does not arise out of a process of production or engineering, whether social or economic or political. The word "désoeuvrée" in Nancy's title distances the notion of community from that of product, art or artifice. Community is not a product, work or "oeuvre", as such. Like dissensus, it cannot be planned or programmed. No reform, no change management, no rational choice can bring them about. Both Jean-Luc Nancy's thinking on community and Rancière's work on dissensus resonate clearly in Bill Readings's comments on the university of dissensus: "dissensus cannot be institutionalised. The precondition for such institutionalisation would be a second-order consensus that dissensus is a good thing, something, indeed, with which Habermas would be in accord".[79]

Rancière's reflection on the question of equality in relation to education is an integral part of his overarching concern with the dangers posed for equality by the contemporary shrinkage of the political and the attack on democracy. The title of his principal work on education, *Le Maître ignorant*,[80] is an apparent oxymoron; it cancels the aura of mastery and knowledge surrounding the teacher or (school)master. By casting the "master" as "unknowing", Rancière's title indicates the latter's lack of superior knowledge in relation to his pupils. It suggests a certain intellectual equality between master and apprentice; for that equality to be realised, however, the domination of the master must be neutralised, a move underlined, indeed, by the subtitle of the book: "Five Lessons on Intellectual Emancipation". It is not possible to explore fully in this essay the nature of the educational and intellectual relation envisaged by Rancière between master and pupil, beyond pointing out that it is based, not on the teacher's superior knowledge, but rather on his or her "unknowing-ness". This view of education is one

---

77 | Ibidem. Readings devotes a whole chapter (Chapter 3) to "The University of Dissensus".

78 | Jean-Luc Nancy, *La Communauté désœuvrée*, Paris: Christian Bourgois 1986.

79 | Readings, *The University in Ruins*, p.167.

80 | Jacques Rancière, *Le Maître ignorant: cinq leçons d'émancipation intellectuelle*, Paris: Arthème Fayard 1987; *The Ignorant Schoolmaster: Five Lessons in Intellectual Emancipation*, trans. Kristin Ross, Stanford: Stanford University Press 1991.

that Wilhelm von Humboldt had placed at the centre of his idea of the research university. "Just as primary instruction makes the teacher possible, so he [sic] renders himself dispensable through schooling at the secondary level. The university teacher is thus no longer a teacher and the student is no longer a pupil. Instead the student conducts research on his [sic] own behalf and the professor supervises his [sic] research and supports him [sic] in it".[81]

Rancière is well aware that the bi-laterally emancipatory tenor of this relationship is threatened by the status of schools in the new post-political dispensation. Whereas, prior to the onset of our self-proclaimed "post-political" age, education was separate from economics and production, the contemporary "skholè" is, from Rancière's point of view, an integral part of economic striving; it is directly and fully incorporated into the closed economy of knowledge, as the prevalence of the contemporary mantra "the knowledge economy" makes perfectly clear. For Rancière, it is precisely its "separation from productive life" ("la séparation avec la vie productive") that makes education egalitarian.[82]

Critique versus Dissensus: Enter Ressentiment

What is particularly striking in Jacques Rancière's work on equality and democracy is the fact that he avoids all mention of critique. Quite unlike Adorno, he does not present negation in a positive or emancipatory light. For Adorno "awareness that an object might be otherwise than it is constitutes the emancipatory core of linguistic (and other forms of) expression".[83] Moroever, for him, "knowledge does not consist in mere perception, classifcation and calculation but precisely in the determining negation of whatever is directly at hand"; and this "determinative negation of the immediacy of the status quo [...] introduces a speculative dimension into the contemplation of the existent".[84] Although Rancière's dissensus similarly questions the given "partition du sensible", it has none of the critical force of Adorno's determinative negation. Moreover, unlike Foucault, Rancière does not consider critique as a valid or effective countering of the threats, violence and reductions of consensus.[85] Instead, he emphasises the value of action;

---

81 | This reference to Humboldt's thought is taken from Chris Clark, *Iron Kingdom: the Rise and Downfall of Prussia 1600–1947*, London: Penguin 2006, p. 333.

82 | Rancière, *Aux bords du politique*, pp. 100–01.

83 | Adorno and Horkheimer, *Dialectic of Enlightenment: Philosophical Fragments*, Stanford CA: Stanford University Press 2002, p. 39.

84 | Ibidem.

85 | "L'essence de la politique réside dans les modes de subjectivation dissensuels qui manifestent la différence de la société à elle-même. L'essence du consensus n'est pas la discussion pacifique et l'accord raisonnable opposés au conflit et à la violence. L'essence du consensus est l'annulation du dissensus comme écart du sensible à lui-même, l'annulation des sujets excédentaires, la réduction du peuple à la somme des parties du

he foregrounds "singular and precarious acts", ways of being, of relating, of living: "[t]he equal society is simply the entirety of egalitarian relations that are formed in the here and now through unique, precarious actions" ["La société égale n'est que l'ensemble des relations égalitaires qui se tracent ici et maintenant à travers des actes singuliers et précaires"].[86] Neither democracy nor equality is founded, according to Rancière, on any particular institutional form or on any specific historical necessity : instead, "it is entrusted exclusively to the constancy of its own actions" ["elle n'est confiée qu'à la constance de ses propres actes"]. In the context of the academy, it is perhaps by circumventing or "ignoring" the planned, standardised, pre-scripted uniformity of formatting, language, idiom that removes agency and responsibility, that academics can create dissensus through the constancy of their own, owned, "singular and precarious" actions.

Why does the author of *Le Maître ignorant* seem to lean so far away from critique, in his approach both to education and to politics? There is an obvious link between Rancière's abjuration of the hierarchical relation between master and pupil on the one hand, and his apparent suspicion or even rejection of critique as a foundational intellectual attitude on the other. This link can be seen with particular clarity in his explicit comments on Ressentiment and *a fortiori* on "Ressentiment criticism". For this thinker of radical equality, every conflict of ideas is at the same time a battle of feeling, affect or emotion. And Ressentiment is the dominant affect characterising the (usually affronted) sense of superiority informing not just anti-democratic thinking (and the Ressentiment associated with it), but to a certain extent, critique *per se*:

> Every intellectual battle is a battle of perceived worlds and therefore a battle of affects. One of the dominant affects of the hatred of democracy is, for example, ressentiment. It is obvious that an entire generation whose hopes for radical change have been frustrated cannot stop ruminating on its ressentiment, constantly stoking up this apocalyptic vision of a society peopled by petty individuals who can think of nothing but consuming Coca Cola and buying Nike shoes and who are thereby threatening the grandiose visions of the future that they were supposed to bear. This vision is marked by a deep gloom. And that gloom – and this is more or less the lesson of the *Ignorant Schoolteacher* – is peculiar to those who think themselves superior. But I am not really concerned here with affects in themselves: what I am trying to do is, rather, to articulate questions of affect with basic political choices, the choice of inequality or equality.[87]

---

corps social et de la communauté politique aux rapports d'intérêts et d'aspirations de ces différentes parties", Rancière, *Aux bords du politique*, p. 251–2.

86 | Rancière, *Haine de la démocratie*, p.106, *passim*.

87 | Rancière, *Haine de la démocratie*, "Toute bataille des idées est en même temps une bataille des mondes perçus et donc une bataille des affects. Un des affects dominants de cette haine de la démocratie c'est, par exemple, le ressentiment. On voit bien comment toute une génération qui a été frustrée dans ses espérances de transformation radicale n'en finit pas de ruminer son ressentiment en entretenant cette vision apocalyptique

Rancière recognises that democracy was – from its very coining – a target for political hostility: "[i]t was to begin with a term of abuse invented in Ancient Greece by those who equated unnameable government by the multitude with the complete ruination of legitimate order".[88] Indeed, it was treated as an abomination by all those "who thought that power belonged by right to those destined for it by their birth or called to it by their abilities" ['qui pensaient que le pouvoir revenait de droit à ceux qui y étaient destinés par leur naissance ou appelés par leurs compétences"].[89] All of Rancière's writings on democracy counter this false premise that power and government should be based on birthright, wealth or on *putatively superior merit or ability*.

Rancière quite specifically distinguishes between two forms of critique of democracy. He cites the American constitution as the first form of critique, arguing that it constitutes a compromise aimed at protecting two principles of superiority, intellectual and material: "government by the best and the order of property". The other form of critique seeks to distinguish, as Karl Marx did, between true and false democracy. Rancière may not explicitly say so, but it is clear that, for him, both critiques are rational, intellectual moves that are nonetheless indissociably linked (as Rancière says of all battles of ideas) to emotion, in this case to the affect of Ressentiment. Again, however, what is important in Rancière's thought is the fact that far from limiting his rejection of critique to the extreme of "Ressentiment criticism", he distances himself from critique per se as a means of upholding equality and of defending or realising democracy.

There is no denying the inherently reactive, or even the borderline negative, direction of critique, regardless of its object or context. Indeed, despite the fact that he identifies it as a moral attitude and even as "virtue", Michel Foucault fully acknowledges its reactive cast in "What is Critique":

> After all, critique only exists in relation to something other than itself: it is an instrument, a means for a future or a truth that it will not know nor happen to be, it oversees a domain it would want to police and is unable to regulate. All this means that it is a function which is subordinated in

---

d'une société peuplée de petits individus ne pensant qu'à consommer du coca et des Nike et qui mettent en péril les grandes visions d'avenir dont ils étaient porteurs. Cette vision est marquée par une morosité fondamentale. Celle-ci — c'est un peu la leçon du *Maître ignorant* — est le propre de ceux qui se pensent supérieurs. Mais ma question ne porte pas directement sur les affects pour eux-mêmes : ce que j'essaye de faire, c'est d'articuler les questions affectives aux grands choix politiques, ceux de l'inégalité et de l'égalité," pp. 9–10.

88 | "Il a d'abord été une insulte inventée, dans la Grèce antique, par ceux qui voyaient la ruine de tout ordre légitime dans l'innommable gouvernement de la multitude.", Rancière, *Haine de la démocratie*, p. 7.

89 | Ibid., p. 8.

relation to what philosophy, science, politics, ethics, law, literature etc. positively constitute.[90]

It is worth reviewing in some detail the terms of Foucault's definition. Critique is, according to him, a secondary, inherently subordinate activity, since it "only exists in relation to something other than itself". Not only does it depend on the prior existence of its object, but it is a wholly tentative operation, ignorant of its outcome. It is a straining towards a "future or a truth" that cannot be known in advance. Critique thus operates not just in ignorance of its actual ends, but also in a certain impotence and even thwarted capability: "it oversees a domain it would *want to police and is unable to regulate.*" We note how Foucault locates critique in a frustrated or at least impossible desire for authority and indeed in incapacity or impotence. He further distinguishes it from academic disciplines such as "law", "philosophy" and "science", identifying it instead as a mobile "function" that is subordinated not only to the discursive domains of those disciplines but also to the similarly, "positively constituted" domains of politics, ethics and poetics.

Not only is critique an inherently subordinate move because it is negatively constituted, but it is also a floating function marked by lack: it has no positive constitutional foundation and possesses no defined object or end of its own. While this free-floating quality could be construed positively as an openness and freedom of action, its reactive basis does imprint upon it a constitutive dependency or secondariness which, along with the aforenoted connotations of impotence, bring it close to, or right into, the emotional territory of Ressentiment. As Nietzsche describes it, Ressentiment is marked by reactivity, secondarity and impotence. Instead of gaining expression in actions or deeds, it constitutes a purely reactive disposition which only attains to action insofar as it founds a "transvaluation" or indeed an inversion, of positive values or virtues. Thus, in the "slave revolt" associated with Christianity, the goods, positions, properties, qualities etc. esteemed, desired and possessed by those marked as "superior" are rejected by those who are deprived of, or excluded from, them. The latter disparage those goods, qualities or virtues, not just emotionally, but also intellectually.

The question that immediately arises in the present study in relation to Ressentiment is as follows: given the difficulty of disentangling struggles of affect from struggles of ideas, when can one be entirely sure that critique is not in fact underwritten by Ressentiment, and if/when it is so underwritten, is the critique thereby entirely vitiated? It was Max Scheler who developed the idea of "Ressentiment criticism".[91] At first sight, this concept appears almost tautological. One wonders, in other words, to what extent the terms "criticism" and "Ressentiment" refer to one and the same thing. In intellectual life or the life of the mind in general, Ressentiment is often clearly very clearly and very busily at work. It comes to the fore in the envy of creativity felt towards the artist by the

---

90 | Foucault, "What is Critique?", p. 42, *passim.*

91 | Max Scheler, *Ressentiment*, p. 51.

critic; in the envy of the verbal power of the critic by the creative artist; in the envy of academic's credentials by the maverick intellectual or journalist; in the envy of the academic for the journalist's greater public appeal and impact.

It would seem, however, that, while all criticism is not informed by Ressentiment, Ressentiment always involves criticism and, as Max Scheler's work shows, "Ressentiment criticism" demonstrates a particular, excacerbated reactivity and negativity. Scheler dwells in particular on the place of envy in the emotional complex of Ressentiment, noting that the envy that gives rise to Ressentiment often involves a sense of injustice based on frustrated entitlement. In other words, Ressentiment, which arises from a feeling of unfairly thwarted entitlement, finds an outlet in the angry diminishment of the object of envy. What makes Ressentiment problematic is not, however, the emotional tangle itself, but rather the repression of emotion and its channeling instead into poor intellectual judgment. For the way in which the volatile emotional state of envy-frustration-resentment is stabilised is by an intellectual operation through which the object of envy is re-interpreted as being, in reality, unworthy of that sentiment. At some level, the subject is not entirely deluded by this sleight of hand. Clearly, a certain self-deception or even a certain reasoning *error* is implicit in the "transvaluation"; after all, the worth of the values in question has not been assessed in its own right, but is rather distorted by being envisaged exclusively in terms of the subject's relation or situation in respect of those (reductive binary) values: possession or deprivation, winning or losing, strength or weakness, success or failure.

It is as a secret pathology of impotent vengefulness that Nietzsche discredits Ressentiment. He links its dark, self-deceiving twistedness to prolonged brooding or "gloomy" (the term that Rancière uses) inaction. Scheler too highlights the importance of the static dimension of the emotion. The impossibility of change, the "continual" or repeated "reliving" of the envy/resentment and the lack of hope all reinforce the impotence that is so characteristic of Ressentiment: "[...] ressentiment is the *repeated experiencing and reliving* of a particular emotional response reaction against someone else".[92] Indeed the importance of duration is further emphasised when Scheler notes that "revenge tends to be transformed into ressentiment the more it is directed against *lasting situations* which are felt to be "injurious" but beyond one's control – in other words, the more the injury is experienced as a destiny."[93]

For Scheler, resolutely and openly unequal societies such as caste systems are not as prone to spawning Ressentiment as those in which there is a legitimate hope or even an expectation of equality, which is, however, disappointed or thwarted. As Scheler puts it, although inequality is the breeding ground for Ressentiment, conditions are perfect when *de jure* equality is contradicted by *de facto* inequality. For in that situation, since the battle of principle has already been fought and won, the inequality will seem all the more impossible to right

---

92 | Ibid., p. 39. Emphasis mine.

93 | Ibid., p. 50.

and the victim's sense of powerlessness is proportionately increased. In a further reflection on the link between Ressentiment and felt powerlessness or impotence, Scheler observes that any (political) change of regime will inevitably inspire "a remnant of absolute opposition against the values of the new ruling group. This opposition is spent in Ressentiment the more the losing group feels unable to return to power. This is why the 'retired official' is a 'typical ressentiment figure".[94] In other words, Ressentiment is often caused by a loss of (proximity to) power and is particularly favoured when there is no perceived possibility of a "return to power".

The contemporary academy is an integral part of the post-historical, post-political world-view described by many thinkers including historian Tony Judt,[95] but also Jacques Rancière, as problematically and paralysingly predominant today. For those who adopt this perspective, there are no alternatives to "what is", or there is at least a belief that "what is, is *all* there is".[96] This sense of inevitability produces an effect or affect of impotence that can only be magnified by the fact that in all situations of inequality that are perceived as overpoweringly inevitable or entrenched, as, for example, when the state involves itself or even directs academic (self-) command and control exercises such as the UK's REF and NSS, any expression of reactive affect, such as resentment, will be regarded as futile. The failure or blockage of the discharge allowed by action or expression can only heighten the sense of impotence associated with Ressentiment. This point is crucial for the current academic setting where "parliamentary" debate and deliberation have been replaced by transmission (usually by email) of information about top-down decisions and other *faits accomplis*.[97]

It is the sense of impotence, of passive inaction, of repressed rather than expressed feeling, so crucial to the timbre of Ressentiment, that resonates, then, in "Ressentiment criticism". Like all criticism (and critique), "Ressentiment criticism" is reactive, secondary, parasitical, subordinate to that to which it reacts. But while not all criticism or critique is necessarily (purely) negative, "Ressentiment criticism" is inherently more negative insofar as it has no positive end in view. In fact, not only does it have no positive end in view, but it would appear to have no end or purpose whatsoever aforethought. Its negativity seems, indeed, to be entirely without purpose: it is, so to speak, constitutionally anti-teleological:

---

94 | Ibid., p. 64.

95 | Tony Judt, *Ill Fares the Land*, New York: Penguin, 2011.

96 | Rancière, *Chronicles*, p. x. See also Rancière, *Haine de la démocratie*, p.94.

97 | Scheler, *Ressentiment*, p. 68: "[Therefore] parliamentary institutions, even when they harm the public interest by hampering legislation and administration, are highly important as discharge mechanisms for mass and group emotions. Similarly, criminal justice (which purges from revenge), the duel, and in some measure even the press— though it often spreads ressentiment instead of diminishing it by the public expression of opinions. If the affects are thus discharged, they are prevented from turning into that psychical dynamite which is called ressentiment".

The more a permanent social pressure is felt to be a "fatality," the less it can free forces for the *practical transformation* of these conditions, and the more it will lead to *indiscriminate criticism without any positive aims.* This peculiar kind of "ressentiment criticism" is *characterized by the fact that improvements in the conditions criticized cause no satisfaction,* — they merely cause discontent, for they destroy the growing pleasure afforded by invective and negation. *Many modern political parties will be extremely annoyed by a partial satisfaction of their demands or by the constructive participation of their representatives in public life, for such participation mars the delight of oppositionism.*[98]

However, the main reason why Scheler's "Ressentiment criticism" pushes criticism *per se* to its negative limit is not so much because it is – inevitably – futile or aimless, as because of its supremely bad faith in *actively desiring* the lack of an issue in terms of a positive outcome.

It is peculiar to "ressentiment criticism" that it does not seriously desire that its demands be fulfilled. It does not want to cure the evil: the evil is merely a pretext for the criticism. We all know certain representatives in our parliaments whose criticism is absolute and uninhibited, precisely because they count on never being ministers. Only when this *aversion from power (in contrast with the will to power)* becomes a permanent trait, is criticism moved by ressentiment. Conversely, it is an old experience that the political criticism of a party loses its pungency when this party becomes positively associated with the authority of the state.[99]

Scheler provides a very clear answer to the question raised at the start of this section: namely the question of the axiomatic link between Ressentiment and criticism:

To a lesser degree, a secret ressentiment underlies every way of thinking which attributes creative power to mere negation and criticism. Thus modern philosophy is deeply penetrated by a whole type of thinking which is nourished by ressentiment. I am referring to the view that the "true" and the "given" is not that which is self-evident, but rather that which is "indubitable" or "incontestable," which can be maintained against doubt and criticism.[100]

In this blanket criticism of "modern philosophy", Scheler suggests that Ressentiment inevitably underlies any type of thinking that overvalues "mere negation and criticism", attributing to it a "creative power". However, his diagnosis of the limitations of "Ressentiment criticism" goes much further, in that he argues that the emotional denial that is part of Ressentiment results in a serious distortion or incapacitation of intellectual judgment: Scheler describes this phenomenon as

---

98 | Ibid., p. 51. Emphasis mine.

99 | Ibid., pp. 51–2. Emphasis mine.

100 | Ibid., p. 67.

the indiscriminate, unfounded, irrational extrapolation of Ressentiment-founded criticism to objects that are not assessed rationally in themselves, but only by association (analogical or contrastive) with others.[101] He stresses, then, the indiscriminate and often purely metonymic nature of judgements associated with Ressentiment, highlighting also their absolutist tenor. He shows how this "general" negativism is linked to a serious rational deficit. The Ressentiment critic's judgment is likely to be deeply flawed due to a *lack of real consideration of things in themselves*; due, that is, to a prejudicial lack of "real contact with the world". This indirect focus and inadequate consideration of things "for themselves" leads not just to extreme, but also to unreasoned or unfounded evaluations:

> Whenever convictions are not arrived at by direct contact with the world and the objects themselves, but indirectly through a critique of the opinions of others, the processes of thinking are impregnated with ressentiment. The establishment of "criteria" for testing the correctness of opinions then becomes the most important task. Genuine and fruitful criticism judges all opinions with reference to he object itself. Ressentiment criticism, on the contrary, accepts no "object" that has not stood the test of criticism. In a different sense, ressentiment is always to some degree a determinant of the romantic type of mind. [...] The formal structure of ressentiment expression is always the same: A is affirmed, valued, and praised not for its own intrinsic quality, but with the unverbalized intention of denying, devaluating, and denigrating B. A is "played off" against B. I said that there is a particularly violent tension when revenge, hatred, envy, and their effects are coupled with impotence."[102]

In pointing out the systematic and derivative nature of the values of "ressentiment criticism", Scheler further emphasises that they are values by comparison or association only. They are arbitrary extrapolations, mere proxies, and he thus stigmatises the lack of independence and of authenticity of judgment that leads to their formation and defence.

Scheler's comments on the figure of the apostate further develop his thinking on the delusions and self-deception of Ressentiment. Rather than being "primarily committed to the positive contents of his [new] belief", the apostate remains motivated by the "struggle against the old belief", living "only for its negation".[103] Clearly, then, "Ressentiment criticism" is distinguished from non-Ressentiment criticism, and even more so from what one might prefer to term "critique" rather than "criticism", by its greater, if not extreme, negativity; that is, by its greater, if not blanket reactivity and by its general wrongness.

---

101 | Ibid., p. 70: "When the repression is complete, the result is a general negativism—a sudden, violent, seemingly unsystematic and unfounded rejection of things, situations, or natural objects whose loose connection with the original cause of the hatred can only be discovered by a complicated analysis."

102 | Ibid., pp. 67–8.

103 | Ibid., p. 66.

Instead of considering directly and rationally the intrinsic worth of certain values or properties, Ressentiment criticism is so overpowered by the emotion of envy founded on lack that its critical *ratio* is multiply vitiated.

It would appear that the contemporary university envisions itself and is also envisioned by the state as having superseded or transcended the realm of, or the need for, (self-)critique as its guiding principle. What, then, of those who persist in such critique, who dissent from this consensus, criticising the current form or format of the academy? Are they not inevitably seen as being motivated primarily by Ressentiment? In such a view, Ressentiment would be, for example, an anti-democratic reaction in the face of the increased democratisation of the university. This seems to be one of the views that Jacques Rancière is suggesting in his book, *Le Maître ignorant*. The Ressentiment studied by Rancière is indeed attributed to those who "think themselves above others." On one side, he notes, lie the "grandiose visions" ["grandes visions"] of radical transformation (entertained in relation to politics, sociology, education, art, etc); and on the other lies the apocalyptic vision of the "little people" ("petits hommes") who in their demotic "critical mass" prevent those visions from being realised.[104] The former are depicted by Rancière as the disappointed, disillusioned critics of democracy; they are "accustomed to exercising the magisterium of the intellect" ["sont habitués à exercer le magistère de la pensée"][105] and so they cannot accept that the narrative of political transformation has been terminated and that the grand revolutionary dream of radical liberation or transformation has been overtaken by a democracy that they do not recognise as a positive value and that they, indeed, execrate. Their criticism can be dismissed as the incontinent, impotent Ressentiment of those who have been disempowered, and who cannot easily foresee a return to power of the values that they espouse.

In his *Homo Academicus*, the French sociologist Pierre Bourdieu gives a "critical insider" account of the French academy of the mid-to-late twentieth century. In his preface to the 1988 English translation of his book on academe, he notes in relation to May 1968 in France that "those consecrated by a bankrupt institution were obliged, if they were to be worthy of the ambitions which it had inculcated in them, to break with the derisory and henceforth untenable roles which it assigned to them, and were led to invent new ways of playing the part of the teacher (all based on adopting a reflexive distance from practice and from the ordinary definition of their functions), by lending him [sic] the strange features of an intellectual master of reflection who reflects on himself, and in so doing, helps destroy himself qua master".[106] This view of the academic who critiques his/her own position of mastery directly echoes, despite its reliance on the value of critique, Rancière's thinking on pedagogy.

In fact, Bourdieu seems to anticipate Rancière's anti-critique position and even attributes to himself – at least to a certain degree – the resentment of the

---

104 | Rancière, *Haine de la démocratie*, p. 100.

105 | Ibid., p. 106.

106 | Bourdieu, *Homo academicus* [English translation], 1988, p. xxvi.

"oblate". This is not, he insists however, Ressentiment in the Nietzschean sense. It is not the Ressentiment of the envious outsider, but is rather the resentment of the disillusioned insider whose investment in academic values and ideals has been disappointed.[107] In fact, Bourdieu refers to *Homo academicus* as a "treatise on the academic passions" and in his preface comments on the "peculiar force with which I felt the need to gain rational control over the disappointment felt by an 'oblate' faced with the annihilation of the truths and values to which he was destined and dedicated rather than [to] take refuge in feelings of self-destructive resentment".[108] Here, rational control or mastery of emotion (in other words, rational critique) is presented as an alternative to resentment, and *a fortiori*, to Ressentiment. However, it is precisely the restorative and regressive reflex reaction not just of "knowing", but of "knowing better", that Rancière would reject in Bourdieu's thinking on education and equality. For it rests, of course, on the position of the intellectually superior critic, trapped in a sterile reactivity from which there is no escape.

Clearly, the shutdown of debate and discussion within the contemporary managerialist structures of academe and the disengaged and irresponsible model of being and thinking that this shutdown serves, do need to be critiqued. However, it would seem that even critique is an inadequate response. And as for dissensus, it is not a response at all, because it lies outside or beyond the "action/reaction" paradigm: it cannot be programmed or commanded into existence. What is paradoxical, however, in any hypothetical levelling of the charge of Ressentiment against critique of the academy is that Ressentiment is itself associated both by Nietzsche and by Scheler with a derivative order of value and with the subordination of authentic fulfillment, strength and action. As currently configured, however, the academy is entirely aligned on proxy values. After all, what critics of the neo-liberal university are particularly concerned to analyse and expose are not just the circular, indiscriminate, derivative values currently measuring and driving academic endeavour, but also the fearful, submissive, slave or zombie mentality that corrals the individual inside the intellectually anaemic and unfree framework of groupthink.

Critique of *Ressentiment*

Although states worldwide are both instrumentalising the public academy as a competitive engine and pressuring it to privatise its costs and risks, it remains the case that it is the university's internal governance and more specifically the *internalised* governance of academics, or their own alignment with this "govern-mentality", that poses the biggest threat to the place of critique or dissensus in academia, *pace* those academics flying too high above their local institutions to get caught in the corporate and bureaucratic glue that most visibly

---

107 | Ibid. p. xvi.

108 | Ibidem.

forecloses critique. Certainly, across the arts and humanities, the Social and Human Sciences and no doubt beyond, and not just in the obvious disciplines such as feminist studies, gender studies, postcolonial studies, globalisation studies, transcultural studies, migration studies, etc., individual academics and the colleges and universities in or for which they work will claim that they are exercising a critical role. Yet increasingly, these claims are incompatible with three factors: firstly, the worldwide consensual operation of Higher Education as a global business; secondly, the input/output driven model of Higher Education within the so-called "knowledge economy"; thirdly, the regressive "schooling" of Higher Education. The revolutionary educationalist, Joseph Jacotot whom Rancière resurrects as the "unknowing schoolteacher", showed illiterate parents that they could teach their own children to read. Rancière uses the example of Jacotot to show that equality functions, as his translator Kristin Ross notes, in a logic of "division rather than consensus, in a multiplicity of concrete acts and actual moments and situations, situations that erupt into the fiction of inegalitarian society without themselves becoming institutions. And in this, my [Ross's] rendering of the title of the book as the *Ignorant Schoolmaster* is perhaps misleading. For Jacotot had no school. Equality does not, as they say in French, faire école".[109]

The author of the *Critique of Cynical Reason*, Peter Sloterdijk, diagnoses a smouldering Ressentiment at work in the contemporary world. According to one of his commentators, Sjoerd van Tuinen, it is the timeless portrait of the man of Ressentiment that lies at the heart of Sloterdijk's polemical commentary on our contemporary capacity for critique. For van Tuinen, Sloterdijk wants to move beyond Ressentiment, or at least beyond a "ressentiment that appears as method".[110] What is particularly convincing in this reference to Ressentiment is the observation made in relation to two successive generations of the Frankfurt School of critical theory, both drowning in Ressentiment. For van Tuinen, "[a]lready at the time of the first generation of the Frankfurt School, the only plausible standpoint of critique was a paralysing ressentiment to which Adorno referred as a sentimental 'concernedness' [Betroffenheit]"; but, as van Tuinen argues, all that "kept this 'ressentiment criticism' (Max Scheler] from becoming cynical was its self-annulling aversion from practical life and power".[111] This aversion could be seen indeed as motivating the commonplace, quasi-pejorative use of the term "academic" as an antonym of 'practical', 'meaningful', 'useful' or 'powerful'. It also marks the distinction that Sloterdijk makes between the first and second generation of Critical Theorists: "with second generation Critical Theory [...] the rat-race of career critics prevails over the cultivation of a feeling

---

109 | Kristin Ross's preface to Rancière, *The Ignorant Schoolmaster*, p. xxiii.

110 | Sjoerd van Tuinen, "From Psychopolitics to Cosmopolitics: The Problem of Ressentiment", in S. Elden (ed.), *Sloterdijk Now*, Cambridge: Polity Press 2012, pp. 37–57.

111 | Ibid., p. 38.

of injustice."[112] Here, Foucault's disdain for the petty polemics of professional critics comes to mind. It is clear that, for the author of Sphere-Critique, this critical bad faith can only be challenged outside the safe circuits of the academy, but also beyond the stridency, amplified in the mass media, of those victim groups that would "restrict our relations to others to moral indignation, anti-elitism, vandalism, scape-goating, and a constant call for more security".[113] This is why Sloterdijk argues for the extra-academic role of the philosopher, for a thinking "at-home-in-the-world" (a "Weltbegriff" or world-liness) instead of a "thinking-confined-to-the-academy" (a "Schulbegriff" or school-ishness).

Sloterdijk, like Rancière, perceives an almost unlimited contemporary intensification of Ressentiment, as rage is dispersed or diffused in a post-historical or post-political vacuum, as the Left collapses and as economics and morality converge in spiralling reflexes of naming, shaming and claiming. This has resulted, according to Sloterdijk, in populist claims to the carefree consumption of acquired rights and in a stridently anti-academic and anti-intellectual consensus of putatively "common sense" economics. These claims are the antithesis of Rancière's equality imperative and are based, instead, on policing. Sloterdijk's "thymotic sovereignty", which offers resistance to economic and religious compensation reflexes, represents action, or at least particular kinds of action (the gifting of life or other gestures of generosity, for example) as interrupting not just the reactive dead-end of "Ressentiment criticism" but also the reactionary chain of retribution and escalation.

In confronting the realities of Ressentiment and its discontents, contemporary social theory tends to focus on how to avoid or preempt it, by working, for example, on the ethics of competition and on standards of fairness, equity and transparency. Yet concentration on such tinkering misses the point, certainly in relation to the values of the academy. To a certain extent, intrinsic academic and intellectual values were always accorded a certain exchange value or currency, in terms of success, promotion, prestige, power, property rights, etc. Even Friedrich Nietzsche was sensitive to the fact that none of his books sold more than 2000 copies in his lifetime, with most of them selling only a few hundred copies. In the contemporary setting, however, where international university rankings have gained global traction and where academic value is more and more often constituted exclusively, explicitly and massively in relation to proxy exchange values, typically money, the distinction between intrinsic and exchange value becomes critical. As we have seen, Ressentiment entirely disables this distinction. Indeed Ressentiment carries, constitutionally, a serious and general cognitive risk: that of systematically underestimating real complexity and of mistaking a partial picture for absolute reality. In the academic context specifically, this is particularly problematic. As Foucault's definition of critique cited above reminds us, critique is partly about correcting error. Rational critique, in theory, allows

---

112 | Sloterdijk, *Critique of Cynical Reason*, p. xxxv–vi.

113 | Sloterdijk, *Die nehmende Hand und die gebende Seite: Beiträge einer Debatte uber die demokratische Neubegrundung von Steuern*, Berlin: Suhrkamp 2010, p. 156.

us to recognise spurious claims to (total) knowledge or (absolute) understanding. Similarly, Lyotard's "ideal" philosopher knows above all what (s)he does not know. Ressentiment is, however, as we have seen, by definition deeply implicated in error, since transvaluation involves a simple inversion of the terms of what are essentially crude binary codes: powerful/impotent, strong/weak, healthy/sick, winner/loser, equal/hierarchical, etc. The risks of cognitive reduction, simplification, reification etc. are self-evident in this context. The academy cannot, therefore, shy away from critique of Ressentiment.

However, the two fundamental questions raised in this volume remain as compelling at the end of the present essay as they were at the outset: firstly the question of how to circumvent the moral and epistemic limits of critique, insofar as these relate both to the implication of Ressentiment in the critique in question, and to the fact that Ressentiment is associated with extreme reactivity, negativity and reductivity, along with a deficit of critical reason; and secondly the question of how to avoid, disarm, deflect, or defuse the charge of Ressentiment used to discredit or to dismiss responsible and careful critique or as an excuse not to engage in it.

The answers to this question are open. They are as numerous as the languages, idioms, styles, discourses, actions etc. that can not so much refuse or refute the binaries and reifications of "Ressentiment criticism" as present the alternative to the monological machine of consensus; that can act against injustice; that can show how things are not (simply) what they are but can (also) be less and more and what they are not, or not yet; that can unsettle the consensus that "we are where we are" and even the consensus regarding who and what "we" are; that can question values of expertise, superiority, certainty, success and mastery. In acting, sharing and responding rather than repressing or reacting, in respecting threatened boundaries (and moving across threatening limits) between disciplines, languages, cultures or ways of thinking, in taking responsibility rather than in avoiding it: in all these ways we might to some extent make responsible critique possible and avoid making dissensus impossible.

About the Authors

VICTORIA FARELD is Associate Professor of the History of Ideas in the University of Stockholm. Her research is in the areas of historical theory, historicity and ethics, political philosophy and modern intellectual history. Her publications include: "The re- in recognition: Hegelian returns", *Distinktion: Scandinavian Journal of Social Theory*, 13 (1) 2012: 125–138, "Hegel and Exposure", *Translating Hegel: The Phenomenology of Spirit and Modern Philosophy* (eds. B. Delaney/ S.O. Wallenstein), Södertörn University 2012: 131–145, "History and Mourning", *Rethinking Time: Essays on History, Memory, and Representation* (eds A. Ers/H. Ruin), Södertörn University 2011: 235–244.

HELEN FINCH is Associate Professor in German at the University of Leeds. She is the author of *Sebald's Bachelors: Queer Resistance and the Unconforming Life* (Oxford: Legenda, 2013), and has published widely on W. G. Sebald and H. G. Adler, as well as on gender and sexuality in German literature. Recent essays have addressed Kafka's influence in H. G. Adler's work, and the metaphysics of history in W. G. Sebald's writings. She is currently working on a monograph on "Holocaust Literature in German: Canon, Witness, Remediation," and is co-editor, with Lynn L. Wolf, of the volume *Witnessing, Memory, Poetics: H. G. Adler and W. G. Sebald* (Rochester, NY: Camden House 2014).

MARY GALLAGHER teaches French and Francophone Studies at University College Dublin. She has published on Caribbean writing, most notably *La Créolité de Saint-John Perse* (Paris: Gallimard 1998) and *Soundings in French Caribbean Writing since 1950* (Oxford: OUP 2002) and on postcolonial positionings more generally: *World Writing: Poetics, Ethics, Globalization* (University of Toronto Press, 2008). She has also published many studies on migrant writing and on the ethics of Emmanuel Levinas. She is most recently the author of *Academic Armageddon: an Irish Requiem for Higher Education* (Dublin: Liffey Press, 2012) and is completing a book on Lafcadio Hearn's Creole trajectory.

DOMINIQUE JEANNEROD is a Lecturer in French Studies in the School of Modern Languages at Queen's University Belfast. His principal areas of interest are in the international circulation of popular fiction, in the theory of the literary field, and in crime fiction writing in Europe. He leads the ICRH International

Crime Fiction research Group and the AHRC international collaborative project Visualizing European Crime Fiction: New Digital Tools and Approaches to the Study of Transnational Popular Culture He is in 2014–2015 Senior Research Fellow in the Institute for Collaborative research in the Humanities. He has taught at Freiburg and at Strasbourg Universities, and at Trinity College and University College (Dublin), before taking up his present appointment at Queen's. He is the author of *San-Antonio et son double* (puf: 2010), and the editor of the anthology Frédéric Dard, *Romans de la nuit* (Omnibus, 2014).

CHRISTINE A. KNOOP is a Research Fellow at the Max Planck Institute for Empirical Aesthetics in Frankfurt. Her research interests include experimental approaches to aesthetic properties of literary texts, prose rhythm, travel literature, non-mother tongue writing, and conceptions of authorship. She is the author of *Kundera and the Ambiguity of Authorship* (London: Maney 2011) and co-editor of *Cumaná 1799. Alexander von Humboldt's Voyage Between Europe and the Americas* (Bielefeld: Aisthesis 2013), and has published a number of articles on works by Milan Kundera, Jean Genet, Paul Scheerbart, Rainer Maria Rilke, and Abbé Prévost.

CAROLINE MANNWEILER studied German and French in Mainz (Germany), St. Louis (USA) and Paris. She received her PhD. in French Literature with a study on Samuel Beckett (*L'éthique beckettienne et sa réalisation dans la forme*). She is currently working as a post-doctoral researcher at the Department of General and Comparative literature at the Johannes Gutenberg-University Mainz.

ERIC S. NELSON is Associate Professor of Philosophy at the Hong Kong University of Science and Technology. He has published over sixty articles and book chapters on Chinese, German, and Jewish philosophy. He is the co-editor with François Raffoul of the *Bloomsbury Companion to Heidegger* (London: Bloomsbury, 2013) and *Rethinking Facticity* (Albany: SUNY Press, 2008). He has also co-edited with John Drabinski, *Between Levinas and Heidegger* (Albany: SUNY Press, 2014); with G. D'Anna and H. Johach, *Anthropologie und Geschichte. Studien zu Wilhelm Dilthey aus Anlass seines 100. Todestages* (Würzburg: Königshausen & Neumann, 2013); and with A. Kapust and K. Still, *Addressing Levinas* (Evanston: Northwestern University Press, 2005).

JEANNE RIOU is Lecturer in German at University College Dublin. She is author of *Anthropology of Connection. Perception and its Emotional Undertones in German Philosophical Discourse,* (Würzburg: 2014) and *Imagination in German Romanticism: Re-thinking the Self in its Environment* (2004), and was joint editor of *Netzwerke. Kulturtechniken der Moderne* (with J. Barkhoff and H. Böhme), (2004) and *Zeichen des Krieges in Literatur, Film und den Medien, Bd. 3: Terror / Signs of War in Literature, Film and the Media, Vol 3: Terror,* (with C. Petersen), (2008). Interested in the relationship of philosophy and literature, her published essays include studies of Viennese Modernism; Freud; Feuilleton-writing in Weimar Berlin; Historiography and Cultural Critique in Schiller and Benjamin.

Index of Names